W9-AGK-123

The Southern Dream
of a Caribbean Empire
1854–1861

The Southern Dream
of a Caribbean Empire

1854–1861

Robert E. May

Louisiana State University Press
Baton Rouge

ISBN 0-8071-0051-X
Library of Congress Catalog Card Number 73-77653
Copyright © 1973 by Louisiana State University Press
All rights reserved
Manufactured in the United States of America
Printed by The TJM Corporation, Baton Rouge, Louisiana
Designed by Albert R. Crochet

To Richard Sewell

Contents

Acknowledgments

In an article in the *Mississippi Valley Historical Review* some years ago, Paton Yoder maintained that the idea of southern hospitality was in part a myth. Yoder's arguments were convincing, yet I must confess to being a captive of that myth. Over the past few years, librarians and archivists throughout the South have helped me tremendously, and many of them have gone out of their way to aid my research. I would particularly like to thank Mary Washington Frazer and Frances Kunstling of the Tennessee State Library and Archives, Jim Bentley of the Filson Club, Laura Harrell of the Mississippi State Archives, Barbara Pegg of the Texas State Archives and Library, Margaret Fisher of the Department of Archives and Manuscripts at Louisiana State University, and William Ray of the University of Virginia Library. In addition, I would like to express my appreciation to the following people, who have either read and criticized part of my manuscript, or provided helpful research leads: William Collins, Spencer Leitman, and Harold Woodman of Purdue University, Ronnie Tyler of the Amon Carter Museum of Western Art at Fort Worth, Texas, and Frank Klement of Marquette University. I will never forget Mr. and Mrs. John Cheadle of Nashville, who graciously allowed me to look at their family collection of DeBow papers at the shortest notice. Richard Current guided the initial stages of this study in his research seminar at the University of

Wisconsin some seven years ago, and his willingness to let me embark on what was a vague and ambitious project for a master's thesis is well appreciated. My debt is deepest to Richard Sewell, who was my adviser through most of my years of graduate study at the University of Wisconsin. His meticulous reading of my dissertation, and his constant prodding and suggestions, helped me invaluably. I am also greatly indebted to Joyce Good, Grace Dienhart, Dorothy Mays, Kathryn McClellan, Betty Pizzagalli, and Brenda Matthews of the Purdue History Department secretarial staff for their help. Finally, my wife Jill's enthusiasm for this study, her understanding of some rather late hours put in at my desk, and her proofreading merit her special mention.

The Southern Dream
of a Caribbean Empire
1854–1861

I

The Awaiting
Paradise

Although Americans had previously expressed interest in annexing Mexico, parts of Central America, and some of the islands of the Caribbean, the urge to extend the national domain southward intensified significantly during the 1850s. Americans became increasingly excited about the potentialities of expansion into the tropics. College students debated the pros and cons of annexation. Merchants in port cities supplied illegal arms and ships to American adventurers—then known as filibusters—who were frequently setting out from American soil to conquer Caribbean lands. The front pages and editorial columns of newspapers rallied public opinion to imperialism. People throughout the country wrote their friends and relatives about possible acquisitions as if they were inevitable, turned out in mass meetings to cheer filibusters and buy their bonds, and pressured their congressmen to initiate expansion legislation. Political party platforms endorsed the spread of the United States southward. Politicians presented expansionist bills, resolutions, and programs in Congress, state legislatures, and county conventions, as well as on the stump. The State Department ordered diplomats in Europe to negotiate for Caribbean acquisitions— even, on occasion, to engage in activities bordering on subversion when it was thought that such activities might lead to territorial gain.

After the Mexican War, American expansionists argued that it was only natural that their country should turn to the tropics since the United States had reached the westward limit of expansion and countries in the Gulf region were more vulnerable than Canada to the north. Many of the Caribbean countries had long suffered from internal revolutions, retarded economies, and political strife. Expansionists contended that the United States should take advantage of their weakness. Many white Americans felt superior to the generally darker people inhabiting lands to the south, and expansionists catered to these prejudices, claiming that it was the United States' duty to uplift those people through annexation. Peoples to the south were thought to be incapable of self-rule; their only hope lay in exposure to American institutions, since the United States was more stable and prosperous.

This haughty attitude gained its widest acceptance in the American South, although it was prevalent in the North and West also. Southern expansionists took the lead in proposing American intervention to help the "ignorant, bigoted and miserable" inhabitants of the Caribbean region. A constant refrain was that the United States should "regenerate" her neighbors. Sam Houston's comment that it was America's mission to bring "law and order" to Mexicans—a people "utterly incapable of framing a government and maintaining a nationality"—typified this school of thought.[1]

Many southerners agreed that Mexico was in desperate straits. A Virginia newspaper depicted Mexicans as the "most brutal, the most barbarous, the most ignorant of all the people who claim the right of being civilized—cowardly, treacherous, ferocious half-Indians—white men

1. Baltimore *Clipper*, May 19, 1856, clipping in John Heiss Scrapbook, John Heiss Papers, Tennessee State Library and Archives, Nashville; Randal McGavock Journal, December 19, 1857, in Herschel Gower and Jack Allen (eds.), *Pen and Sword: The Life and Journals of Randal W. McGavock* (Knoxville, 1959), 447; Dallas *Herald*, August 21, 1858, January 11, 1860.

even worse than they—robbers, murderers, fugitives from justice of all descriptions." To southerners, the "damn" Mexicans were "greasers" and their republic an "abortion." Central Americans and Caribbean islanders were similarly belittled: "The miserable republics of Central America, peopled by a degraded half race of humanity, will yet bow to the rule of the Anglo-American." An Alabama newspaper predicted that Americans would carry "moral and material well being to the disintegrating communities and decaying races of Spanish America." [2]

According to expansionist rationale, the peoples of the tropics would offer little nationalistic resistance to amalgamation because they had the common sense to appreciate the benefits that American rule would bring. The Louisville *Daily Courier*, for example, claimed that Cuba, a Spanish possession, was weary of oppressive rule and yearned for annexation to the United States so that it could "learn a sure system of government." A southern congressman expressed the same confidence about all the republics of the tropics: "With swelling hearts and suppressed impatience they await our coming, and with joyous shouts of 'Welcome! welcome!' will they receive us." [3] Anti-American sentiment and incidents were either ig-

2. Richmond *Whig*, January 19, 1858, January 4, 1859; Wily Morgan, Jr., to Sam Houston, March 24, 1860, in Governors' Letters, Sam Houston, Texas State Archives and Library, Austin; Jay Max Maisel, "The Origin and Development of Mexican Antipathy Toward the South, 1821–1867" (Ph.D. dissertation, University of Texas, 1955), 278–79; Dallas *Herald*, August 21, 1858; Fayetteville *Arkansian*, October 18, 1860; Tuskegee (Alabama) *Republican*, January 7, 1858. For similar comments, see photocopy of Ben McCulloch to Sam Houston, April 6, 1860, in Sam Houston Papers, Barker Texas History Center Archives, University of Texas, Austin; John Ford to Edward Burleson, Jr., February 15, 1856, in Edward Burleson, Jr., Papers, Barker Texas History Center Archives, University of Texas, Austin; Augustus Chapman Allen to Sam Houston, September 19, 1859, in Governor's Letters, Sam Houston.
3. Louisville *Daily Courier*, February 19, 1859; *Congressional Globe*, 35th Cong., 2nd Sess., 705.

nored or discounted as irrelevant. "Lower" races simply
did not have the right of self-determination:

> This is the greater movement, before which all minor
> moral rights disappear. Who in England talks of the moral
> rights of the Sepoys?... Where in Europe are the defend-
> ers of the moral rights of the Tartar?... We have almost
> found our western limit. The shores of the Pacific and the
> great central desert of North America already bound our
> development westward, and it must turn southward, where
> decaying nations and races invite our coming. Small phi-
> losophers may harp upon moral rights here, as they do in
> Europe, but it will produce no more effect upon the march
> of races in America, Europe, Africa, or Asia, than whis-
> tling has upon the wind.[4]

While southern expansionists portrayed American extension as beneficial to the peoples who would be encompassed, they also indicated that they expected acquisitions
to bring rich bounties to the United States itself. Although
expansionists had little respect for the inhabitants and
governments of the Caribbean region, they held the land,
climate, and resources in high esteem. The tropics were described as an undeveloped paradise—a veritable Garden
of Eden—anxiously awaiting the enterprise and appreciation that only Americans could bestow. There was an
almost unreal character to their effusive praise of the
Caribbean soil and climate.

This dreamlike outlook was especially manifest in respect to Cuba, whose sugar plantations were enjoying
boom times. Cuba was said to be "redolent with the rich
odors of its budding flowers and tropical fruits and pro-
ductions, girt with her spreading waters and covered with
her genial climes." Red flamingoes, standing by Cuba's
lagoons, peered into the island's clear waters; and fish,
"emulating the tints of precious stones and the prismatic
hues of the rainbow," inhabited the surrounding seas.

4. Tuskegee *Republican*, January 7, 1858.

Southerners commonly referred to the island as the "Pearl
of the Antilles," the "Queen of the Antilles," or the "Gem
of the Antilles"; and poets sang her praises:

> Isle of the Ocean! jeweled on the breast
> Of waters fragrant with thy tropic breath,
> Thou seem'st alike some happy dream at rest
> In the calm sea of mind! But underneath
> Those clear, blue skies there lurks despair and death.
> How long, Oh righteous Heaven! shall Freedom weep
> O'er such fair lands as these—the Eden of the deep?

Occasionally southerners got so carried away by their
own rhetoric about Cuba that their prose became erotic:
"[Cuba] admires Uncle Sam, and he loves her. Who shall
forbid the bans? Matches are made in heaven, and why not
this? Who can object if he throws his arms around the
Queen of the Antilles, as she sits, like Cleopatra's burning
throne, upon the silver waves, breathing her spicy, tropic
breath, and pouting her rosy, sugared lips? Who can object? None. She is of age—take her, Uncle Sam!" [5]

Other Caribbean countries were equally paradisical. A
Texan raved that Mexico was an "enchanted land of gor-
geous mines and jeweled mountains, whose beautiful sce-
nery, and strange, stirring annals, are alike tinted with
the hues of a wild and wondrous romance." A transplanted
southerner reported that Nicaragua enjoyed "perpetual
summer. Trees here are all green ever vegitating and cast-
ing forth their luscious fruits[.] Were it not for the civil

5. *Congressional Globe*, 35th Cong., 2nd Sess., 705; Tuskegee *Republican*, February 25, 1858; George H. Reese (ed.), *Proceedings of
the Virginia State Convention of 1861* (4 vols.; Richmond, 1965), I,
469; *Southern Literary Messenger*, October, 1860; Louisville *Daily
Courier*, January 11, February 19, 1859. Franklin Knight points out
that by 1838 Cuba was the "foremost producer of the world's sugar,"
attributing this to the decline of sugar production in Haiti and the
overuse of soils in the British West Indies. The growth of Cuba's
railroad network further stimulated the boom. See Franklin W.
Knight, *Slave Society in Cuba during the Nineteenth Century* (Madison, 1970), 3, 28–41.

wars that are continually raging ... it would rank with
any of the terrestrial paradises which dot our world." A
Kentuckian claimed that Nicaragua's soil could produce at
least three times as much corn as soil in the United States
and twice the amount of sugar per acre. Nicaragua's indigo crop, when "properly handled," was comparable to
"any in the world," and the country was rich in wood and
mineral resources. A Texan believed that the fertility of
Nicaragua's coastal area surpassed that of the Nile Delta,
and an Arkansas newspaper predicted that Nicaragua
could become "one of the richest countries in the world
within a few years." The Tuskegee *Republican* contended,
however, that the "magnificent" "terrestrial paradise" of
Haiti was "worth a dozen Nicaraguas." [6]

Heaven could be found almost anywhere in the tropics
of the Western Hemisphere, and many southern expansionists argued that the United States would be foolish to
rest content with anything less than the annexation of all
of Mexico, Central America, and the Caribbean Islands;
some southern imperialists even extended their hopes to
South America. Such men felt little strain in reeling off a
list of countries ready for the taking. A Georgian wrote
Stephen Douglas, "Strike a giant blow for *Cuba, Porto
Rica [sic], Sonora* and *Chihuahua.* ... Point the South to
the West Indies Mexico and Central America." A United
States representative urged that the Gulf of Mexico be
made into a "great American lake" by the annexation of
Mexico, Central America, and Cuba. And to an influential
Texan, Mexico, Central America, and South America were

---

6. *Congressional Globe*, 34th Cong., 1st Sess., Appendix, 1296;
John S. Brenizer to his sister and brother-in-law, October 27, 1855,
from Granada, Nicaragua, in John Brenizer Papers, Tennessee
State Library and Archives, Nashville; J. L. Richmond to Governor
[Charles] Morehead of Kentucky, October 30, 1856, published in the
Frankfort (Kentucky) *Commonwealth*, clipping in John Heiss
Scrapbook, John Heiss Papers; account of R. J. Swearingen in
Texas State Gazette, May 17, 1856; *Arkansas State Gazette and
Democrat*, October 10, 1857; Tuskegee *Republican*, May 20, 1858.

"ripe fruit." So breathtaking and limitless was the expansionist perspective that one can safely assert that some southerners had become possessed by a dream of Caribbean empire. Expansionists often used the very word "empire" to characterize their tropical aspirations.[7] Vital to this dream of empire was the expectation that slavery would be intrinsic to its realization. Although most of the countries of the Caribbean, Central America, and South America had abolished slavery, southerners believed that it could and should be reestablished. United States Senator Albert Gallatin Brown put the case bluntly to some of his Mississippi constituents: "I want Cuba, and I know that sooner or later we must have it. . . . I want Tamaulipas, Potosi, and one or two other Mexican States; and I want them all for the same reason—for the planting or spreading of slavery. And a foothold in Central America will powerfully aid us in acquiring those other States. . . . Yes, I want these Countries for the spread of slavery." Proslavery spokesman George Fitzhugh envisioned slaves throughout South America, Mexico, and the West Indies producing the cotton, rice, sugar, coffee, and tobacco that whites in the North and in western Europe so urgently needed.[8]

Some annexationists even contended that the very scar-

7. Barton Pringle to Stephen Douglas, February 22, 1859, in Stephen Douglas Papers, University of Chicago; manuscript in John Henry Brown's hand, dated 1860, in John Henry Brown Papers, Barker Texas History Center Archives, University of Texas, Austin; *Congressional Globe*, 35th Cong., 1st Sess., Appendix, 458–61; William Walker, *The War in Nicaragua* (Mobile, 1860), 280; Memphis *Daily Appeal*, December 30, 1860; Dallas *Herald*, February 20, 1861; Montgomery *Daily Confederation*, March 21, 1860; Louisville *Daily Courier*, January 11, 1859; Edward A. Pollard, *Black Diamonds Gathered in the Darkey Homes of the South* (New York, 1859), 108, 111.

8. M. W. Cluskey (ed.), *Speeches, Messages and Other Writings of the Hon. Albert G. Brown* (Philadelphia, 1859), 588–99; George Fitzhugh, *Cannibals All, or Slaves Without Masters*, ed. C. Vann Woodward (Cambridge, Mass., 1960), 202; Fayetteville *Arkansian*, October 18, 1860; Montgomery *Daily Confederation*, March 20, 1860.

city of slavery was the cause of the region's poverty. White men were unfit for work in a hot tropical climate; but blacks, because of their African origins, were physically suited, and could labor effectively with white guidance. *De Bow's Review* explained: "Think you the Caucasian race can stand to toil and labor under the burning rays of a tropical sun, and sleep in vigor and prosperity under the miasma of its exuberant and mighty plains and swamps? No! Its resources are to be finally and fully developed by that race which God in his mercy formed and created for just such regions." [9]

Southern expansionists hoped that the extension of slavery southward would take place quickly. During the 1850s the South failed to make Kansas a slave state; and, as the decade waned, prospects for the establishment of the institution elsewhere in the American West were dismal. For the South to maintain sectional balance of power, new slave territory would have to be acquired to counterbalance free states regularly being admitted to the union. New slave states, and new slave-state congressmen, would enable the South to protect the institution of slavery and

9. *De Bow's Review*, XVII (1854), 281. For similar arguments, see *Congressional Globe*, 35th Cong., 2nd Sess., 290; Mobile *Daily Register*, July 31, 1856; Walker, *War in Nicaragua*, 262; Reese (ed.), *Proceedings of the Virginia State Convention*, I, 652–53; Montgomery *Daily Confederation*, March 20, 1860; manuscript in John Henry Brown's hand, dated 1860, in John Henry Brown Papers. The theory that only Negroes could work effectively in tropical regions was widespread throughout the United States in the antebellum period because of racial misconceptions. An unlikely exponent of exporting slavery to the tropics was Hinton Helper, generally regarded as a leading antislavery spokesman in the Old South. Helper viewed the tropics as an escape valve for American slaves, in a manner reminiscent of Robert Walker's suggestion during the annexation of Texas controversy that Texas would serve as a funnel through which slaves would go to Mexico and freedom. The difference was that Helper expected slavery to permanently survive in the tropics. See Hinton R. Helper, *The Land of Gold* (Baltimore, 1855), 221–22; Frederick Merk, "A Safety Valve Thesis and Texan Annexation," *Mississippi Valley Historical Review*, XLIX (1962), 413–36.

"Southern rights." Jefferson Davis expressed such reasoning when he supported a congressional bill to acquire Cuba on the basis that it would "increase the number of slaveholding constituencies." Governor Wickliffe of Louisiana endorsed the acquisition of Cuba and Mexico because of Louisiana's "political" interest "in the speedy admission of new Southern States." John Ford of Texas felt that Mexico was a "political necessity" for Texas and the South; and a Texas newspaper made the same point: "The Southerners are looking for new fields of enterprise, and for the means of carrying into execution some plan by which they can restore the lost balance of power. Mexico furnishes the means." The same phrase, "balance of power," was used by another Texan to explain the support that "extreme Southern rights men" gave to filibustering in the 1850s.[10]

Southerners wanted to boost slave-state representation in the United States Senate.[11] They had abandoned hopes of retaining power in the House of Representatives: representation in that body was based on population, and the North had outdistanced the South in population because immigrants were attracted to the North's free-labor system and climate. But the South could hope to retain a balance of power in the Senate. This had been a "cardinal principle of Southern political policy" ever since the Missouri Compromise debates, and John C. Calhoun and Jefferson

10. Jackson *Weekly Mississippian*, July 27, 1859; *Texas State Gazette*, October 9, 1858; *Texas Republican*, January 28, 1859; John Ford to Edward Burleson, Jr., February 15, 1856, in Burleson Papers; John H. Reagan, *Memoirs: With Special Reference to Secession and the Civil War* (New York, 1906), 70. See also *Congressional Globe*, 35th Cong., 2nd Sess., 347; Alexandria *Gazette*, May 20, 1859; James C. Pickett to John Quitman, March 20, 1854, in John Quitman Papers, Mississippi Department of Archives and History, Jackson; Pollard, *Black Diamonds*, 107–108.

11. *Documents of the First Session of the Fourth Legislature of the State of Louisiana, 1858*, 13; *Brownlow's Knoxville Whig*, February 20, 1858.

Davis had both stressed the principle in their speeches during the sectional crisis of 1850. Some expansionists supplemented these political arguments for tropical slave lands with rationales that appealed particularly to southerners. New soils, for instance, offered an escape from lands depleted by one-crop agriculture. Some expansionists contended that tropical expansion would alleviate threats of race revolt and slave competition for white labor opportunities—threats posed by a disproportionate Negro population in some regions. The concept of tropical expansion, as William Barney has pointed out, occasionally even provided a hypothetical, if visionary, escape from the paradox of rationalizing the existence of slavery in a society committed to egalitarianism. Southerners could claim that the tropics were so conducive to slave labor that virtually their entire black population would ultimately emigrate there. The South left behind would be a society rid of the burden of slavery, yet also free from problems of race revolt and racial friction that might accompany emancipation if there were no territorial outlet.[12]

The emphasis upon political benefits to be gained from tropical acquisitions led many southern politicians to spurn annexation of Canada and the other provinces of British North America at the very time that they were urging southward expansion. Acquisitions in the north would offset annexations in the tropics, and the South would have nothing to show for its effort. Although northern congressmen occasionally noted the two-faced nature of southern expansionism, and charged hypocrisy, southern expansionists felt that their inconsistency was justi-

12. Charles S. Sydnor, *The Development of Southern Sectionalism, 1819–1848* (Baton Rouge, 1948), 132–33; Holman Hamilton, *Prologue to Conflict: The Crisis and Compromise of 1850* (Lexington, 1964), 71–72, 139; William Barney, *The Road to Secession: A New Perspective on the Old South* (New York, 1972), 4–21, 65–78.

fied.[13] Congressman Evans of Texas answered northern attacks with this burst of rhetoric:

> It is sometimes made a matter of complaint, and we have listened to it even on this floor, that all our acquisitions, or, as they are opprobriously styled, aggressions, have australized towards the tropics, while no annexations seem inclined to advance us any nearer to the ice of the Arctic Circle. Such objectors must surely have forgotten their readings in history. All nations endowed with even savage liberty, or the power of free locomotion, are, and ever have been, urged towards the summer-lands of the South. . . . The tide of emigration is repelled by the frozen snows of the wintry north, by its gloomy forests, the howling of its angry winds, and the thick-ribbed ice of its polar lakes. On the contrary, the eye as well as the imagination must always dwell with delight and enthusiasm on the fragrance, beauty, and emerald verdure of those sunny groves where the golden light lives forever on the grass, and the glory of fruit and flowers never fades from the green of the leaf which no frost withers. Hence all great migrations . . . have flowed . . . in the direction of the equator.[14]

13. *Congressional Globe*, 34th Cong., 1st Sess., Appendix, 668; *ibid.*, 35th Cong., 1st Sess., 711; *ibid.*, 35th Cong., 2nd Sess., 543.

14. *Ibid.*, 34th Cong., 1st Sess., Appendix, 1298. The movement in the United States to annex Canada passed through a relatively dormant period during the 1850s, particularly after the signing of the Canadian Reciprocity Treaty of 1854. Even during the late 1840s, when there had been a significant movement in Canada for amalgamation with the United States, Americans expressed little interest in the idea. The reciprocity treaty allayed Canadian unrest with the British Empire and ushered in a "period of golden contentment" for ten years. One of the reasons southerners supported the reciprocity agreement may well have been an expectation that it would dampen the possibilities of annexing Canada. See Donald F. Warner, *The Idea of Continental Union: Agitation for the Annexation of Canada to the United States, 1849–1893* (Lexington, 1960), 4–39; Charles Tansill, *The Canadian Reciprocity Treaty of 1854* (Baltimore, 1922), 76–77; James Morton Callahan, *American Foreign Policy in Canadian Relations* (New York, 1937), 259. Some southern expansionists, however, expressed a willingness to accept Canada during the 1850s. See an 1859 speech by Robert Toombs in *Congressional Globe*, 35th Cong., 2nd Sess., 540–41.

Economic benefits were expected to accrue dispropor-
tionately to the South because of its geographic proximity
to the proposed tropical acquisitions. Such expectations
heightened the sectional dimension of the movement. Gulf
states leaders, in particular, expected their region to profit
from the development of land, minerals, trade, and transportation. Governor Wickliffe's argument for the acquisition of Cuba stressed Louisiana's "especial commercial
interest" in the island; and expansionist propaganda for
Cuba rarely failed to cite possibilities for exploitation:
"Were Cuba annexed, Havanna [sic] would speedily become the great *entrepot* of southern commerce, and in a
few years be the rival of New York itself. It would be
the nucleus around which would cluster the trade of all the
Gulf and many of the South American ports; of all the
North and South American Pacific ports, as it passes over
the Isthmus; and also of the Asiatic and East Indian
ports. . . . There is no telling what an immense city Havanna [sic] would become. And she would be a southern
city, a slaveholding city." Visions of commercial advantage also affected opinion in the upper South. The Louisville *Daily Courier* argued that the acquisition of Cuba, in
conjunction with the construction of a southern transcontinental railroad, would guarantee "the future prosperity
of the South." [15] And the attention that southern commercial conventions and *De Bow's Review* (the South's most
trade-conscious periodical) bestowed upon countries such
as Mexico and Nicaragua indicates that businessmen
throughout the South were interested in the benefits of
expansion.

Sectionalism, in relation to the Caribbean, was a relatively novel development. Before the 1850s the Caribbean
had not been a salient possibility for most southern expan-

15. *Texas Republican*, January 28, 1859; Tuskegee *Republican*,
May 13, 1858; Louisville *Daily Courier*, January 11, 1859.

sionists, and what interest they had shown usually had not been slavery oriented. Southerners disagreed among themselves as to whether slavery could expand southward, as did northerners. This disagreement especially affected discussions of annexing Mexico. During the Mexican War, when there was a distinct possibility that American armies might conquer all or most of Mexico, or that a good slice of Mexico might be ceded in a peace treaty, southerners divided over whether acquisition should be an American policy. Mexico had abolished slavery in 1829, and many southern leaders doubted that it could ever be reestablished. Waddy Thompson, a South Carolinian who had recently been American minister to Mexico, warned that climatic and geographic factors determined that slavery "never can exist" in Mexico; and many southerners shared his views. Prominent southern spokesmen such as John Calhoun, Robert Toombs, and Alexander Stephens all spoke out against acquiring Mexican territory, as did the influential Charleston *Mercury*. Calhoun warned that the United States Constitution could not effectively function in respect to such extensive acquisitions, that an inevitable political struggle over whether the acquisitions should be slave or free would break the union, and that Mexicans, as a "race," were incompatible with Americans: "More than half of the Mexicans are Indians, and the other is composed chiefly of mixed tribes. I protest against such a union as that! Ours, sir, is the Government of a white race." [16]

16. *Niles' National Register*, October 30, 1847, p. 137; *Congressional Globe*, 30th Cong., 1st Sess., 26, 96–100; Robert Toombs to John C. Calhoun, April 30, 1847, and George H. Hatcher to Calhoun, January 5, 1848, both in Chauncey S. Boucher and Robert P. Brooks (eds.), "Correspondence Addressed to John C. Calhoun, 1837–1849," *Annual Report of the American Historical Association for the Year 1929* (Washington, D.C., 1930), 373, 416; Frederick Merk, *Manifest Destiny and Mission in American History* (New York, 1963), 210; John D. P. Fuller, *The Movement for the Acquisition of All Mexico, 1846–1848* (Baltimore, 1936), 42.

Some prominent southern leaders during the Mexican War, such as Alexander Sims of South Carolina and General John Quitman of Mississippi, believed that if Mexico entered the union, it would do so as a slave state. But the evidence belies accusations by a number of northern antislavery leaders that the war was being fought for the benefit of a "slave power." It has been shown conclusively that opinion in both North and South as to the slave potential of Mexico was sharply split, that the West gave the all-Mexico movement its strongest backing, and that "Southeastern slave-holders were never very enthusiastic supporters of extensive annexations of Mexican territory." [17]

Prior to 1850, Cuba was the only tropical country with slavery that intrigued southerners to any great extent. However, the proposed annexation of that country attracted significant support throughout the United States. Strategic and commercial considerations dictated that all Americans give thought to the value of controlling Cuba.

Ever since Spain had relaxed its restrictions on foreign trade with Cuba during the Napoleonic wars of the late eighteenth and early nineteenth centuries in order to take advantage of neutral shipping, the island had functioned as a depot for American trade. Though the growth rate of United States-Cuba trade declined after the War of 1812, American exports to and imports from Cuba between 1835 and 1865 still ranked third or fourth compared to trade with other countries. The United States became especially dependent on shipments of Cuban sugar, for Louisiana plantations in the early nineteenth century could only accommodate about one third of the national

17. Said Sims: "We may rightfully, and without any great danger, looking to an overruling Providence and to the patriotism of our people, permanently occupy this country Mexico. And I have no doubt . . . that every foot of territory we shall permanently occupy south of thirty-six degrees thirty minutes, will be slave territory." See *Congressional Globe*, 29th Cong., 2nd Sess., 291; Fuller, *All Mexico*, 114–15.

demand for the product.[18] Not only did this trade contribute significantly to the commercial growth of New York City—which became a center for sentiment favoring the annexation of the island—but commercial interests all over the eastern United States were dependent on it.[19]

Cuba's location—only ninety miles from the coast of Florida—concerned Americans of all sections. Although there was little apprehension that Spain, by now a weak power, would ever use Cuba as a base for aggression against the United States, there was always the danger that the island would fall into the hands of a mightier European power, particularly England. John Quincy Adams, Henry Clay, Albert Gallatin, and other prominent early American leaders shared this fear of England, which emerged as the United States' main political and economic rival in the Caribbean area, and preferred that Cuba remain a Spanish colony until the United States could annex it or establish its independence. In 1810 James Madison instructed his minister to tell the British government that the United States would not sit idly by should England try to gain possession of Cuba; and Secretary of State John Quincy Adams established "no-transfer" as a cardinal tenet of American foreign policy in an 1823 dispatch to the American minister to Spain: "The transfer of Cuba to Great Britain would be an event unpropitious to the in-

18. John H. Coatsworth, "American Trade with European Colonies in the Caribbean and South America, 1790–1812," *William and Mary Quarterly*, XXIV (1967), 245–47, 254; Roland T. Ely, "The Old Cuba Trade: Highlights and Case Studies of Cuban-American Interdependence during the Nineteenth Century," *Business History Review*, XXXVIII (1964), 458 and *n*; Lester D. Langley, *The Cuba Policy of the United States* (New York, 1968), 4, 21–24. Langley points out that by 1854 the United States was sending $8,551,752 worth of exports to Cuba.

19. Ely, "Cuba Trade," 460; Coatsworth, "Trade with European Colonies," 248. Coatsworth specifically mentions grain farmers in the Chesapeake and eastern Pennsylvania regions, the flour-milling industry in Baltimore and Philadelphia, New England fisheries, livestock producers, meat processors, and lumber interests as being dependent on the American export trade to the West Indies.

terests of this Union. . . . The question both of our right and our power to prevent it, if necessary by force, already obtrudes itself upon our councils, and the administration is called upon, in the performance of its duties to the nation, at least to use all the means within its competency to guard against and forefend it." [20] The "no-transfer" principle did not preclude eventual American ownership. If it had, this would have been remarkable for an age of "manifest destiny" in which the United States acquired Florida, Louisiana, Texas, and other territory. The annexation of Cuba gradually became an unofficial national policy.

Many American leaders took it for granted that sooner or later the island would gravitate toward the United States. Annexation, it was argued, would eliminate Spanish tariffs; prevent, in the spirit of the Monroe Doctrine, the extension of European influence in the Western Hemisphere; and perhaps lead to more effective suppression of the African slave trade, since Cuba was a key station in that traffic. And, as the years passed, some influential Americans argued that possession of the island was necessary for the protection of a future Isthmian canal. Thomas Jefferson, Henry Clay, John C. Calhoun, James Monroe, and John Quincy Adams all stressed the importance of eventually acquiring Cuba for the national welfare. They considered the "no-transfer" policy only a stopgap measure to hinder European aggression against the island, or European pressure on Spain to sell it, until the United States was prepared to accept the challenge of annexation.

20. John Quincy Adams to Hugh Nelson, April 28, 1823, in Robert Smith (ed.), *What Happened in Cuba?* (New York, 1963), 29; Langley, *Cuba Policy*, 4; Philip Foner, *A History of Cuba and Its Relations with the United States* (2 vols.; New York, 1962–63), I, 127. A month before the dispatch, however, Adams had been willing to let England seize Cuba rather than contest such an action. See Allan Nevins (ed.), *Diary of John Quincy Adams* (New York, 1928), 295. The policy was boldly reaffirmed in December, 1852, by Secretary of State Edward Everett in a message to the French minister to the United States. See Edward Everett to Count Sartiges, December 1, 1852, in Smith (ed.), *What Happened?*, 50–55.

In his "no-transfer" dispatch, Adams indicated that "in looking forward to the very probable course of half a century, it is scarcely possible to resist the conviction that the annexation of Cuba to our federal republic will be indispensable to the continuance and integrity of the Union itself." [21]

Sectional overtones were never entirely absent in the national dialogue over Cuba. Philip Foner has suggested that as early as the 1820s southern slaveowners led in advocating acquisition because they feared that slavery might be abolished in Cuba and that this might negatively affect slavery in the South.[22] Sectional motivation, however, was subordinate to national interest during these early years. Even in the 1850s, when the questions of slavery and Cuba became virtually inseparable, two northern presidents—Franklin Pierce of New Hampshire and James Buchanan of Pennsylvania—made determined efforts to purchase Cuba from Spain.

Before 1850, the major division over the question of Caribbean expansion was between Whigs and Democrats rather than between the North and South. The expansionist wing of the Democratic party showed interest in the absorption of Caribbean lands, whereas Whigs often balked at such proposals. Democratic President James K. Polk was the only American president who tried to buy Cuba before 1850, and western Democrats led the all-Mexico movement during the Mexican War. Whigs, on the other hand, headed opposition to war with Mexico in 1846, to the all-Mexico movement during the war, and to Polk's plan to acquire Yucatan in 1848.[23]

Northern Whigs often opposed tropical expansion because they were hostile to slavery; but this does not ac-

21. Adams to Hugh Nelson, April 28, 1823, in Smith (ed.), *What Happened?*, 27–28.
22. Foner, *History of Cuba*, I, 139.
23. Merk, *Manifest Destiny and Mission*, 94, 153, 206–97. Whigs and Democrats also disagreed on the propriety of expeditions from the United States to conquer Caribbean countries, Whigs generally

count for southern Whig antagonism. Actually Whigs of both sections were traditionally conservative concerning expansion: "Whigs, as a party, were fearful of spreading out too widely. They adhered to the philosophy of concentration of national authority in a limited area, as contrasted with the Democratic philosophy of dispersion of authority over wide spaces."

Democrats like Stephen Douglas, John L. O'Sullivan, and George Sanders, rather than Whigs, were the most visible crusaders for the expansionist "Young America" movement of the late 1840s and early 1850s. They believed that young American leaders had a mission to spread freedom and democracy in both the New and Old World. The example of enlightened American institutions would inspire peoples of Old World nations to break free from despotic governments, and countries in the Western Hemisphere could realize their potential by incorporation into the United States. The movement derided as "Old Fogies" Democratic moderates who advocated restraint in expansion and caution in European involvement. At times, its nationalistic zeal passed beyond mere speech. Sanders, for instance, tried to provide muskets for revolutionary leaders in Europe during the 1848 uprisings. Years later, as the American consul-designate to London, he publicly advocated the assassination of Louis Napoleon III and gave a dinner party for Mazzini, Garibaldi, Kossuth, and other famed European revolutionaries. O'Sullivan, a New York editor, championed European dissidents in his *Democratic Review* and became party to intrigues intended to bring Cuba into the American union.[24]

---

opposing such expeditions and Democrats sometimes forming the backbone of support for them. See James Fred Rippy, "Anglo-American Filibusters and the Gadsden Treaty," *Hispanic American Historical Review*, V (1922), 172–76; Langley, *Cuba Policy*, 29; Durwood Long, "Alabama Opinion and the Whig Cuban Policy, 1849–1851," *Alabama Historical Quarterly*, XXV (1963), 277–78.

24. The "Young America" movement derived from an address of

Thus, before 1850, American expansionists looked southward with a nationalistic vision. Political party affiliation characterized the movement far more than regionalism. But in the 1850s manifest destiny became sectionalized. Northerners and southerners could still agree on the feasibility of new territory, but they could not agree as to which foreign countries were acceptable or as to what institutions would be permitted in the new acquisitions. A once broadly based movement became seriously divided. This division originated in the debate over the status of slavery in the Mexican Cession, but did not crystallize until the passage of the Kansas-Nebraska Act in 1854, which insured that the question of slavery expansion would be a major national problem for years to come. Following the act, there arose a concerted southern movement to extend slavery into the tropics—particularly Nicaragua and Mexico—and to annex Cuba as a new slave state. Simultaneously, northern antislavery leaders, many of them expansionist in principle, bridled themselves against what they considered further concessions to a "slave power." The dispute over Caribbean expansion became an important element in the matrix of events that led to the American Civil War.

Ralph Waldo Emerson to the Boston Mercantile Association in 1844. John L. O'Sullivan adopted Emerson's phrase of "Young America" in the *Democratic Review* and connected the idea with the concept of "Manifest Destiny." See Julius Pratt, "John L. O'Sullivan and Manifest Destiny," *New York History*, XIV (1933), 219; Merle Curti, "Young America," *American Historical Review*, XXXII (1926), 36–37; Albert K. Weinberg, *Manifest Destiny: A Study of Nationalist Expansionism in American History* (Baltimore, 1935), 111–29; Merle E. Curti, "George N. Sanders—American Patriot of the Fifties," *South Atlantic Quarterly*, XXVII (1928), 79–87; Robert W. Johannsen, "Stephen Douglas and the American Mission," in John G. Clark (ed.), *The Frontier Challenge: Responses to the Trans-Mississippi West* (Lawrence, 1971), 112–17, 123–32; Willis Frederick Dunbar, *Lewis Cass* (Grand Rapids, 1970), 53–71.

II

From Manifest Destiny to Sectional Destiny

Mid-nineteenth century American expansionists had no compassion for formerly great nations, such as Spain, which were now in a state of decline. Earlier in the century Spain had lost an empire in the New World; but expansionists insisted that she now be deprived of Cuba, her remaining valuable possession in the Western Hemisphere. To the "manifest destiny" generation, Spain had become the "sick man" of Europe, and sympathy for underdogs was not part of expansionist sentiment. A southerner expressed these attitudes in a letter to an acquaintance who had been reluctant to support American acquisition of the island: "Spain, poor old Spain, who once covered the surface of the great deep with her Armada, once the seat of pomp and power and grandeur, finds herself stripped of all her jewels, save one, which nought but *family* pride prevents her parting with. Our destiny is onwards." [1]

Given the nature of events between the Mexican War and the Civil War, it is remarkable that Cuba never became United States property. American presidents during this period supported annexation of the island, and three of them made determined efforts to purchase it. American diplomats in Europe devised complex schemes to force Spain to cede the island; in fact, it was an un-

1. William H. Smith to James Foster, January 3, 1853, in James Foster Papers, Louisiana State University Department of Archives and Manuscripts, Baton Rouge.

official axiom that to secure appointment as minister to a European power one had to be a fervent believer in America's mission to obtain Cuba. A large segment of Congress supported that goal, as did most Americans. Considerable public support could even have been mustered for going to war with Spain for Cuba. In addition, a number of filibuster expeditions to invade Cuba were planned in the United States, and some actually left American soil for that purpose.

Not surprisingly, expansionist James K. Polk opened the extended American campaign for Cuba. Urged on by many of the "Young America" stalwarts of his party—including Stephen Douglas, John L. O'Sullivan, and Lewis Cass—the president pressured a skeptical James Buchanan (his secretary of state) in June of 1848 to approach the Spanish government concerning a possible sale of the island. Buchanan authorized American Minister to Spain Romulus Saunders to offer up to $100 million for Cuba. The Spanish government, however, sharply rebuffed the initiative, thereby giving Polk's expansionism an uncommon defeat. Polk left office in 1849, and the succeeding administration of Zachary Taylor (and of Millard Fillmore after Taylor's death) de-emphasized diplomacy to obtain Cuba—although Secretary of State Edward Everett claimed that the United States would eventually acquire Cuba when he rejected an English-French proposal for a tripartite convention that would establish a British-French-American guarantee of Spanish control of Cuba.[2]

2. Milo Milton Quaife (ed.), *The Diary of James K. Polk* (4 vols.; Chicago, 1910), III, 446–93; St. George Leakin Sioussat, "James Buchanan," in Samuel Flagg Bemis (ed.), *The American Secretaries of State and Their Diplomacy* (10 vols.; New York, 1927–29), V, 298–300; Edward Everett to Count Sartiges, December 1, 1852, in Smith (ed.), *What Happened?*, 50–55. The tripartite proposal was initiated by Spain, apprehensive at the time about potential filibuster movements against Cuba from the United States. See Robert Benson Leard, "Bonds of Destiny: The United States and Cuba,

The federal government would once again bid seriously for Cuba in 1854, when Franklin Pierce was president. But in the interim, the diplomats were superseded by a group of Cuban revolutionaries and their American sympathizers. These agitators argued that the Cuban people anxiously awaited American aid to throw off Spanish rule and that the only way to free Cuba from the grasp of Spain would be to attack it from American soil.

The idea of independence and possible annexation to the United States actually attracted only a limited following on the island itself. Strongest backing came from some of the creole sugar planters, particularly the wealthy members of the *Club de la Habana*. Many Cuban creoles felt that Spanish trade restrictions hurt them financially; in addition, creoles resented the favored position of Peninsular Spaniards in the corrupt colonial bureaucracy. Some creoles, moreover, feared that continued Spanish rule portended the abolition of slavery and perhaps a dominant status for Cuba's blacks.

These planters were only slightly troubled by abolitionism in Spain. Although abolition had been proposed in the Spanish Cortes as early as 1811, the emancipation movement had traditionally been weak. What they did fear, however, was that Spain might bow to persistent antislavery pressure from the British government, which over the past half century, had wrested numerous concessions from Spain in this direction. In 1817, for instance, Spain had agreed reluctantly to a treaty with Britain that theoretically eradicated Cuba's African slave trade. Subsequent agreements imposed by Britain attempted to make this treaty more binding than it proved to be. Particularly alarming to Cuban slave interests were the activities of

1848–1861" (Ph.D. dissertation, University of California, 1953), 105–18. See also *Congressional Globe*, 29th Cong., 1st Sess., 92, 96, for resolutions of Senator David Levy of Florida in 1845 requesting Polk to initiate negotiations for Cuba.

David Turnbull, British consul in Havana from November, 1840, to June, 1842. Turnbull labored for a treaty between Britain and Spain that would allow a mixed Spanish-British commission to take a census of slaves illegally introduced into Cuba since 1820, with the result that these slaves would be freed. Since illegally imported slaves made up the bulk of the plantation slave force in Cuba, such a treaty would have tremendously undermined the island's slave system. Cubans who favored annexation to the United States argued that it would reduce the British threat to slavery in Cuba. In addition, should Britain succeed in curtailing the slave trade, the surplus of slaves in the upper slave states in the American South would take care of the deficiency.[3]

In the late 1840s, these proannexation elements were investigating a number of ways of getting Americans involved in their cause. In 1848, for instance, they approached the American Mexican War general, William Worth, concerning a possible movement of discharged veteran soldiers to Cuba. They also opened channels of communication with John L. O'Sullivan and other expansionist Democrats, as well as with the Cuban exile population in the United States. Narciso López, an unlikely candidate for subversive activity, emerged as their leader in the late 1840s.

Venezuelan by birth, López at a young age had participated in Spanish army operations against the revolutionary, Simon Bolívar. Later López served the Spanish government in various administrative posts in both Spain and Cuba. But he lost his posts, suffered business failures, and cast his fate with the anti-Spanish faction in Cuba. In 1848 he fled to the United States during a Spanish arrest of revolutionaries. López quickly began plan-

3. Knight, *Slave Society in Cuba*, 25–26, 88–90, 102; Arthur F. Corwin, *Spain and the Abolition of Slavery in Cuba, 1817–1886* (Austin, 1967), 19–28, 53–55, 69–70.

ning for a United States-based invasion to liberate Cuba and attracted considerable support, particularly among the exiled Cubans in New York City. By 1849 he was ready for action. Coordinating his activities with the Havana Club, he recruited men and by July stood poised for a two-pronged attack on Cuba. López's main body of troops was with him in New York, while another eight hundred men gathered in the area of Round Island, near New Orleans.

Word of López's preparations, however, reached the federal government. Even Polk, the opportunistic expansionist, had disparaged filibustering as a means of acquiring Cuba. The purchase plan had been partly intended to forestall such attempts. Zachary Taylor, Polk's successor, proved even more adamantly opposed to filibustering. Taylor issued a proclamation against the expedition, had his secretary of state, John Clayton, alert district attorneys in key port cities, dispatched naval vessels to blockade Round Island, and had López's two ships in New York seized.[4] Many of López's followers temporarily abandoned the cause.

The Cuba agitators were not dissuaded by the government's show of power. John L. O'Sullivan began organizing another expedition from New York, but his plans to clear a ship for Cuba *before* picking up filibuster passengers went awry when the Spanish consul was informed of his activities by a disloyal follower. O'Sullivan's steamer was seized, and he and some of his followers were brought to trial.[5]

López, married to the daughter of a Cuban aristocrat and strongly proslavery, switched his focus to the South

4. Foner, *History of Cuba*, I, 53–55, 177, II, 10, 42–44; Robert G. Caldwell, *The Lopez Expeditions to Cuba, 1848–1851* (Princeton, 1915), 8–12, 16–17, 43–56; Anderson G. Quisenberry, *Lopez's Expeditions to Cuba, 1850 and 1851* (Louisville, 1906), 28–30; Quaife (ed.), *Diary of Polk*, III, 475–77, 499–500; Leard, "Bonds of Destiny," 51–57.

5. Leard, "Bonds of Destiny," 81–82.

following his initial disappointment. After his 1849 expedition dissolved, he transferred his headquarters from New York to New Orleans. López also approached prominent southerners and offered to cede leadership to one of them in order to win increased southern support. He failed in his quest—Robert E. Lee, Jefferson Davis, and John Quitman (the governor of Mississippi) declined the offer —but he did succeed in winning endorsements from influential southerners. Quitman apparently gave serious thought to heading the movement; he contributed money, gave López military advice, and suggested recruits. Laurence J. Sigur, exiled Cuban and editor of the New Orleans *Delta*, also gave money to the cause, provided newspaper endorsements, and permitted López to use his home as headquarters. John Henderson, a Mississippi cotton planter and former United States senator, gave López substantial backing.[6]

Less than a year after his abortive first attempt at conquest, López prepared to try again; and in the spring of 1850 he and some six hundred adventurers, almost exclusively Americans, moved against the town of Cárdenas, Cuba. They captured the town easily, but failed to get the local populace actively involved in their support and decided to withdraw when faced with formidable Spanish military opposition. The return to Key West, Florida, aboard their steamboat *Creole* proved harrowing. The filibusters narrowly escaped capture by the Spanish vessel *Pizarro* and later barely avoided detention by United States officials at Key West for violation of the Neutrality Law of 1818, which prohibited private military expeditions from United States soil to foreign countries. The adventurers avoided arrest by completely disembarking

6. C. Stanley Urban, "The Idea of Progress and Southern Imperialism: New Orleans and the Caribbean, 1845–1861" (Ph.D. dissertation, Northwestern University, 1943), 272*n*, 284; Henry S. Foote, *Casket of Reminiscences* (Washington, D.C., 1874), 356; Foner, *History of Cuba*, II, 47–49.

from the *Creole* within ten minutes after arrival at the Key West pier—including the vacating of wounded from the ship. This must rank as one of the more successful accomplishments in filibuster history.

The United States government again interceded. Federal officials confiscated the *Creole*, and a federal grand jury in New Orleans indicted sixteen of the movement's leaders, including López, Henderson, and Quitman. Quitman, a committed states' righter, refused at first to surrender to federal officials on the grounds that his prosecution would infringe on Mississippi's sovereignty; but he eventually resigned his governorship and went to New Orleans. Three hung juries, however, stymied the government's case, and all suits were dismissed.[7] López immediately resumed expedition preparations.

López intended for his next expedition to coincide with an uprising in Puerto Principe, a city in central Cuba. Spanish officials, however, became aware of the conspiracy and began arresting suspects. In addition, a rebel challenge near Trinidad, on the south side of Cuba, was put down. Early reports in the American press on these developments were not clear; and López, anxious to proceed, optimistically determined that the rebellion was in progress. On August 3, 1851, he departed from New Orleans with over four hundred men. He arrived in Cuba on August 11 by way of Key West and divided his men into two groups. One group accompanied him on the march inland, while the second, under Colonel William Crittenden (nephew of United States Attorney General John Crittenden), guarded supplies. Aid from sympathetic Cubans

7. Caldwell, *Lopez Expeditions*, 57–82; Ray Broussard, "Governor John A. Quitman and the Lopez Expeditions of 1851–1852," *Journal of Mississippi History*, XXVIII (1966), 113–17; Henry G. Connor, *John Archibald Campbell: Associate Justice of the United States Supreme Court* (Boston, 1920), 91; Leard, "Bonds of Destiny," 79n.

again failed to materialize, and government troops quickly overwhelmed both parts of López's force. Most of the filibusters, including López, were killed in battle or executed afterward. Some of those taken prisoner were sentenced to labor in Spain's quicksilver mines and were later pardoned. Crittenden, one of those executed, wrote to his uncle about López's miscalculation of the extent of his popular support in Cuba: "I was deceived by Lopez. He, as well as the public press, assured me that the island was in a state of prosperous revolution." [8] Such unfounded optimism would plague other filibusters in coming years.

In spite of López's dismal end, his expeditions served as an initiation ceremony for a persistent American filibuster movement in the 1850s. Virtually every year up to the Civil War, American adventurers would formulate schemes to invade, or would actually invade, some part of the Caribbean region. Many of the leaders of these escapades had either fought with López or helped in planning. John Quitman of Mississippi, who assumed charge of the Cuban movement after López's death, is a prime example. John Henderson and L. J. Sigur transferred their allegiance to Quitman. John Thrasher, an American resident of Cuba, member of the Havana Club, and editor of a Cuban industrial journal that published implicitly proannexation sentiments, proceeded to the United States and joined Quitman after his pardon for support of López's invaders. Many of López's men, such as Roberdeau Wheat, Theodore O'Hara, Louis Schlessinger, and Achilles Kewen, later involved themselves in William Walker's intervention in Nicaragua in the middle and late 1850s. Callender Fayssoux, mate of the *Creole* on López's Cárdenas expedition, later served as Walker's naval commander. For the

8. Leard, "Bonds of Destiny," 87–90; Caldwell, *Lopez Expeditions*, 83–113; Broussard, "Quitman and the Lopez Expeditions," 119; Quisenberry, *Lopez's Expeditions to Cuba*, 90.

rest of the 1850s, veterans of López's campaigns kept each other posted on new filibuster expeditions to Cuba and elsewhere. Frequently they became leading officers or recruiters for later filibustering.

When word reached New Orleans that Spanish authorities had executed Crittenden and his men, pro-López mobs responded by gutting the office of the local Spanish newspaper, *La Union,* destroying property in the Spanish consulate, and raiding various Spanish coffeehouses and cigar shops. This was the most extreme reaction in the United States to the news. But the executions aroused considerable resentment in many parts of the country,[9] for López's cause transcended American sectionalism. Although he had directed his most recent recruiting efforts to the South, he had gained considerable support in New York City and elsewhere in the North. Northerners, as well as exiled Cubans and European revolutionary refugees, had made substantial contributions to his movement in terms of manpower and financing.

Nevertheless, events following López's thrusts at Cuba had significant sectional implications. Rumors were rife in the South, and in the rest of the United States, that Spain, at Britain's urging, was considering emancipating Cuba's slaves. These rumors were partly based on a misunderstanding of the new Spanish contract-labor policy. In 1847 Spain had inaugurated a policy of importing Chinese into Cuba on an eight-year contract-labor basis; and in 1849 this labor system was extended to include the Yucatecan Indians. From 1847 to 1853 an estimated thirty thousand Chinese laborers had entered Havana. Many Americans viewed these actions as an attempt by Spain to gradually replace the Cuban slave system. Actually the

9. New Orleans *Daily Picayune,* August 22, 1851; Leard, "Bonds of Destiny," 92–101.

Spanish government had implemented the policy in response to the fears of many Cuban whites that the percentage of Africans in Cuba had grown to such dangerous proportions that race revolt threatened.

However, Americans had valid cause to believe an emancipation policy for Cuba was being considered. British diplomatic pressure against slavery in Cuba reached an all-time high in the early 1850s. Lord Palmerston, British foreign secretary, issued a virtual ultimatum to Spain demanding the enforcement of agreements to suppress the slave trade. Members of Parliament proposed that Spain surrender Cuba to England in compensation for defaulted Spanish bonds held by Britishers. And special emphasis was put on the need for Spain to finally free the Cuban emancipados—blacks taken from captured slave vessels. According to the treaty of 1817, such Negroes were supposed to get a certificate of emancipation, then work for the Spanish government as either servants or free labor, and gain freedom after four years. The emancipados, however, had traditionally been reenslaved, despite the treaty's stipulations.

British pressures in this direction were nothing new, but in the early 1850s the Spanish government demonstrated an unusual willingness to seriously consider British demands. Though Spain had thoroughly crushed the López invasion, the experience of being invaded induced Spanish officials to investigate means to prevent a repetition. The solution chosen involved more defense preparation and partial compliance with British demands. Spanish officials intimated in various ways that should invasion occur, they would free Cuba's slaves and arm them rather than have the island fall to the United States. To demonstrate that they were serious, Spanish officials took a few steps in the direction of abolition, especially after Juan de la Pezuela became captain general of Cuba in 1853.

Pezuela, a known abolitionist from his term as governor of Puerto Rico (1849–1851), issued orders calling for emancipados imported since 1835 to be freed and called for the punishment of people who had organized slave-trading expeditions. He also instructed the Cuban press to discuss emancipation, allowed intermarriage between black women and white men, and enabled free blacks to participate in his militia.

The Spanish government hoped that these halfway steps, with the implied threat of full emancipation, would prove enough to deter any future filibustering. Certainly southerners would look askance at any plans risking such an outcome. These actions would also help reduce what had become the "high-water mark of British abolitionist pressure" against Spain.[10]

The Spanish plan functioned to the extent that Americans, particularly southerners, recognized the threat of abolition. As early as December, 1852, American Minister to Spain Daniel Barringer reported to the United States government that orders had been delivered to the captain general of Cuba to arm the slaves and give them control over Cuba in the event of an American invasion. Pezuela's activities reinforced the report. Pierre Soulé, the "Young American" who succeeded Barringer as minister to Spain in 1853, wrote Secretary of State William Marcy that Cuba would soon be lost "to the civilized world" because of emancipation, barring American intervention. Soulé asserted that Spain, with England's backing, planned to free all Africans imported into Cuba since 1821. William H. Robertson, acting United States consul in Havana, confirmed the alarms of Barringer and Soulé. In a series of letters to Marcy in late 1853 and early 1854, Robertson

10. Corwin, *Spain and the Abolition of Slavery*, 112–15; Urban, "The Idea of Progress," 450; Caldwell, *Lopez Expeditions*, 22–27; Allan Nevins, *Ordeal of the Union* (2 vols.; New York, 1947), II, 348.

reported that emancipation had already commenced, that Pezuela was arming the Cuban blacks, and that Cuban whites were waiting in desperation for American help since they expected that Negro rule would be a calamity both for the island and for the United States. Congressman Alexander Stephens, the future Vice President of the Confederacy, complained to his brother about alleged British and French involvement in Spanish emancipation policy, and said about Cuba: "We must and will have it and we can not permit them to go on with their policy of filling it with Africans first." A Texan annexationist warned that England had "the beautiful queen of the Antilles by the throat" and would not relinquish her grip "until her bleeding victim lies writhing and dying in the dust suffocated by a million negro hands!" [11]

Spain had struck a sensitive nerve. Southerners remembered all too vividly the bloody rebellion in the French West Indies colony of Saint-Domingue around the turn of the century. They viewed that rebellion and its consequence—the creation of a black republic—in the worst possible light: the very word "Haiti" evoked images of black slaves devastating property and torturing and murdering their former masters. Southern whites commiserated with the many white Haitians who fled to the United States, shuddered at their horror stories, and feared that the revolution would eventually infect their own slaves. That Haiti's economy stagnated in subsequent years—

11. Soulé to Marcy, December 23, 1853, Robertson to Marcy, February 14, March 20, April 21, 25, May 7, 10, 11, 1854, and Marcy to Alexander M. Clayton, October 25, 1853, all in William R. Manning (ed.), *Diplomatic Correspondence of the United States: Inter-American Affairs, 1831–1860* (12 vols.; Washington, D.C., 1932–39), II, 733–34, 737, 748–49, 765–66, 768, 772, 782–83, 785–86; Basil Rauch, *American Interest in Cuba, 1848–1855* (New York, 1948), 275; Alexander Stephens to Linton Stephens, May 9, 1854, in Alexander Stephens Papers, University of North Carolina Library, Chapel Hill; *Congressional Globe*, 34th Cong., 1st Sess., Appendix, 1294.

sugar, cotton, and cocoa production all declined—contributed to the negative image.[12] Reports that Spanish officials were arming blacks in Cuba frightened a society already worried that the example of Haiti might influence Negroes on southern plantations. Reports that Spanish officials were encouraging intermarriage between the races alarmed a people who disparaged racial amalgamation as "mongrelization." Rumors of an impending total emancipation and a British-Spanish treaty to secure that end increased southern anxieties even more.

Instead of intimidating southern expansionists, however, Spain succeeded only in provoking calls for a preventive invasion. The *Arkansas State Gazette and Democrat*, for instance, urged suspension of the neutrality laws to facilitate an invasion of Cuba before Spain could enact its emancipation program. John Quitman accelerated his military preparations because he feared "a negro or mongrel empire" near the southern border would touch off slave revolts in the Gulf states. A correspondent in the office of the New Orleans *Daily Delta* informed Secretary of War Jefferson Davis that people in the Deep South felt Cuba had to be conquered quickly if she were to be secured "in such a state as to make her valuable to the South." [13]

Many southern expansionists failed to see that Spain threatened emancipation simply as a means to curtail filibustering. Instead, they concluded that complete abolition was imminent and that only American acquisition, through filibustering or some other means, could prevent "another

12. Winthrop Jordan, *White Over Black: American Attitudes Toward the Negro, 1550–1812* (Chapel Hill, 1968), 380–84; James G. Leyburn, *The Haitian People* (Rev. ed.; New Haven, 1966), 23–95, 250–62.

13. *Arkansas State Gazette and Democrat*, May 26, July 21, 1854; Quitman to B. Dill, February 9, 1854, in John Quitman Papers, Mississippi Department of Archives and History; Alexander Walker to A. G. Haley, June 15, 1854, in Jefferson Davis Papers, Library of Congress.

Haiti" off the southern coast. Action was needed: "With Cuba as a free negro colony but a few leagues distant from our most populous Slave States it would not be difficult to destroy the efficiency of that class of our population and render abolition desirable with us. It therefore behooves our government to step in between these ambitious propagandists and their prey." [14] The Louisiana General Assembly on March 16, 1854, approved resolutions inviting the United States government to act in respect to Cuba, saying that it viewed "with regret and alarm the policy recently inaugurated by the government of Spain in the Island of Cuba, the manifest object and effect of which must be the abolition of slavery in that colony and the sacrifice of the white race." Politicians and the press throughout the South invoked the term "Africanization" to describe what they assumed to be the Spanish program for Cuba, and few southerners needed anyone to tell them that the word meant Negro rule as in Haiti.[15]

The specter of emancipation brought a sense of immediacy and crisis to the annexation question in the South. Time suddenly became crucial. In the past many expansionists had assumed that if the United States were patient, the island, like "ripe fruit," would fall into its hands. Now the possibility of American ownership might slip away forever, if action were not taken immediately.

Many northerners also were concerned over possible abolition in Cuba. Few of them believed in racial equality, and the thought of Negro rule was anathema. The Demo-

14. Clarksville (Tennessee) *Jeffersonian*, January 29, September 28, 1853; See also *De Bow's Review*, XVII (1854), 222, XVIII (1855), 311; *Texas State Gazette*, June 24, September 9, 1854, May 19, 1855; Richmond *Daily Dispatch*, May 10, 1854; Edward B. Bryan, "Cuba and the Tripartite Treaty," *Southern Quarterly Review*, IX (1854), 16.

15. "Abolition of Slavery in Cuba," *House Miscellaneous Documents*, 33rd Cong., 1st Sess., No. 79; *Texas State Gazette*, May 27, June 24, 1854; John Quitman to Franklin Pierce, undated, in John Quitman Papers, Mississippi Department of Archives and History.

cratic New York *Herald,* for instance, fulminated that it would be "suicidal on our part to tolerate the erection of a free negro State, in so rich and fertile an island as Cuba, within a few miles of our Southern frontier." [16] But northerners rarely felt that their immediate interests would be threatened by an end to slavery in Cuba. After all, few northerners owned slave plantations that could be affected by "another Haiti." In the sense that the threat of "Africanization" caused southerners to feel that Cuban acquisition was urgent, it helped sectionalize the issue.

A more tangible factor than the vague, but persistent, emancipation threat also contributed to the sectionalizing of the Cuban annexation question. The heightening of tension between North and South caused by Stephen Douglas' controversial Kansas-Nebraska Act of 1854 intensified sectionalism concerning Caribbean expansion, particularly in respect to Cuba. The territorial issue had been somewhat dormant since the Compromise of 1850; but when Douglas opened the Kansas and Nebraska territories to slavery—territories that had been closed to slavery by the Missouri Compromise of 1820 (which had prohibited slavery in the territory of the Louisiana purchase above the parallel 36°30'), sectional disputes broke out. Northern antislavery interests claimed that their section and cause had been cheated and vowed that they would intensify their efforts against slavery expansion. Congressman Benjamin Pringle of New York remarked to his colleagues that the Kansas-Nebraska Act would be "the last advantage that slavery will gain over freedom in this country." The moderate New York *Times,* on May 26, the day after Congress passed the act, noted "a growing and profound determination among the masses of the free States that slavery shall not extend itself." Although antislavery concern focused on Kansas, Cuba was such a visible target for

16. New York *Herald,* July 4, 1854.

southern expansionists that antislavery interests increasingly disavowed interest in annexing the island: "There was a time when the North would have consented to annex Cuba, but the Nebraska wrong has forever rendered annexation impossible." [17]

Conversely, the Kansas-Nebraska Act encouraged southerners in their desire to expand slavery; and the more antislavery interests railed, the more determined southern expansionists became. While many southern leaders fought for the admission of Kansas to the union as a slave state, they also found the prospect of expansion into Cuba increasingly attractive. There was a significant burst of enthusiasm in the southern states for acquiring the island as a means of combatting the antislavery movement.

The Democratic convention for the Arkansas second congressional district resolved in May, 1854, that Cuban annexation would do more to protect slavery than "compromise with fanatics and abolitionists." A. Dudley Mann, a Virginian who was assistant secretary of state and a close friend of Secretary of War Jefferson Davis, wrote a southern congressman that Cuba was "essential to the South both in a political and geographical point of view." Some southerners even asserted that the significance of the Kansas-Nebraska Act was not so much that slavery would ever find a home in those territories, but that the act recognized the *principle* of slavery expansion and would facilitate the extension of slavery into the tropics. The New Orleans *Daily Picayune* claimed that the Kansas-Nebraska debate, ostensibly concerned with the Northwest, was actually a struggle over Cuban acquisition, and that the act had ratified the broad principle "upon which alone, if Cuba is ever acquired, it can be received safely

17. *Congressional Globe*, 33rd Cong., 1st Sess., Appendix, 889; New York *Times* and New York *Courier and Enquirer*, quoted in James Ford Rhodes, *History of the United States from the Compromise of 1850* (9 vols.; New York, 1900–28), II, 33n.

to the Southern States." Alexander Stephens termed Cuba a greater issue than Kansas.[18] Some southern newspapers such as the Natchez *Daily Courier* and the Charleston *Courier* payed more attention to the Cuba movement than to the debate over Kansas in the spring of 1854. Many southern leaders thought that Cuba offered a greater opportunity to the expansion of slavery than did the American West because Cuba's climate and topography were better suited to plantation agriculture. Cuba's proximity to the South and distance from the North gave southerners an added advantage. And since Cuba was settled, whereas the western territory was undeveloped, it could be brought into the union more quickly.

Following the Kansas-Nebraska Act, an impressive number of influential southerners gave strong support to the Cuba movement both privately and publicly. Governor James Broome of Florida advocated Cuba's acquisition to his state's legislature. Congressman Lawrence Keitt of South Carolina confided, "I am for Cuba—and leave the consequences," and exclaimed to a Lynchburg, Virginia, audience that Cuba "must be ours." The Southern Commercial Convention of January, 1855, called for the acquisition of Cuba. John Cunningham, a Charleston Know-Nothing, tried to get a resolution through the South Carolina house calling for the acquisition of Cuba. The prominent Robert Toombs, senator from Georgia, wrote

18. *Arkansas State Gazette and Democrat*, May 19, 1854; A. Dudley Mann to Lawrence Keitt, August 24, 1855, in Lawrence Keitt Papers, Duke University Library, Durham, North Carolina; New Orleans *Daily Picayune*, June 9, 1854; Alexander Stephens to W. W. Burwell (the editor of the Baltimore *Patriot*), May 7, 1854, in Ulrich B. Phillips (ed.), "The Correspondence of Robert Toombs, Alexander H. Stephens, and Howell Cobb," *Annual Report of the American Historical Association for the Year 1911* (2 vols.; Washington, D.C., 1913), II, 344. See also Josiah James Evans to Benjamin Perry, January 19, 1858, in Benjamin Perry Papers, Alabama Department of Archives and History, Montgomery; Caleb G. Forshey to John Quitman, May 20, 1857, in John Quitman Papers, Harvard University Library.

in a private letter of his desire for Cuba; and the Richmond *Enquirer* declared: "The acquisition of Cuba is the only measure of policy in regard to which the people of the South feel any special and present interest." [19]

Many of these expansionists were arguing not only that the acquisition of Cuba would strengthen slavery and the South, but also that circumstances had never been so propitious for incorporating the island into the union. Urging an all-out crusade for Cuba, they warned that the South should not pass up this opportunity.

Expansionists felt confident that an immediate effort would succeed primarily because England and France had become embroiled in a war against Russia in the Crimea. Since Americans commonly believed that both countries had designs on Cuba, and since many Americans feared that an attempt to acquire Cuba would be countered by English and French force (or perhaps even preemptive annexation), the distraction of a European war was an asset to the United States. Expansionist southern newspapers such as the Yazoo City *Weekly Whig* and the widely read New Orleans *Daily Picayune* urged action before England and France disengaged themselves from the war. One of John Quitman's cofilibusters wrote him: "I think whilst the allied powers are fighting for Turkey, we might take a more substantial breakfast." Alexander Stephens emboldened Quitman: "You are right, sir; now is the time to act—Now is the time to move while England and France have their hands full in the East." American officials in Europe asserted that it was an appropriate time to strike.

19. *Journal of the Proceedings of the House of Representatives of the State of Florida, 1856*, Appendix, 17; Keitt to Susanna Sparks, February 14, 1855, in Keitt Papers; New York *Times*, October 7, 1856; New York *Herald*, January 16, 1855; New Orleans *Daily Picayune*, July 4, 1855; *Journal of the House of Representatives of the State of South Carolina, 1854*, 114; Robert Toombs to Howell Cobb, August 1, 1854, in R. P. Brooks (ed.), "Howell Cobb Papers," *Georgia Historical Quarterly*, VI (1922), 154; Richmond *Enquirer*, June 20, 1854, quoted in New York *Herald*, June 22, 1854.

E. B. Buchanan, United States consul to La Rochelle, France, advised Secretary of War Jefferson Davis that the Crimean War and revolution in Spain gave the United States a free hand regarding Cuba. American Minister to England James Buchanan apprised his political ally John Slidell, United States senator from Louisiana, that Britain would avoid war with the United States over Cuba at all costs. The British public was even "preparing for such an event." [20]

The apparent receptivity to expansionism of the Democratic administration also encouraged proannexationists to consider the time appropriate for an initiative toward Cuba. President Franklin Pierce had informed the nation of his position on expansion in his inaugural address a year earlier: "The policy of my administration will not be controlled by any timid forebodings of evil from expansion. Indeed, it is not to be disguised that our attitude as a nation and our position on the globe render the acquisition of certain possessions not within our jurisdiction eminently important for our protection, if not in the future essential for the preservation of the rights of commerce and the peace of the world."

Known expansionists dominated Pierce's cabinet. Secretary of State Marcy had supported Polk's Cuban pur-

20. Yazoo City (Mississippi) *Weekly Whig*, April 21, 1854; New Orleans *Daily Picayune*, March 23, 1854; R. A. Love to Quitman, May 24, 1854, and F. R. Witter to Quitman, October 17, 1854, both in John Quitman Papers, Mississippi Department of Archives and History; typewritten copy, Stephens to Quitman, February 24, 1855, in Quitman Family Papers, Mississippi Department of Archives and History, Jackson; E. B. Buchanan to Davis, August 1, 1854, in Davis Papers, Library of Congress; copy of James Buchanan to Slidell, May 23, 1854, in James Buchanan Papers, Historical Society of Pennsylvania, Philadelphia. Northern expansionist newspapers uttered similar sentiments. The New York *Herald* of May 3, 1854, stated: "The day has come for a positive and conclusive settlement with Spain concerning the island of Cuba. We may have it now, and avoid war; but if we hesitate . . . till the European war is over, we may be driven for our security and our rights in the Gulf of Mexico, into a collision with England and France."

chase scheme in 1848 and would support the annexation of Hawaii in 1855. Jefferson Davis had endorsed annexation of Cuba while in Congress and was widely believed to have influence with the president. Attorney General Caleb Cushing was notoriously expansionistic. A. Dudley Mann expressed southern confidence in Pierce, even though the president was from New Hampshire: "I feel confident that the President will succeed in purchasing Cuba. This will be glory enough for his administration."

Pierce also packed the European diplomatic corps with expansionists. He appointed Senator Pierre Soulé, the fiery Louisianian, to the crucial post of minister to Spain. James Buchanan, whose outlook toward annexation of Cuba had improved since his service in Polk's cabinet, was designated minister to England. None other than John L. O'Sullivan, "manifest destiny's" mouthpiece, became minister to Portugal. August Belmont, a leading New York financier and nephew of expansionist Senator Slidell of Louisiana, held the ministry at The Hague. In addition, known expansionists held minor diplomatic posts throughout Europe. "Young America" was elated with these choices, although many expansionists discounted William Marcy as being too cautious and labeled him the administration's "Old Fogy." The movement's enthusiasm was well expressed by Senator Soulé, who lauded Narciso López and called for Cuba annexation, and by the crowd of exiled Cubans in New York who serenaded Soulé in August, 1853, before he departed for Madrid.[21]

Pierce, therefore, had formed his administration for

21. James D. Richardson (comp.), *Messages and Papers of the President* (20 vols.; Washington, 1897–1917), VI, 2731–32; *Congressional Globe*, 30th Cong., 1st Sess., Appendix, 599; Ivor Spencer, *The Victor and the Spoils: A Life of William L. Marcy* (Providence, 1959), 180n, 335, 388–93; Hudson Strode, *Jefferson Davis, American Patriot* (New York, 1955), 210–11; A. Dudley Mann to Judge Nicholson (editor of the Washington *Union*), October 2, 1854, in Virginia Letters Collection, University of Virginia Library, Charlottesville; Amos Ettinger, *The Mission to Spain of Pierre Soulé, 1853–1855* (New Haven, 1932), 98–100, 174–76.

expansion. By the spring of 1854 he was in the advantageous position of having a number of means by which to pursue Cuba, if he so desired. He could, for instance, renew Polk's efforts to purchase the island from Spain. American representatives in Europe were urging such a course, suggesting that revolt in Spain, political intrigue in Europe, and the Spanish debt made a purchase attempt more feasible than in 1848.

Even before he left Washington for his overseas post, Buchanan told the president that the holders of Spanish bonds might be elicited to put pressure on Spain to sell Cuba so that the value of their bonds would increase. From London, the minister reinforced these ideas in a letter to William Marcy: "The great capitalists of Europe might be easily enlisted in its favor and probably the Queen mother." Buchanan further enunciated his faith in this method in letters to Slidell. Slidell, despite connections with Quitman's filibuster movement, responded to Buchanan's optimism and urged Marcy to cooperate fully with the minister to England. It would be foolish, warned the senator, to exclude either Belmont or the Rothschild financial interests from any negotiations to this end.[22]

Belmont, a strong purchase advocate, similarly informed Secretary of State Marcy that the "political-financial condition of Spain" was "preparing the way" for American acquisition of Cuba and that the Spanish minister to The Hague favored the sale. Soulé, who had been pursuing a course independent of Buchanan and Belmont, reasoned along similar lines in a dispatch to Marcy. Soulé detailed a complex plan that would have taken advantage of the bankruptcy and factional politics ever present in Spain. Soulé predicted that with $300,000 he could give the democratic party of Spain the financial means to take over the government, which would then cede Cuba to the

---

22. Buchanan to Marcy, April 18, 1854, in William Marcy Papers, Library of Congress; Buchanan to Slidell, May 23, 1854, and Slidell to Buchanan, June 17, August 6, 1854, in Buchanan Papers.

United States. An "elevated source" had told him so! Soulé also thought it possible that a serious revolt in Cuba would force Spain to sell the island to salvage part of the "cherished jewel." And the Queen Mother of Spain, who had spent her year's salary and needed funds, was a perfect subject for a bribe. With money in hand he could work wonders. The idea of taking advantage of Spain's financial weakness was also being discussed in expansionist circles back in the United States and was picking up support. The Richmond *Dispatch* commented: "The best course that Spain can take to replenish her exchequer is to sell the island of Cuba to the United States. It is obviously impossible that the weakest power of the old world can long retain the richest island of the new. Let her yield gracefully to her 'manifest Destiny,' sell Cuba before it is taken from her 'without a consideration,' and apply the proceeds to her 'system of railways,' the diffusion of education among her people and the promotion of morality in her Court." [23]

But should Pierce feel that war with Spain would be a better way to acquire Cuba, and that Cuba was worth a war, he had a perfect pretext for inaugurating such a conflict. On the morning of February 28, 1854, the American steamer *Black Warrior* entered the port of Havana while on its regular Mobile-New York run, with more than nine

23. Belmont to Marcy, May 31, 1854, in Marcy Papers; Soulé to Marcy, February 23, July 15, 1854, in Manning (ed.), *Diplomatic Correspondence*, XI, 739, 798; Richmond *Dispatch*, January 20, 1854. See also A. Dudley Mann to Marcy, September 4, 1854, and James Buchanan to Marcy, December 8, 1854, both in Marcy Papers. Philip S. Klein states that the holders of the Spanish bonds (including the Barrings and the Rothschilds) were ready to sell Cuba for something over $100 million if the money could be used to build up the country. The Church, too, which was threatened by confiscation of its property for government financial reasons, looked upon the sale of Cuba as feasible. See Philip S. Klein, *President James Buchanan: A Biography* (University Park, 1962), 235. The Queen Mother, Maria Christina, was interested in selling the island to build up the Spanish treasury and to avoid a future war with the United States. See Ettinger, *Mission of Pierre Soulé*, 708.

hundred bales of cotton in its hold, and was seized by Spanish authorities. Havana justified confiscation by pointing out that the vessel had failed to comply with a harbor regulation, even though the regulation was obscure and had traditionally been ignored by foreign vessels. The New York and Atlantic Steamship Company, owner of the vessel, protested the incident, which was not the first of its kind in Cuban waters.[24] Pierce unquestionably commanded an issue that could have been used to instigate a war; and some expansionists, especially in the South, urged him to do just that. The New Orleans *Daily Picayune* exclaimed: "It only remains to be seen whether our Government and people will submit to this, or make it a cause of war." A Mississippi newspaper suggested that incidents such as the *Black Warrior* seizure could only result in the United States "tearing that jewel from the Spanish crown."[25]

Should Pierce reject war and purchase as ways to acquire Cuba, he had a third alternative: he could reverse the policy of his predecessors against filibustering and endorse the widely publicized John Quitman expedition, which was nearly ready for its planned intrusion into Cuba.[26] The last Democratic president, James K. Polk, had not hesitated to use questionable methods to further

24. Samuel Bemis describes the regulation and its relation to the *Black Warrior* thus: "By informal oral agreement it was the understanding of her owners that, like similar American steamers of her class—packet ships carrying passengers and mails, in command of naval officers—she should touch at Havana free from the necessity, demanded of merchant vessels by Spanish law, of making manifest of her cargo. This was a special concession." See Bemis (ed.), *American Secretaries of State*, VI, 189. See also Henry L. Janes, "The Black Warrior Affair," *American Historical Review*, XII (1907), 280–98; New York *Herald* March 12, 1854. The *Herald* reported that one of the proprietors of the company had even gone to Washington to meet with Pierce about the problem.
25. New Orleans *Daily Picayune*, March 11, 1854; Natchez *Daily Courier*, March 10, 1854. See also *Texas State Gazette*, May 27, 1854.
26. For examples of publicity about Quitman's plans, see Richmond *Whig*, June 21, 1854; Charleston *Daily Courier*, May 29, 1854.

his expansionist goals in Oregon and Texas, and he had been very successful. A profilibuster policy, like war proposals and purchase schemes, had its adherents in the United States, particularly in the South.

Whatever action Pierce decided to take that spring of 1854, a lot would depend on whether he and southern leaders like Slidell and Quitman could come to some sort of understanding, or whether they would work at crosspurposes. It would be hard enough for the administration to overcome northern antislavery opposition to the addition of Cuba as a slave state. But a disagreement over policy between Pierce and southern expansionists would divide the movement, and this could be a fatal blow.

III

The Cuba Movement
1854–1855

◤◥◤◥◤◥◤◥◤◥◤◥◤◥◤◥◤◥◤◥◤◥◤◥◤◥◤◥◤◥◤◥

To the mobile American people of the pre-Civil War era, place of birth often bore little relation to the sectional loyalties they ultimately adopted. Origins were quickly forgotten by many who moved from their native states, even by those who migrated from the nonslaveholding states of the North to the slave regions of the South.

John Quitman was one of the more prominent Americans who quickly discarded loyalty to his original state and section. Born the son of a Lutheran pastor in Rhinebeck, New York, in 1799, Quitman taught school for a while and then studied law in Ohio. But when he traveled to Natchez, Mississippi, to practice law, he soon became a southerner. He married a girl with a small fortune in 1824 and quickly gained election to the state legislature. By 1835 he owned a cotton and sugar plantation, including some hundred and fifty slaves, and later acquired holdings in Louisiana as well as forty thousand acres in eastern Texas. In no time a prominent figure in Mississippi politics, Quitman served a short term as governor of the state (1835). Participation in the Texas revolution and Mexican War gained Quitman a considerable military reputation. As brigadier general of volunteers, he played a conspicuous role in Winfield Scott's conquest of Mexico City, and he earned further recognition when Scott appointed him military governor of the Mexican capital. Military fame furthered his career in state and national politics, compensating for his rather lackluster speaking abilities.

Even before the Mexican War, Quitman had committed himself to extremist southern politics. He supported John Calhoun and nullification in 1832, and he rarely vacillated about states' rights thereafter. In November, 1850, when he was again serving as governor, he urged the Mississippi legislature to summon a secession convention; and during his abbreviated 1851 campaign for reelection he stood for rejection of the Compromise of 1850. One historian has termed Quitman the "father of secession in Mississippi."

To Quitman, annexation of Cuba was a means of strengthening the South and states' rights within the union, given the unwillingness of the southern states to secede in 1850. He wanted Cuba to enter the union as a slave state to balance the admission of California as a free state in 1850, and he gave his support to the López movement to achieve that end. The limits that Quitman put on his involvement with López apparently were motivated by a conviction that his service to the South as governor during the crisis of 1850 was of more importance than the advantages that would accrue from his presence in the invasion force. Once the California crisis receded, however, he became more interested in actively leading an invasion of Cuba, especially when emancipation became a threat.[1]

Quitman resumed his Natchez law practice after resigning from the governorship in 1851 and opened negotiations with the Cuban Junta in New York, headed by former cohorts of López. From the summer of 1853, until April, 1854, Quitman bickered with the organization about his terms for leading the expedition. Remembering López's fate, Quitman demanded a million dollars "at his disposal" before assuming command and eventually agreed to a compromise figure of $800,000. Once agreement was achieved,

1. John K. Bettersworth, *Mississippi: A History* (Austin, 1959), 214; C. Stanley Urban, "The Abortive Quitman Filibustering Expedition, 1853–1855," *Journal of Mississippi History*, XVIII (1956), 56–57; Urban, "The Idea of Progress," 272*n*, 284.

supporters started to sell bonds; and on April 30, 1854, Quitman formally accepted leadership.[2]

Despite the professed intention of the Junta to liberate Cuba, Quitman's sights were set on annexation; for he regarded Cuba as vital to the South. He and his close associates expected that in the brief interval between Spanish rule and incorporation into the union, the Cuban planters could satisfactorily resolve the indeterminate status of the emancipado blacks. Once they were conclusively relegated to the status of slavery, Cuba could apply for admission to the union as one or more slave states, much as Texas had a decade earlier. Quitman and his friends ruled out purchase as a means to acquisition because this intermediate period would be skipped. Not only would Cuba become United States territory following purchase—in which case the free status of emancipados would be legally protected—but Pezuela would have time to free more slaves before the formal transfer of the island. In addition, if Cuba assumed a territorial status, northern antislavery forces could contest its admission as a slave state and might even succeed in incorporating it as a free state, as they already had done with California.[3]

Word quickly spread throughout the South of Quitman's firm commitment to lead a Cuba expedition. Even before his agreement with the Junta, the Mississippian

2. Urban, "Abortive Quitman Expedition," 177–79; Urban, "The Idea of Progress," 530–32; Louis Schlessinger to Quitman, November 7, 1853, in John Quitman Papers, Mississippi Department of Archives and History.

3. Quitman to Franklin Pierce, undated, in John Quitman Papers, Mississippi Department of Archives and History; unsigned circular in Quitman's hand, dated New Orleans, July, 1854, Alexander Clayton to Quitman, November 10, 1853, Samuel Walker to Quitman, July 31, 1854, A. G. Haley to Quitman, June 14, 1854, and J. W. Lesesne to Quitman, June 8, 10, 1854, all in Quitman Papers, Harvard University Library. After Quitman severed his relationship with the Cuban Junta in 1855 he publicly anounced the annexationist goal in a speech in Old Fellow's Hall in New Orleans. See New Orleans *Daily Picayune*, August 18, 1855.

received many letters of inquiry concerning rumors that he was involved in such an enterprise. Now Quitman and his lieutenants were inundated with requests for information as to how one could become part of the movement. Mexican War veterans longing for the sound of battle, holdovers from the López movement, and southern military academy graduates anxious to prove their worth all wanted to be a part of what a Texan called the "paramount enterprise of the age." Nonmilitary people also found the design appealing. A Louisianian, for instance, declared that he loved surgery, possessed a "chest of assorted medicines" as well as "everything necessary in the way of surgical Instruments," and wanted to join Quitman's medical staff.[4] A highly disproportionate number of applicants expected to be officers—which must have created headaches for Quitman. Nothing "less than the head of a Brigade" was the way an Alabamian explained his availability. A Kentucky senator's brief parody of filibusters a number of years later flawlessly described their inflated view of their own potentialities : "If we get into a war about Cuba, these are not the men who are going to do any fighting unless you make up a regiment of colonels or majors. They would join that, but they will never go in the rank and file. . . . Go down to the taverns and look at some of them as you see them strutting about." [5]

An arresting number of prominent southerners, however, also offered their support. A list of the general's Texas backers reads like a minor *Who's Who* of Texas

4. William Mason to Quitman, July 15, 1854, Horatio Nunes to Quitman, July 7, 1854, Robert Farquharson to Quitman, February 7, 1855, Henry Gillespey to Quitman, February 9, 1855, and J. F. Mitchell to Quitman, February 10, 1855, all in Quitman Papers, Harvard University Library.

5. *Congressional Globe*, 35th Cong., 2nd Sess., 1059; Robert Farquharson to Quitman, February 7, 1855, William Mason to Quitman, July 15, 1854, G. Chandler to Quitman, May 18, 1854, and J. W. Lesesne to Quitman, June 10, 1854, all in Quitman Papers, Harvard University Library.

politics in the 1850s. His foremost organizer in the Lone Star State was John Ford, who had served in the Texas congress and as mayor of Austin, had fought in the Mexican War (where he received his nickname "Rip"), and had led campaigns against Indians throughout the 1840s and 1850s. He had also been editor of both the Austin *Texas State Times* and the *Texas State Gazette* and had gained prominence in the Texas Rangers. Other Texas adherents included Hiram Waller, Hugh McLeod, L. D. Evans, James P. Henderson, and John Marshall. Waller was in the Texas legislature; McLeod had been adjutant-general of the Texan army and a United States congressman; Evans served as a district court judge and United States congressman; Henderson had been a leader of the Texas Republic and later served as governor of Texas and as United States senator; and Marshall edited a newspaper.

In Alabama, Governor John Winston worked actively in Quitman's behalf. J. F. H. Claiborne, a leading planter and politician and former member of the United States House of Representatives, supported Quitman in Mississippi. A number of Mississippi newspapermen labored for Quitman, as did some members of the Mississippi legislature. Alexander Stephens boosted Quitman's cause in Georgia.

Many of these men did more than merely orate or encourage prospective recruits. Some made significant financial contributions; and a few, including Ford and Marshall, intended to accompany the invasion force. Mississippian Robert J. Walker, who had endorsed the purchase of Cuba while secretary of the treasury under Polk, told Marshall he would put his life and income on the line for Quitman if he were not so deeply involved in Texas railroad schemes.[6]

This ground swell of support from influential southern-

6. John S. Ford to Quitman, June 5, August 12, December 17, 1854, in John Quitman Papers, Mississippi Department of Archives

ers well reflects the fact that annexation of Cuba had become a sectional goal around the time of the Kansas-
Nebraska Act. Because of his well publicized antipathy
to the Compromise of 1850, Quitman's reputation as an
extreme defender of southern rights was unchallenged.
Southerners flocked to his standard trusting that the
movement would enhance the strength of the slave states.
A Jackson, Mississippi, supporter disclosed that the "desire that Cuba should be acquired as a Southern conquest
is almost unanimous among Southern men in this part of
the State." Another follower called acquisition of Cuba
"the only hope of the South." John Ford wrote that possession of the island would secure the South "against ma-
lign influences from any quarter" and would "place an
immoveable keystone in the arch of the Union." Quitman
and other key organizers such as Henderson, Thrasher,
and Samuel Walker emphasized the sectional importance
of their activities when eliciting support. Quitman, for instance, wrote a Georgia backer, "I hope Georgia will do
something for this great Southern movement so vital to
our common interests." [7] Genuine concern for the welfare
and rights of Cuba's population motivated few of the
filibusters.

and History; John Ford to Hugh McLeod, January 24, 1855, in Hugh
McLeod Papers, Texas State Archives and Library, Austin; John
Marshall to Quitman, June 14, 18, 1854, in John Quitman Papers,
Mississippi Department of Archives and History; Quaife (ed.),
Diary of Polk, III, 469.

7. F. Jones to Quitman, June 10, 1854, and John Ford to Quit-
man, August 12, 1854, both in John Quitman Papers, Mississippi
Department of Archives and History; William Langley to Quitman,
January 13, 1855, and Quitman to C. A. L. Lamar, January 5, 1855,
both in Quitman Papers, Harvard University Library. See also Dr.
F. R. Witter to Quitman, October 17, 1854, C. H. Mott to Quitman,
April 2, 1854, and J. McDonald to Quitman, March 10, 1854, all in
John Quitman Papers, Mississippi Department of Archives and His-
tory; I. Boyd to Quitman, August 10, 1855, in John Quitman Papers,
Louisiana State University Department of Archives and Manu-
scripts, Baton Rouge; W. Gowan to Quitman, June 1, 1854, and
Samuel Walker to Quitman, July 31, 1854, both in Quitman Papers,
Harvard University Library.

Quitman occasionally received unsolicited letters of inquiry from northern adventurers, but he apparently ignored most of them.[8] He did, however, work in conjunction with a few prominent northerners, such as John L. O'Sullivan and New York Congressman Mike Walsh. Both O'Sullivan and Walsh had southern proclivities. O'Sullivan strongly defended states' rights; and in the Civil War he would side with the Confederacy. Walsh, a leader of the radical labor-reform, anti-Tammany faction within the New York Democratic party, frequently denounced abolitionists. He complained to Quitman that "northern hypocrites and demagogues" stymied the interests and rights of "Southern men." Louis Schlessinger, the exiled Hungarian patriot, also involved himself in Quitman's plans.[9]

Quitman and his followers, therefore, were not only committed to annexing Cuba, but also regarded Cuba as a sectional objective. They were well aware, however, that their success would depend in part on a favorable, or at least neutral, attitude on the part of the national government. Should Pierce invoke the neutrality laws against filibustering, the chances for leaving the United States with a formidable expedition would be greatly reduced. Even before Quitman accepted leadership, Pierce had publicly denounced such expeditions.[10] Given Quitman's conviction that Cuba had to be invaded with overwhelming force, the president's opposition was unbearable. The filibusters were counting on a change of policy.

8. See, for instance, R. M. Garner (of Indiana) to Quitman, August 1, 1854, and Will Morris (of Philadelphia) to Quitman, April 13, 1854, both in John Quitman Papers, Mississippi Department of Archives and History.

9. John L. O'Sullivan to Quitman, August 29, September 8, 1853; Mike Walsh to Quitman, October 3, 1853, May 25, 1854, and Louis Schlessinger to Quitman, May 18, 1853, all in Quitman Papers, Harvard University Library; Louis Schlessinger to Quitman, November 3, 1853, September 9, 1854, in Quitman Family Papers.

10. Richardson (comp.), *Messages and Papers of the President*, VI, 2742.

In the spring of 1854, Quitman and his supporters believed that Pierce and Jefferson Davis' commitment to annexing Cuba would ultimately outweigh their obligation to enforce the neutrality laws. Mike Walsh informed Quitman from Washington that his soundings in administration circles revealed that although the president and cabinet disapproved of filibustering, "they would not ... dare attempt to take any part against us, after the expedition was once started." In June, Quitman heard indirectly from Representative Philip Phillips of Alabama that the president would not significantly interfere with filibustering, despite public pronouncements. The pro-Quitman Natchez *Daily Courier* was speaking for Quitman when it proclaimed confidently on June 3: "At all events, our filibusters will be enabled without hindrance to carry out their own plans until Congress can be dragooned into the measure." [11]

The *Daily Courier*'s reference to Congress alluded to Quitman's trump card. In the unlikely event that Pierce should prove a formidable antagonist, support had been lined up in Congress to eliminate the law on which the president's power of intervention was based. Senator John Slidell of Louisiana, who was in close touch with Quitman, introduced a motion on May 1 to suspend the neutrality laws, and he was pledged to fight for its passage if necessary. Other southern senators, including Judah P. Benjamin of Louisiana and Albert Gallatin Brown of Mississippi were also committed to the scheme.[12]

11. Mike Walsh to Quitman, May 25, 1854, and J. W. Lesesne to Quitman, June 8, 1854, both in Quitman Papers, Harvard University Library; Natchez *Daily Courier*, June 3, 1854. See also [?] to Quitman, February 27, 1853, and [?] to Quitman, July 13, 1854, both in John Quitman Papers, Mississippi Department of Archives and History. Both Walsh and Lesesne intimated that the quieter Quitman kept his mobilizing activities, the less likely it was that public pressure would force Pierce to intervene. See also Claude M. Fuess, *The Life of Caleb Cushing* (2 vols.; New York, 1923), II, 176.

12. Samuel Walker to Quitman, July 31, 1854, and John Slidell to

Pierce, indeed, was in the process of rethinking his Cuba policy by the time Quitman assumed command. The island attracted Pierce's attention almost immediately after his inauguration and long before the *Black Warrior* affair. Pierce was as much concerned about possible emancipation as most Southerners; and in May, 1853, he appointed Alexander Clayton of Delaware special agent to Havana to investigate the legitimacy of the abolition rumors. Secretary of State Marcy instructed Clayton to ascertain whether there was a treaty between England, France, and Spain stating that Spain would "Africanize Cuba if England and France would guarantee her control of the island." He was also to investigate a reported substitution of African and Chinese laborers for slaves. Clayton found no evidence of such a treaty and reported this to the State Department in December.[13]

Unconvinced, Pierce dispatched a second agent, Charles W. Davis, in March, 1854, to reinvestigate the abolition rumors. Davis' mission came in the wake of the *Black Warrior* incident. The bellicosity of Marcy's instructions to Davis reveal how strained United States-Spanish relations had become and hint that the administration might have been considering going to war for Cuba. Marcy portrayed the president as "impatient" to hear from "unquestionable authority" whether Spain was abolishing slavery in Cuba. The secretary threatened: "Unless a change of policy ensue, whereby our rights are to be rigorously respected and our future completely guarded against the in-

Quitman, October 5, 1854, both in Quitman Papers, Harvard University Library; *Congressional Globe*, 33rd Cong., 1st Sess., 1021. More exactly, Slidell's motion asked for the Committee on Foreign Relations to consider the expediency of authorizing the president to suspend the neutrality laws during recesses of Congress.

13. See Clayton's report on his mission, in Folder 34, J. F. H. Claiborne Papers, University of North Carolina, Chapel Hill. See also Marcy to Clayton, October 26, November 8, 1853, in Manning (ed.), *Diplomatic Correspondence*, XI, 166–68; Urban, "The Idea of Progress," 490–91; Spencer, *Victor and Spoils*, 322.

fluences of bad neighborhood, the day of retributive justice must soon arrive. Injury to our citizens and insult to our flag, have been of such frequent occurrence that our forbearance is ceasing to be a virtue." Davis reported in May that Pezuela had abolitionist tendencies, that, while in Havana, he saw black regiments being raised, and that Spain was doing England's bidding in respect to slavery. And he called for United States intervention.[14]

The administration, well aware that acquiescence in Cuban emancipation would alienate its southern support, let it be known in diplomatic circles that the United States would not tolerate Negro rule in Cuba. In July of 1853, Marcy wrote to James Buchanan in England that the danger of abolition in Cuba was real, that England supported it, and that England ought to be aware that "she is concurring in an act which, in its consequences, must be injurious to the United States." Buchanan later replied that, in his talks with British Foreign Minister Lord Clarendon and with English society, "whenever a proper opportunity afforded" he had expressed his "confident conviction that if there *should be a rising* in the Island against intolerable opposition, and any *third Power* should render material aid to the Spaniards it would be impossible to prevent the United States from rushing to the assistance of the oppressed." Marcy sent similar instructions to Soulé in Spain.[15]

Pierce was uncertain, however, as to how far he should go beyond diplomatic protest on both the emancipation and *Black Warrior* issues. Certainly the situation demanded action. His personal desires for Cuba aside, Pierce knew

14. Marcy to Davis, March 15, 1854, and Davis to Marcy, May 22, 1854, both in Manning (ed.), *Diplomatic Correspondence*, XI, 170–73, 789–95.
15. Marcy to Buchanan, July 2, 1853, in "The Ostend Conference," *House Executive Documents*, 33rd Cong., 2nd Sess., No. 93, p. 10; Buchanan to Marcy, March 31, 1854, and Marcy to Soulé, April 3, 1854, in Marcy Papers.

that acquisition could only strengthen his political position in the South and please the expansionist wing of the Democratic party in the North. Ultimately he would accept his European ministers' suggestion that manipulation of Spain's financial difficulties would force her to cede Cuba. But for months he wavered, apparently toying with the idea of war.

Congressional debates over the *Black Warrior* affair probably contributed to Pierce's decision to reject an extreme course of action such as war or filibustering. Comments by some northern senators and representatives made it painfully obvious that should Pierce initiate war or approve a southern-oriented invasion of Cuba, he would face strong antislavery opposition and would not have a united country behind him.

The first indication of growing antislavery irritation with the idea of Cuba as a new slave state came when Representative Philip Phillips called for Pierce to transmit to the House any information he possessed concerning the *Black Warrior* incident. On March 15 the president responded with documents and a message saying that the United States was seeking a peaceful solution to the problem. However, he added a comment that instructed Congress to consider the possibility of war with Spain: "In case the measures taken for an amicable adjustment of our difficulties with Spain should unfortunately fail, I shall not hesitate to use the authorities and means which Congress may grant to insure an observance of our just rights, to obtain redress for injuries received, and to vindicate the honor of our flag. In anticipation of that contingency, which I earnestly hope may not arise, I suggest to Congress the propriety of adopting such provisional measures as the exigency may seem to demand." [16]

The House disregarded Pierce's suggestion. But before the Cuba debate subsided, veteran antislavery representa-

16. *Congressional Globe*, 33rd Cong., 1st Sess., 601, 636–37.

tive Joshua Giddings of Ohio applauded the Spanish seizure of the *Black Warrior* and castigated Pierce and the
southern press for wanting to retard emancipation in
Cuba. To Giddings, Pierce's policy was the "support of
slavery in Cuba, and its extension in the territories of the
United States," and he notified southerners that he would
wage an "unmitigated, unceasing warfare" against it.
Thomas Bayly of Virginia, chairman of the Committee
on Foreign Affairs, defended the president, as did a number of representatives. Bayly warned that the government
should take action before filibusters tried to take the island. If the government did not do something, "there will
arise a feeling difficult to be restrained." Unable to reach
a consensus, the House temporarily dropped the Cuba
issue.[17]

The Senate devoted more attention to the question of
Cuba. Slidell followed his motion to suspend the neutrality
laws with a speech citing the danger of "Africanization"
of Cuba and hinting that he was well informed of Quitman's activities and that Quitman was waiting for a revolution in Cuba as the signal for putting his expedition
under way. "I desire no movement on the part of our citizens, until the Cubans shall have put their own shoulders
to the wheel.... One thing is certain, that in despite of all
your statutes, your collectors, your marshals, your Army
and Navy, if the revolutionary standard be once hoisted in
Cuba, and maintained for a few short weeks, no Administration can prevent our citizens rushing to the rescue in
such numbers as will secure its triumph—a Democratic
President would not desire to do it." [18]

Stephen Mallory of Florida and Judah Benjamin reiterated Slidell's charge that slavery was about to be abol-

17. *Ibid.*, 646–51.
18. *Ibid.*, 1021–24. For the connection of the expedition and an expected revolution in Cuba, see also Samuel Walker to Quitman, May
30, 1854, in Quitman Papers, Harvard University Library.

ished in Cuba; then Salmon Chase of Ohio gave a speech that must have been as chilling to southern senators as Giddings' unquestionably was to southern representatives. Chase applauded the trend toward emancipation in Cuba, even if instigated by England or France. Such measures commanded his "sympathy" and "best wishes." Slidell, Mallory, and Benjamin avoided responding to this provocative attack, knowing well that a response would make it politically difficult for expansionist northern Democrats to support the acquisition of new slave territory. Further debate ensued in mid-May when Senators Mallory and Benjamin again tried to arouse the Senate over "Africanization." Their cries for American intervention provoked resistance not only from William Seward of New York and other northern senators, but also from former secretary of state John Clayton of Delaware, who denied that Spain intended to destroy Cuba by abolishing slavery and challenged Benjamin to produce proof to the contrary. The Senate took no action on Slidell's resolution and referred the emancipation question to the Committee on Foreign Relations, which in turn merely requested information from the president.[19]

Given Congress' indecisiveness, as well as the increasing evidence that sectionalism was undermining the possibility of legislative accord, it is little wonder that Pierce emphasized diplomatic means to acquire Cuba. Pierce's initial strategy was to emphasize American anger over the *Black Warrior* incident in order to exert pressure on Spain to cede the island. Later he would broaden his approach.

Though Spanish authorities released the *Black Warrior* on March 16, after payment of a fine of $6,000, Marcy apprised Soulé the next day that the seizure of the ship and its cargo was a "flagrant wrong." It was the Spanish government's duty to correct the error: "The damages to the owners of the *Black Warrior* and her cargo are estimated at three hundred thousand dollars, and this amount you

19. *Ibid.*, 1024, 1194, 1199, 1298–1300.

will demand as the indemnity to the injured parties."
Soulé did so and Spain delayed an answer. On April 3
Marcy increased the pressure on Spain to sell Cuba in a
nineteenth-century version of "brinkmanship." He wrote
Soulé that unsettled conditions in Spain and the danger
of emancipation in Cuba made the present a proper time
to accomplish an "object so much desired by the United
States." Marcy cited Spanish infringements on American
commerce and informed Soulé that he could offer up to
$130 million for Cuba. If Spain refused to accept the of-
fer, the minister was to direct his efforts "to the next
most desirable object, which is to detach that island from
the Spanish dominion and from all dependence on any
European power." Marcy had long advocated the liberation of Cuba should cession to the United States prove
impossible.[20]

Despite Marcy's aggressive language, the administration pondered for weeks about what further action should
be taken if Spain would not accept Soulé's offer, and about
how it should respond to pressure to support filibustering.
As late as May 25 and 26, 1854, Marcy was writing Buchanan and Minister to France John Y. Mason that the
administration's course of action on Cuba was "under ad-
visement" but "unsettled." On May 30 the Democratic
majority of the Senate foreign relations committee met
with Pierce and urged him to support Slidell's motion to
repeal the neutrality laws.[21] Mike Walsh's optimistic letter to Quitman was mailed during this period.

The administration seems to have been preoccupied with

20. Marcy to Soulé, July 23, 1853, March 17, April 3, 1854, in
Manning (ed.), *Diplomatic Correspondence*, XI, 160–65, 174–75.
The Spanish minister of foreign affairs, Calderón de la Barca, wrote
Soulé on May 7 that the $6,000 fine would be remitted. See Leard,
"Bonds of Destiny," 190.

21. Draft of letter, Marcy to James Buchanan, May 26, 1854, and
draft of letter, Marcy to Mason, May 25, 1854, both in Marcy
Papers; Spencer, *Victor and Spoils*, 322–23; [?] Whitman to Quitman, July 13, 1854, in John Quitman Papers, Mississippi Department of Archives and History.

the Kansas-Nebraska bill, which was the subject of tortured debate at the very time the Cuba crisis came to a head. Pierce was reluctant to simultaneously embroil his administration in two major sectional conflicts, and was marking time until the debates ran their course. Marcy wrote Mason that the "Nebraska bill has not yet but will shortly become a law—From this which has proved a very troublesome matter we shall at once enter upon another still more embarrassing—the Cuba question." And he informed Buchanan on the very day the Kansas-Nebraska bill passed: "The Nebraska question being now disposed of, the next important matter to come up will be Cuba." [22]

Pierce found it difficult to dismiss the "Nebraska question" as easily as Marcy, for the bill's passage restricted his Cuba options. Because the Kansas-Nebraska Act incensed northerners, Pierce had to proceed gingerly. Marcy explained the problem to John Mason: "The Nebraska question has sadly shattered our party in all the free states and deprived it of the strength which was needed & could have been much more profitably used for the acquisition of Cuba." [23] Pierce was already under strong antislavery attack for his support of the Kansas-Nebraska bill, and he realized that if he urged war for Cuba or supported Quitman and his filibusters, he would be even more open to the charge that he was a tool of the South, and this in turn would undermine his political position in the North. Congressional debates and commentaries in the press revealed that northern opposition to slavery expansion had stiffened over the last few months. Quiet diplomacy for Cuba would be much less likely to reawaken the slavery controversy than would war or filibustering.

Furthermore, administration leaders may have simply felt that the purchase of Cuba through diplomatic chan-

22. Draft of letter, Marcy to Mason, May 25, 1854, and draft of letter, Marcy to Buchanan, May 26, 1854, both in Marcy Papers.
23. Quoted in Spencer, *Victor and Spoils*, 324.

nels was more feasible and that the use of force would gravely endanger the diplomatic efforts being made. From the bitter Spanish reaction to López's expeditions, it would have been easy for Pierce to conclude that diplomacy would fail in the event of further filibustering. Horatio Perry, secretary of the American legation in Spain, asserted that the cession of Cuba would be "highly probable" once Spain and the United States were on friendly terms. And he cautioned: "Genl Quitman and the Cuban Junta cannot do it. The states of Louisiana, Mississippi & Alabama can do little towards it. They may ruin this natural, fair & fruitful policy of the United States, but they cannot aid it. They may precipitate the nation into a war for the conquest of Cuba, but they cannot purchase it so long as they threaten that alternative." Marcy claimed that filibusters encouraged Spanish hostility and that if the United States carried out the "robber doctrine," it would be degraded in the eyes of the civilized world and would lose in self-respect.[24]

Pierce took a significant step toward a diplomatic strategy for Cuba, on the day after he signed the Kansas-Nebraska Act, when he issued a proclamation warning that the government would prosecute illegal expeditions. It is unclear whether this was Pierce's own decision, or whether it was prompted by Jefferson Davis. Davis and Quitman were rivals in Mississippi politics, and Davis might have had personal motives for intervening against the filibuster. Davis also felt that Albert Gallatin Brown, an ally of Quitman, had pushed him out of Mississippi politics.

Even before the administration reached a final decision on a Cuba policy, charges filled the air that Davis would be responsible for a forthcoming administration attack on the filibuster movement. While Quitman's agent in Wash-

24. Perry to Marcy, September 4, 1854, and Marcy to Lorenzo B. Shepard, April 12, 1855, both in Marcy Papers.

ington confided that Davis was a "bitter" and "unmanly opponent," intent only on destroying Quitman's reputation, the Natchez *Daily Courier* publicly uttered the same thoughts. In June, 1854, the secretary of war was told that such charges were widespread and that his position in the Deep South would be injured unless he gave evidence that Cuba was to be taken and "fully appreciated the importance of the measure to the South." [25]

Whether or not Davis was culpable, Quitman supporters had good reason to complain that the federal position against filibustering was hardening; for Secretary of State Marcy quickly acted to enforce Pierce's proclamation. Apparently feeling that the administration would provoke anger in the South if it took a vigorous stand against Quitman, Marcy first attempted to persuade Quitman to defer his invasion plans. He urged Slidell to telegraph New Orleans (where Quitman's movement was centered) that the administration was taking "immediate" measures in respect to Cuba. But Slidell refused. Marcy then acted forcefully. He contacted the United States district attorney in New Orleans, and soon Quitman and five supporters were facing a United States circuit court. Although a sympathetic grand jury failed to find evidence of an invasion plot, Judge John Campbell braved New Orleans profilibuster sentiment by compelling Quitman and two associates—Thrasher and A. L. Saunders—to post bonds of $3,000 as a pledge that they would not disobey the neutrality laws for the next nine months.

Although Quitman continued recruiting and planning his expedition, thus violating the spirit of Campbell's or-

25. Richardson (comp.), *Messages and Papers of the President,* VI, 2769–70; James Byrne Ranck, *Albert Gallatin Brown: Radical Southern Nationalist* (New York, 1937), 124; Natchez *Daily Courier,* March 10, 1854; Alexander Walker to A. G. Haley, June 15, 1854, in Davis Papers, Library of Congress; New York *Herald,* January 9, 1855; Urban, "The Idea of Progress," 560–61; Spencer, *Victor and Spoils,* 320; Rauch, *American Interest in Cuba,* 266.

der, he soon felt the sting of this ruling. Instead of hoping that their actions would attract government support, filibusters now knew that they were running afoul of the law. Many had felt that at the least a neutral administration was necessary for success. Suddenly their hopes vanished. Quitman received reports from Jackson, Mississippi, that people were in a "fog" about the expedition and that many had "abandoned all care of any thing being done." And, from Austin, John Ford reported: "The arrests in New Orleans had a very bad effect here." [26] But Quitman could compensate for manpower losses. A. L. Saunders, who had gone to Kentucky after Judge Campbell's decision, reported that he could muster one thousand men in Kentucky alone. Quitman constantly received letters from men anxious to join, and he only wanted three or four thousand men for the invasion force.[27]

Financial difficulties plagued Quitman to a far greater degree. "The want of money is the obstacle in the way of prompt and quick action," he explained to a Georgia supporter. "If you or any of our friends in Georgia can aid us in this, it will be more acceptable than in any other way." Quitman had particular problems trying to finance trans-

26. Slidell to James Buchanan, June 17, 1854, in Buchanan Papers; Connor, *Campbell*, 91–98; Urban, "The Idea of Progress," 567–68; Urban, "Abortive Quitman Expedition," 183–84; Foner, *History of Cuba*, II, 90; William Langley to Quitman, January 13, 1855, in Quitman Papers, Harvard University Library; John S. Ford to Quitman, August 12, 1854, and F. Jones to Quitman, June 10, 1854, both in John Quitman Papers, Mississippi Department of Archives and History. John Campbell at this time was associate justice of the United States Supreme Court, fulfilling his duty of presiding over the United States circuit court at New Orleans.
27. A. L. Saunders to Quitman, February 4, 1855, and Quitman to C. A. L. Lamar, January 5, 1855, both in Quitman Papers, Harvard University Library. Many of the letters Quitman received were from groups of men offering to volunteer together. See James Bickell to Quitman, September 28, 1854, William Estelle to Quitman, December 19, 1854, W. A. Lacy to Quitman, February 19, 1855, and J. McRagh to Quitman, March 2, 1855, all in Quitman Papers, Harvard University Library.

ports for the invasion army. To overcome his problems, he required that each enlistee for the expedition pay fifty dollars plus transportation to the nearest seaport. But the money was not forthcoming in the amount required. Governor John Winston of Alabama reported in June, 1854, that he had found, after a journey in the "country," that lack of funds held back many who would like to support the cause; and the situation had not cleared up a half year later when John Thrasher wrote from Port Gibson, Mississippi, that he had "great difficulty" in getting "even the friends of the cause to promise any thing towards it; and still greater difficulty in getting them to come forward, & fulfill the promise."

Judge Campbell's action had its greatest impact in the realm of finances. Filibustering was a highly speculative investment to begin with, and the government's position persuaded many that Quitman's bonds were a poor risk. One supporter remarked to Quitman: "I cannot promise positively to raise any funds on the sale of Cuban bonds. I find great difficulty in inspiring confidence." And Quitman was inundated with letters from every recruiting front in the South stating that his bonds were not selling.[28]

Compounding Quitman's problems were fissures within his movement. In particular his relationship with the Cuban Junta was unstable. A faction of the Junta, headed by the antislavery Cuban Domingo de Goicuría, broke with Quitman and particularly impaired his Georgia organization. The general's disputes with Cuban exiles troubled him far more than the unfavorable publicity in some southern newspapers, and even in expansionist sheets.

28. John Winston to Quitman, June 3, 1854, in John Quitman Papers, Mississippi Department of Archives and History; John Thrasher to Quitman, January 24, 1855, in Quitman Family Papers; Quitman to C. A. L. Lamar, January 5, 1855, Samuel Walker to Quitman, October 8, 1854, and W. A. Lacy to Quitman, February 19, 1855, all in Quitman Papers, Harvard University Library.

Such newspapers often asserted that while war or diplomacy provided honorable means for expansion, filibustering was immoral and underhanded.[29]

A low point was reached in late 1854. Quitman's followers were asking for their money back, leaving the movement, and complaining that they were going broke while they waited, jobless, for the invasion to begin. Quitman thought of abandoning the whole enterprise; but he gamely persisted, trying to circumvent the neutrality proclamation by planning an expedition that would have neither arms nor officers until after it left United States waters. He received rifles, cash, and the loan of a steamer from New York shipping magnate George Law and promises of a substantial number of recruits from the Texas Rangers. At a small country store at Bayou Boeuf, Louisiana, he purchased a considerable amount of supplies, including $1,300 worth of tobacco, whiskey, brandy, and gin "for the boys"—undoubtedly necessities for the sort of men who enrolled in such expeditions. Potential soldiers were converging on New Orleans and outlying plantations by early 1855.

Quitman planned to invade Cuba by the first week of March, 1855. This time the administration interfered decisively. In a Washington conference, Pierce persuaded Quitman that such an expedition would be a catastrophe. The new captain general of Cuba, José G. de la Concha, had sent proof of the island's invulnerability to attack. Concha also seemed to be more willing to protect the slave system on the island than Pezuela had been. This may have

29. Louis Schlessinger to Quitman, September 9, 1854, in Quitman Family Papers; typewritten copy, Samuel Walker, "The Diary of a Louisiana Planter," entry for December 19, 1859, in Samuel Walker Papers, Tulane University Library, New Orleans; Quitman to C. A. L. Lamar, January 5, 1855, in Quitman Papers, Harvard University Library; Leard, "Bonds of Destiny," 138–39; Charleston *Daily Courier*, May 3, 10, 1854; Yazoo City (Mississippi) *Weekly Whig*, April 21, 1854; North Carolina *Weekly Raleigh Register*, March 22, 1854.

been the decisive point for Quitman, given his sensitivity to the emancipation question. In addition, Quitman had promised many of his followers that the expedition would coincide with a Cuban uprising; but Concha's precautions made such a rebellion unlikely. And Albert Gallatin Brown had failed to get the Senate to repeal the neutrality laws in March. Wanting to avoid López's fate, convinced of Pierce's unalterable opposition, and reassured on the slavery question, Quitman formally resigned from the Junta on April 30.[30] Quitman's future involvement with filibus-

30. C. R. Wheat to Quitman, October 11, 1854, and Quitman to John S. Ford, October 11, 1854, both in John Quitman Papers, Mississippi Department of Archives and History; Quitman to C. A. L. Lamar, January 5, 1855, Charles Cummings to Quitman, November 14, 1854, William Brantly to Quitman, January 17, 1855, H. Forno to Quitman, January 23, February 6, 1855, and Alexander Stephens to Quitman, February 24, 1855, all in Quitman Papers, Harvard University Library; John Thrasher to Hugh McLeod, January 24, 1855, and John Ford to Hugh McLeod, January 14, 1855, both in McLeod Papers; *Congressional Globe*, 33rd Cong., 2nd Sess., 1148; Leard, "Bonds of Destiny," 139–40; Ranck, *Albert Gallatin Brown*, 134; Foner, *History of Cuba*, II, 87–88, 93–94, 104–105; D. Clayton James, "The Tribulations of a Bayou Boeuf Store Owner, 1853–1857," *Louisiana History*, IV (1963), 255; Corwin, *Spain and the Abolition of Slavery*, 115–23.

   Newspapers during that period carried reports of a great military buildup in Cuba. Twenty-three vessels of war were on alert, military arrests were made, new militia companies were formed, and private telegraph messages were prohibited as was the sale of firearms. See Columbus (Georgia) *Enquirer*, February 27, 1855; New Orleans *Daily Picayune*, February 15, 1855; *National Intelligencer*, April 8, 1855. Amelia Murray, an Englishwoman traveling in Cuba, wrote: "Military uniforms are visible in every direction, and fortresses bristle all round this city." See Amelia Murray, *Letters from the United States, Cuba and Canada* (New York, 1856), 258. See also Urban, "The Idea of Progress," 625–29. William H. Robertson warned Marcy from Havana in February, 1855, that any American expedition to Cuba would lead to a "greater sacrifice of life than from any previous expedition" and described Concha's military preparations. In later letters he told Marcy that Quitman's resignation from the Cuban Junta led to the disbanding of Cuba's black regiments and that the new Captain General had no abolition plans. This contributed to the more moderate tone in American diplomacy with Spain that developed in the late stages of Pierce's administra-

tering would be vicarious. He would become a staunch spokesman for other filibusters from the congressional seat to which he was elected later in 1855.

Pierce had opposed the filibusters at least partly because of his confidence in diplomacy as the means to acquire Cuba; and he had acted on his March statement to Congress that he would use diplomacy long before Quitman's enterprise dissolved. Congress, however, proved reluctant to cooperate with the president. On August 1, 1854, Pierce requested a $10 million appropriation from Congress to support a proposed three-man commission that would proceed to Madrid and attempt to persuade Spain to sell Cuba. Pierce refused to specify how the appropriation would be used; and the Senate Committee on Foreign Relations, entrusted with the request, recommended on August 3, 1854, that the matter be postponed until the December session of Congress. The committee suggested that Congress "leave the question with the President"— a suggestion that the Senate accepted. Jefferson Davis later used Congress' refusal to participate as a rationalization for the administration's failure to acquire the island. A number of newspapers agreed with him.[31]

Now that Congress' hesitancy to commit itself was clear, Pierce and Marcy realized that any progress toward acquiring Cuba would have to come from the European diplomatic corps. Less than two weeks after the Senate committee's negative report, Marcy sent fresh instructions to Soulé suggesting that much could be done in London

tion. See William H. Robertson to Marcy, February 14, March 7, May 22, June 20, July 5, 1855, in Manning (ed.), *Diplomatic Correspondence*, XI, 839, 853–54, 869–70.

31. *Congressional Globe*, 33rd Cong., 1st Sess., 2178; New York *Herald*, August 4, 8, 1854; Spencer, *Victor and Spoils*, 322; John J. McRae to J. F. H. Claiborne, June 7, 1855, in J. F. H. Claiborne Papers, Mississippi Department of Archives and History, Jackson; *Texas State Gazette*, April 14, 1855. Davis delivered the speech in question in Vicksburg in June, 1855.

and Paris. He suggested that Soulé arrange a private conference with Ministers Buchanan and Mason to discuss the situation. If a workable plan could be arranged, England would not "interpose" to prevent a Cuba cession.[32]

Marcy and Pierce probably suggested a conference because Buchanan and Soulé had not been corresponding with each other. Although the ministers differed on details, they had remarkably similar ideas as to how Cuba could be purchased. For some time they had been convinced that financial intrigue would secure Cuba. In addition, Marcy was sensitive to complaints from both Buchanan and Mason that they were not posted on the progress of the negotiations at Madrid for Cuba. With their hands tied in Washington by Congress' refusal to endorse the administration's commission recommendation and with the administration in no position politically to declare war on Spain, Pierce and Marcy were finally responding to their ministers' proposals, which had been reaching the State Department for some time. Ironically, the belated concession pleased neither Buchanan nor Mason, and each protested being forced into the conference. Mason expected it to be a waste of time, and Buchanan insisted to Pierce that treasury funds for Belmont's use with the holders of Spanish bonds would prove far more effective.[33]

Marcy's instructions led to the incredible Ostend Manifesto. Instead of meeting in secret, the three ministers, and some other members of the American diplomatic corps, convened at Ostend, Belgium, amid much excitement and publicity from the European press. After deliberations at Ostend and Aix La Chapelle, they produced a document, dated October 18, that became known as the Ostend Mani-

32. Marcy to Soulé, August 16, 1854, in Marcy Papers.
33. Marcy to Buchanan, May 26, 1854, John Y. Mason to Buchanan, May 31, September 24, 1854, John Slidell to Buchanan, June 17, August 6, 1854, April 3, 1855, John Forney to Buchanan, May 25, 1854, Buchanan to Slidell, May 23, 1854, Buchanan to Marcy, July 14, 1853 (copy), and Buchanan to Franklin Pierce, September 1, 1854, all in Buchanan Papers.

festo. It was actually a dispatch, signed by the three ministers, which strongly implied that the United States should go to war for Cuba if Spain refused to sell it. Pierce and Marcy had abandoned the idea of war months earlier, and Marcy had clearly stated this in a June letter to Soulé. But the instructions for the conference had been so vague, and so many of Marcy's letters to Soulé since the *Black Warrior* incident had been bellicose, that the ministers misread the administration's intent.

The Ostend Manifesto presented a number of reasons why Cuba should be purchased: suppression of the African slave trade, commercial advantages to both nations (Spain could build railroads from the cession money), outrages on the rights of American citizens and on the flag of the United States, and the advantage of obtaining an island so situated as to be a threat to national security. But instead of outlining a feasible financial scheme, as Marcy had expected, the manifesto stated that if Spain would not sell Cuba, it might be necessary to resort to the law of "self-preservation": if "Cuba, in the possession of Spain seriously endanger[s] our internal peace and the existence of our cherished Union . . . then, by every law, human and divine, we shall be justified in wresting it from Spain." Soulé sent a letter with the manifesto reiterating the ministers' hopes for peace, yet adding that if the attempt to acquire Cuba were to "bring upon us the calamity of a war, let it be now, while the great powers of this continent are engaged in that stupendous struggle which cannot but engage all their strength and tax all their energies as long as it lasts, and may before it ends, convulse them all." [34]

The document met rough going in Washington. Pierce and Marcy were willing to countenance virtually anything

34. Marcy to Soulé, June 24, 1854, Soulé to Marcy, October 15, 1854, in Manning (ed.), *Diplomatic Correspondence*, XI, 189–90, 825–26; Leard, "Bonds of Destiny," 197–98; *House Executive Documents*, 33rd Cong., 2nd Sess., No. 93, pp. 124, 126, 128–32.

the European ministers would do on their own initiative to facilitate acquisition, and they had placed this responsibility on the ministers to avoid the very use of force the manifesto advocated. Thus, a strategy that implied conquest was unacceptable. The administration's dilemma was complicated by the criticism that the conference had received in Europe, and United States congressmen demanded that all correspondence relating to the conference be made public. The administration had been badly defeated in the fall election and was in no position to press for an expansionist program that had been impaired, even before the elections, by sectional antagonisms. In fact, Pierce and Marcy were so embarrassed by the conference's results that when the documents were sent to Congress in March, 1855, the letter in which Marcy had suggested to Soulé that the United States might have to "detach" Cuba from Spain was missing.

After receiving the manifesto, Marcy complained to Mason and Assistant Secretary of State A. Dudley Mann (who had been deeply involved in the preliminaries to the conference while in Europe) about the publicity. On November 13 he pointedly told Soulé that he did not interpret the ministers' dispatch as advocating the seizure of Cuba, and he instructed Soulé to refrain from further attempts at purchase of the island. The minister was to concentrate on moderately pressing outstanding *Black Warrior* claims. The implicit repudiation was too much for the hot-tempered Soulé, who soon resigned. Soulé, however, was expendable. His duel over a point of honor with the French ambassador to Spain soon after he reached the country had long since impaired his diplomatic usefulness, and recent involvement in Spanish revolutionary politics had destroyed what was left of his credibility with the Spanish government.[35]

35. Marcy to John Y. Mason, October 19, 1854, in Marcy Papers; Spencer, *Victor and Spoils*, 325–28; *Congressional Globe*, 33rd Cong., 2nd Sess., 9; Leard, "Bonds of Destiny," 202 and *n*.

After Ostend, the Pierce administration made only feeble attempts to purchase Cuba, and all but abandoned the idea of financial intrigue. In a dispatch to Perry in April, 1855, Marcy noted the need to protect American commerce in the West Indies, but said nothing of further negotiations for Cuba. Marcy's instructions to Soulé's replacement, Augustus C. Dodge, described American acquisition of Cuba as "inevitable," but mentioned a recent vote of the Spanish Cortes against a sale and asserted that the United States must respect its decision. Dodge received instructions to try to resolve technical problems such as the captain general's lack of authority to negotiate infringements on American commerce and the need to prevent emancipation of the slaves in Cuba. A later letter (May 12, 1855) suggested that Dodge negotiate for Cuba, but was moderate in tone. Nothing came of these instructions. Dodge informed Marcy in July, 1855, that all parties in Spain opposed the sale of Cuba. Their "false pride" would cause them to refuse "any price." In the spring of 1855 the administration briefly flirted with the possibility of using a new incident involving an American ship as a means to pressure Spain to cede Cuba. A Spanish warship had stopped the *El Dorado* off the Cuban coast and then searched her for filibusters. The administration sent the American Home Squadron to the Cuban coast, but subsequently backed off from a *Black Warrior* type confrontation with Spain.[36] Pierce, like Quitman, had abandoned pursuit of the "Pearl of the Antilles."

Quitman and Pierce's failure to acquire Cuba in 1854–1855 had important political implications. The abortive attempts heightened the sectional controversy and significantly affected the public careers of a number of lead-

36. Marcy to Perry, April 9, 1855, Marcy to Dodge (draft in Cushing's handwriting), dated Thursday, 1855, and Marcy to Dodge, May 12, 1855, all in Marcy Papers; Dodge to Marcy, July 12, 1855, in Manning (ed.), *Diplomatic Correspondence*, XI, 874; Leard, "Bonds of Destiny," 203–209.

ing Americans, including President Pierce, James Buchanan, Pierre Soulé, and, to a lesser extent, Jefferson Davis.

The wily James Buchanan benefited from his involvement. He demonstrated that he stood with the South on the need for Cuba; but unlike Soulé, he had not tarnished his image. Many southern leaders detected his influence in the Ostend Manifesto. Slidell congratulated Buchanan on the document, saying: "I have read with great pleasure your Ostend Manifesto. I say yours, for I think it carries internal evidence of its being the product of your sound judgment and practiced pen." Buchanan's expansionism aided his capture of the next Democratic presidential nomination, and in his 1856 campaign he capitalized on his reputation by running on a platform calling for American "ascendancy in the Gulf of Mexico." Southern expansionists responded to this appeal and endorsed Buchanan partly because of his Cuba position. The Montgomery *Advertiser*, for instance, termed Cuba necessary to the "tranquility" of the South and stated that the "position assumed by Mr. BUCHANAN in the Ostend Manifesto, in regard to the acquisition of Cuba, ought certainly to decide every Southern man to cast his vote cheerfully for him." [37]

Pierre Soulé, however, had left for Spain as the darling of many southern expansionists and had returned discredited. Expansionists asserted, with some justification, that Soulé's various blunders had ruined an excellent chance to obtain the island. A Texas newspaper charged that Soulé had sabotaged his mission even before he left the United States, when he publicly announced that he planned to ac-

37. Slidell to Buchanan, April 3, 1855, in Buchanan Papers; J. W. McDonald to Quitman, December 20, 1855, in Quitman Papers, Harvard University Library; *Official Proceedings of the Democratic Convention ... 1856*, 27, 31; Montgomery *Advertiser*, September 13, 1856, quoted in New York *Daily Times*, October 7, 1856. See also Richmond *Enquirer*, August 15, 1856; Mobile *Daily Register*, June 11, 1856.

quire Cuba. Given the Spanish public's known opposition, Soulé should not have drawn attention to his objective; and when he did, he should have been immediately requested to resign. Instead, the country had to suffer his "disrespectful, pompous and incautious" activities in Europe, which only further undermined Pierce's intentions.[38]

Secretary of War Jefferson Davis escaped lasting political damage, but he was obliged to counter southern charges that he had been responsible for the prosecution of Quitman and that he opposed the annexation of Cuba. Mississippi Governor John J. McRae told J. F. H. Claiborne that Davis had expressed a desire to acquire Cuba. "He says that the Administration has done all that was in its power to acquire the Island, and thinks it would have been done, if Congress had sustained the President." Even now, "no efforts" would be "left unspaired [*sic*]" to take Cuba.[39] McRae probably intended the information to reach Quitman, for Quitman was connected with Claiborne. That Davis felt it imperative to make such a reassurance is indicative of the strong feeling for Cuba in the South. The issue would come up again a few years later, and this time Davis would make his pro-Cuba sentiments much more evident.

The failure of the negotiations probably hurt President Pierce the most. Quitman and his many sympathizers throughout the South blamed their ineffectuality on the president's obstructions, thereby minimizing their own deficiencies. As John Thrasher put it, the "energetic action of the administration against us, together with some other causes," blocked the expedition and forced Quitman

38. Philip Phillips to Collin J. McRae, April 3, 1854, in Collin J. McRae Papers, Alabama Department of Archives and History, Montgomery; rough draft of A. Dudley Mann to A. O. P. Nicholson, October 2, 1854, in Virginia Letters Collection; Clarksville *Standard*, December 9, 1854.

39. John J. McRae to J. F. H. Claiborne, June 7, 1855, in Claiborne Papers.

to resign. John Henderson publicly raised strict construc-
tionist objections to Pierce's action, stating that the United
States Constitution mentioned nothing about presidential
authority to issue neutrality proclamations. An Arkansas newspaper protested the government's prosecution of
Quitman in New Orleans on the grounds that the Mississippian was a "lawyer" and "gentleman" and obviously
was telling the truth when he claimed that he had violated
no law. Southerners who felt the *Black Warrior* affair justified war expressed similar disappointment when Pierce
let the crisis recede. Albert Gallatin Brown summed up
the feeling of many southern expansionists when he described Pierce as lacking "backbone." [40]

The frequent charge of insensitivity to southern needs
especially impaired Pierce's political standing in the South.
Quitman and his followers felt that the president's emphasis on diplomacy proved how unwilling he was to recognize the danger of emancipation, which they felt would be
carried out if Spain agreed to a cession, and could only be
stopped by means of an invasion. The filibusters and the
administration were not speaking in the same language,
and Quitman could find no way to bridge the gap. Samuel Walker wrote from Washington in this vein: "I tell
you the administration trembles before filibusterism—the
word spoken in their office puts them on nettle, but they
still pretend twill be bought. The friends say but for *us*
in N.O. it would have been bought. I told them it was the
worst thing for the South, & the very thing we did *not*
desire—that we would make her independent in spite of

40. John Thrasher to C. A. L. Lamar, May, 1855, in John Quitman
Papers, Mississippi Department of Archives and History; Albert
Gallatin Brown to J. F. H. Claiborne, June 29, 1854, in Claiborne
Papers; John Henderson, "Considerations on the Constitutionality
of the President's Proclamations," (pamphlet dated June 10, 1854,
published by the New Orleans *Daily Delta*), in Southern Filibusters
Collection, Louisiana State University Department of Archives and
Manuscripts, Baton Rouge; *Arkansas State Gazette and Democrat*,
July 21, 1854.

the administration." Quitman said Pierce had given the country a "humbug administration," that the president had ignored a "conspiracy" which existed "between several of the powers of Europe—England, France & Spain to cripple American commerce and American progress by Africanizing Cuba," and that abolition threatened the slave system of the fourteen southern states from which the whole country benefited. According to Quitman, the president's opposition to filibustering revealed that he had surrendered to "antislavery elements." Alexander Stephens charged that Pierce's Cuba policy proved he was trying to court the North. Similar barbs were aimed at William Marcy for his central role in the purchase scheme and its failure.[41] Differences over Cuba endangered the North-South coalition holding the national Democratic party together.

If extreme southern expansionists were troubled by Pierce's actions, they were appalled by the new Republican party's position on Cuba. From the filibuster standpoint, Pierce might have been misinformed, but at least he intended to acquire Cuba, presumably as a slave state. Republicans not only opposed the annexation of Cuba, but spelled out that their opposition was based on their commitment to prevent the addition of any new slave states. Even after the Cuba crisis of 1854–1855 subsided, Republicans kept alarming the country about a southern plot to annex Cuba as a slave state, and frequently cited the Ostend Manifesto as their main evidence. Representative Edward Wade, for instance, talked of the document in these bitter terms: "Go at it wolf-fashion, O slave De-

41. Samuel Walker to Quitman, July 31, 1854, E. L. [?] to Quitman, June 8, 1855, Quitman to B. F. Dill, June 18, 1854, and Quitman to Alexander McClung, February 4, 1855, all in Quitman Papers, Harvard University Library; Alexander Stephens to Linton Stephens, May 9, June 15, 1854, January 21, 1855, in Stephens Papers, University of North Carolina Library; *Congressional Globe*, 34th Cong., 1st Sess., Appendix, 1296.

mocracy, and take Cuba; it will be needed in a little while as medicine for a Union sick of too much freedom and too little slavery." To Henry Wilson the manifesto was a slave plot "that disgraced the diplomacy of the country." When Abraham Lincoln ran for president in 1860, his platform opposed the Ostend Manifesto as a "highwayman's plea" worthy only of "shame and dishonor." [42]

Although acquisition of Cuba remained an official goal of the national government, by the mid-1850s the debate over Cuba had become sectionalized. This would become even more apparent in 1859, when James Buchanan would make a renewed bid for Cuba and would ask Congress for funds. Southerners had come increasingly to feel a special concern for acquiring the island, and many southern expansionists had concluded that northerners were either hostile to the goal of a slave Cuba in the union, or did not understand how profoundly southern security depended on acquisition of the island with slavery intact. At the same time that such feelings were developing, events in Nicaragua and Mexico were embroiling those countries in the controversy over the expansion of slavery southward.

42. *Congressional Globe*, 34th Cong., 1st Sess., Appendix, 641, 1063, 1079, 36th Cong., 1st Sess., 594; New York *Daily Times*, September 26, 1856; Thomas H. McKee (ed.), *The National Conventions and Platforms of all Political Parties, 1789–1900* (Baltimore, 1900), 99.

IV

William Walker
in Nicaragua

In late July, 1856, Purdy's National Theatre of New York opened a new three-act musical set in the Nicaraguan towns of Granada and Rivas. The theater advertised that the play offered romance and an abduction, as well as exciting songs like "I won't die an old Maid." A large cast would perform the various roles including "Jefferson Squash, a roving Yankee" and "Ivory Black, a superior nigger." The main character was "General Walker, the hope of Freedom," and the play was entitled "Nicaragua, or, Gen. Walker's victories." [1]

The theater's directors were capitalizing on the national publicity that attended the exploits of William Walker, a Tennessean who had recently gained control of Nicaragua through invasion. His audacity had captivated many Americans of the "manifest destiny" generation. The country's expansionist press had reported his progress in minute detail. And already legends about him were circulating. Walker's Nicaraguan newspaper, *El Nicaraguense*, had started the most persistent legend by stating that Walker, who had piercing grey eyes, was the embodiment of an old Nicaraguan Indian folk belief that a "grey-eyed man" would relieve their country from oppression. Throughout the United States supporters of the adventurer hailed the "Grey-Eyed Man of Destiny" advancing American civilization in the tropics. A Tennessean wrote

1. John Heiss Scrapbook, in Heiss Papers.

in his journal that Walker could become "the greatest hero of his age," and a Baltimore paper predicted that he would now proceed to conquer Mexico, the rest of Central America, and Cuba. The New York *Evening Post* termed his achievements part of the "irresistible law of modern colonization." By the summer of 1856, William Walker had become one of the most talked about men of his era.[2]

Today William Walker is anything but a household name, yet his bizarre career has historical significance. His exploits not only fascinated people throughout the United States, but intensified the southern Caribbean movement by encouraging many southern leaders to consider the possibility of expanding slavery into Central America.

Walker was born in Nashville in 1824. His father, a Scotch immigrant and stern Calvinist, employed free Negroes as servants, and this early connection with free Negroes seems to have influenced Walker to oppose slavery as a young man. Walker attended the University of Nashville, where he was apparently a model student, and then went to the University of Pennsylvania, graduating with a medical degree in 1843. After travels and study in Europe, Walker returned to Nashville to set up a medical practice. He found medicine unappealing, however, and moved to New Orleans where he was admitted to the bar. After establishing a mediocre law practice, he again changed professions, this time entering journalism as coeditor and coproprietor of the New Orleans *Crescent*. It was in New Orleans that Walker made one of his few lasting friendships—with Edmund Randolph, a grandson of the founding father—and had his only known romance. He fell in love with a deaf-mute, Ellen Martin, and even

2. William O. Scroggs, *Filibusters and Financiers: The Story of William Walker and his Associates* (New York, 1916), 128–29; Gower and Allen (eds.), *Journals of Randal McGavock* (April 29, 1856), 362–63; Baltimore *Clipper*, May 19, 1856, clipping in John Heiss Scrapbook, Heiss Papers; New York *Evening Post*, quoted in *National Intelligencer*, November 30, 1855.

learned sign-language to communicate with her. When she died from cholera in April, 1849, he was deeply disturbed and soon emigrated to California.

In California Walker became active in newspaper work, law, and Democratic politics. He earned an antislavery reputation when he committed himself to the Broderick faction in state politics; he also fought a number of duels and suffered a jail term for contempt of court for defending freedom of the press. In 1853 he underwent still another occupational transformation, turning filibuster despite his having written editorials against the López expeditions while on the *Crescent* staff. He would become the most successful filibuster in American history.

Walker's exploits and personality intrigued his contemporaries to the point that they felt almost compelled to describe his character and appearance. They differed concerning Walker's hair and eye color. Edmund Ruffin thought that his famous eyes were "light greenish blue" rather than grey. But they agreed that he was freckled, short (no more than five feet, six inches), and skinny. Walker's extreme shyness and lack of pretension attracted the most comment. He spoke sparingly and tended to keep his hands in his pockets, and this reticence may explain his unspectacular law career. Many people expressed surprise at his ambition and wondered how he could gain enough respect to effectively command men. "Strange man and still stranger history" exclaimed one Nashville acquaintance. But he was extremely brave in battle and men followed him under the most dire hardships. They even joined Walker in new filibustering enterprises after participating with him in others that failed.[3]

3. Edmund Ruffin Diary, May 14, 1858, in Edmund Ruffin Papers, Library of Congress; W. Grayson Mann to William Trousdale, June 15, 1857, in William Trousdale Papers, Tennessee State Library and Archives, Nashville; Harrisburg *Weekly Telegraph,* November 20, 1856; Memphis *Daily Appeal,* August 12, 1857; Clarksville (Texas) *Standard,* January 19, 1856; Tuskegee *Republican,*

Why Walker committed himself to so dangerous and illegal a career as filibustering has puzzled his biographers. Walker's own account of his endeavors, *The War in Nicaragua*, published in Mobile the year of his death (1860), is factual for the most part, but offers little insight into his motivations. That few of his personal letters survived his death has further hindered researchers. The attempt of one writer to explain Walker as an agent of slavery expansion is obviously incorrect because it disregards his activities in New Orleans and California.[4]

A recent psychological evaluation of Walker by Albert Z. Carr probes much deeper. Carr maintains that Walker rebelled against his strict Calvinist upbringing, often striking out at authority in an attempt to assert his own power. This rebelliousness led Walker to reject a career in the ministry, which his father favored, and accounts, in part, for his desire to lead men. Moreover, Walker was sexually frustrated throughout his life, and needed outlets for his libidinal drives. Ellen Martin's death is the key to his life according to this interpretation: "His chance of emotional liberation had gone with the death of Ellen Martin. . . .

January 28, 1858; Parker French to Cyrinus Fitzgerald, March 10, 1858, in Mirabeau Buonaparte Lamar Papers, Texas State Library and Archives, Austin; C. W. Doubleday, *Reminiscences of the 'Filibuster' War in Nicaragua* (New York, 1886), 104–105; Gower and Allen (eds.), *Journals of Randal McGavock* (May 27, 1857), 416; John H. Wheeler, *Reminiscences and Memoirs of North Carolinians* (Columbus, Ohio, 1884), 24; Walker to John Berrien Lindsley, March 18, 1848, quoted in John Edwin Windrow, *John Berrien Lindsley: Educator, Physician, Social Philosopher* (Chapel Hill, 1938), Appendix, 191; *Congressional Globe*, 35th Cong., 2nd Sess., 967; Scroggs, *Filibusters*, 12–16, 49; Albert Z. Carr, *The World and William Walker* (New York, 1963), 8–14, 23–24, 36; typescript of H. Royston Lawson, "William Walker: His Early Life," in Tennessee State Library and Archives, Nashville.

4. Edward S. Wallace, *Destiny and Glory* (New York, 1957), *passim*.

His maleness found its outlet in an assault . . . upon the political timidities of his environment." A captive of the romantic ideas of chivalry and virginity, Walker became a worshipper of heroism. A nationalist, he resented European encroachments in Central America. An idealistic activist, he decided that his intervention might aid America's "manifest destiny" and at the same time rally a nation divided over slavery.[5]

W. O. Scroggs, in a much earlier study, emphasized Walker's vision of America's "manifest destiny" and agreed that Ellen Martin's death led to Walker's "daring ambition and a reckless disregard of life." To Scroggs, Walker's actions south of the border were a mutation of the American movement westward. Certainly Walker migrated to California in 1849 because he craved the excitement California offered in that year of the gold boom. Walker's invasions of Nicaragua and Mexico were extensions of his participation in this movement. Scroggs explains filibustering in social-Darwinist terms: "In its final analysis filibustering may be described, in the phraseology of Herbert Spencer, as a process of equilibrium of energy. Whenever a superior or more energetic people are brought into conflict with an inferior or less energetic group, a process of equilibration between the two groups occurs. This equilibrative movement is always some kind of conflict, and in its primitive aspect we call it the struggle for existence." [6] Scroggs, as well as Carr, also mentions specific reasons for Walker's becoming a filibuster such as his knowledge of

5. Carr, *Walker*, 3–7, 14, 74, 76, 81, 95, 123–24. The problem with Carr's study is that it is sparsely annotated, and much of Carr's psychological interpretation seems intuitive to the extreme.

6. Scroggs, *Filibusters*, 2–4, 15. Scroggs also notes that a puritanical spirit reigned at the University of Nashville when Walker went there. Students could not attend balls, horse races, cockfights, or the theater, and they had to participate in compulsory prayers twice a day in the chapel. See *ibid.*, 10–11.

French expeditions in Sonora in the early 1850s, the intervention of Byron Cole in the development of Central American mines in 1854, and Walker's failure in California law and politics.[7]

Except for Scroggs's imposition of Rudyard Kipling and Herbert Spencer on the history of the 1850s, much in both his and Carr's interpretations seems plausible, although in the absence of definitive evidence, Walker's personality remains open to further analysis. A few observations can be forwarded here, none of which detract, necessarily, from previous studies of Walker. Overly sensitive in his youth—one acquaintance recalled how he read to his invalid mother every morning—and perhaps over-idealistic, he seems to have hardened by the time of his filibustering expeditions; for on these expeditions he burned towns, confiscated property, executed rivals and deserters, and established dictatorial rule, with few second thoughts. John Wheeler, who served as American minister to Nicaragua during the Walker years, and who knew Walker well, depicted the filibuster as one who "looked upon men as the mere titulary pawns of the chessboard, to be moved and sacrificed to advance the ambitious plans of others."[8]

Whether such an autocratic person could have loved American democracy is debatable. Walker may have been alienated from democracy by 1853 for some reason or

7. Carr, *Walker*, 75–76, 91–95; Scroggs, *Filibusters*, 16, 82–92. There were many Frenchmen in California in the early 1850s, and a number of expeditions left the new state to conquer Sonora's gold and silver mines. All ended in failure. Walker met the leader of one of the expeditions in San Francisco—Count Gaston Raoul de Raousset-Boulbon—and was impressed by him. See Carr, *Walker*, 74–76; Rufus Kay Wyllys, "The Republic of Lower California, 1853–1854," *Pacific Historical Review*, II (1933), 194–213.

8. Jane Thomas, *Old Days in Nashville, Tennessee: Reminiscences* (Nashville, 1897), 78; Wheeler, *Reminiscences*, 27.

combination of reasons. Certainly democracy on the California frontier did not work entirely to his liking. Carr's interpretation of Walker is perhaps most relevant when it points to Walker's need for personal power. A restless wanderer throughout his early life, Walker may have accidentally discovered filibustering to be the best means of achieving power over a large group of people—perhaps over a country. In the process Walker's democratic inclination may have taken a back seat. One disillusioned follower described him as a "freckled little Despot." [9] There is no conclusive proof that Walker ever wanted to annex Mexico or Nicaragua to the United States or that he wanted to establish a truly democratic system south of the border. It may be that Walker hungered for power and adventure and never intended to extend the democratic institutions invoked in John L. O'Sullivan's concept of "manifest destiny."

William Walker's first intrusion southward came in the fall of 1853, following a refusal by the Mexican government to honor his application for colonizing privileges in the state of Sonora. Set on eventually invading Sonora, Walker and forty-five followers eluded United States military authorities in San Francisco and left for Lower California. Their first target was La Paz, the territorial capital, near the southern tip of Lower California. Using a Mexican flag as a ruse, Walker captured both the governor and the town. He followed up the victory by declaring Lower California an independent republic and himself its president. Then on January 18, while President Pierce over three thousand miles away was issuing his proclamation against filibustering, Walker decreed the yet-to-

9. Parker French to Cyrinus Fitzgerald, March 10, 1858, in Lamar Papers; typewritten copy of Louis Schlessinger to John Quitman, September 3, 1857, in Quitman Family Papers.

be-conquered Sonora annexed to his republic of Lower California.[10]

Walker's stay in La Paz brought the partial ruin of government offices and archives, as well as considerable plundering. His attempts to win over the populace by abolishing the Mexican tariff had little effect, and, following a minor skirmish, the Americans left La Paz and started working their way up the western coast of the peninsula toward Sonora.

By February of 1854, reinforcements had increased Walker's force to about 150 men; but Mexican resistance was coalescing, provoked by Walker's practice of requisitioning horses from the people. In addition, federal authorities in San Francisco, under instructions from Jefferson Davis, arrested Walker's agents and refused to permit Walker's supplies and some of his reinforcements to leave port.

Walker and his band reached Sonora by crossing the Colorado River near the top of the Gulf of California; but beset by internal dissension, desertion, starvation, and lack of clothing, Walker hastily retreated northward to the United States border, then proceeded to San Francisco and was put on trial for violating the neutrality laws. In August a friendly jury acquitted Walker. Although fines were levied on his cohorts, they were never paid. The Tennessean's next expedition would achieve far more success. After a year of California politics, during which time he

10. Walker claimed that the purpose of his Mexican expedition had been to protect American families on the Sonora border against Apaches. See Walker, *War in Nicaragua*, 19, 21. The expedition was not as strong as it might have been because Colonel Ethan Allen Hitchcock, commander of the Pacific Military Division, had seized the ship that Walker planned to use, thus confusing Walker's plans. In the haste to depart from San Francisco before further action was taken, men, supplies, ammunition and weapons were left behind. The expedition's weakened condition was probably what influenced Walker to make Lower California rather than Sonora itself his first target. See Wyllys, "Republic of Lower California," 201–203.

attended the Democratic state convention as a delegate, Walker went south again—this time to Nicaragua.[11]

Nicaragua, bordered by Honduras on the north and Costa Rica on the south, is located in about the middle of Central America and faces both the Caribbean Sea and the Pacific Ocean. It was one of the republics that achieved independence during the breakup of the Spanish empire in the Western Hemisphere early in the nineteenth century. The five republics of Nicaragua, Honduras, Guatemala, El Salvador, and Costa Rica consolidated into a United Provinces of Central America—better known as Guatemala—and abolished slavery. Disputes caused the union to dissolve in 1831.

During the six years prior to the Walker adventure, Americans became increasingly involved in Nicaragua.[12] With thousands of easterners searching for an easy way to reach the California goldfields, American business enterprise focused on Nicaragua as a practical route. If a traveler were to embark on a vessel at Greytown (San

11. *National Intelligencer*, March 13, 1854; James Fred Rippy, *The United States and Mexico* (New York, 1926), 94; Carr, *Walker*, 74–91, 97; Thomas Ray Wilson, "William Walker and the Filibustering Expedition to Lower California and Sonora" (M.A. thesis, University of Texas, 1944), 44–48; Wyllys, "Republic of Lower California," 203–209; John E. Wool to Jefferson Davis, January 10, February 28, March 1, 1854, Jefferson Davis to John E. Wool, January 12, 1854, and John E. Wool to Winfield Scott, May 15, 1854, all in "Correspondence Between the Late Secretary of War and General Wool," *House Executive Documents*, 35th Cong., 1st Sess., No. 88, pp. 6, 9, 10, 19–20, 27ff. Wool asserted that he had helped break up reinforcements for Walker and that "no aid has been rendered to Walker since my arrival in the country." Later Davis modified his stand against filibustering, repudiating Wool for being too stringent in his interpretations of the neutrality laws. See Davis to Wool, April 14, August 18, 1854, in "Correspondence Between the Late Secretary of War and General Wool," *House Executive Documents*, 35th Cong., 1st Sess., No. 88, pp. 52–99.

12. "Nicaragua and the Filibusters," *Blackwood's Magazine*, LXXIX (1856), 316–17.

Juan del Norte) on the Caribbean Sea, follow the San Juan River into Lake Nicaragua to the west, and cross the lake, all that would be left of his journey would be a twelve-mile land trip to San Juan del Sur on the Pacific Ocean. This was the best way to get to California. Travel across the United States desert was extremely dangerous. Transit across Mexico was mostly by land. Panama was further south, and thus a longer trip. Were a canal ever constructed across Nicaragua, the trip would be even easier. In June, 1849, the American consul to Guatemala arranged a treaty with Nicaragua giving the United States government or its citizens the exclusive right to build and fortify a Nicaraguan canal.

Cornelius Vanderbilt, the railroad magnate, had profit in mind when he organized the Accessory Transit Company to compete with a rival company that was working the route across Panama. In 1851 Vanderbilt secured from the Nicaraguan government a contract giving his company a monopoly of transit from Greytown to the Pacific, and the contract proved most lucrative. From 1851–1856, two thousand Americans per month traversed the route, and the company dominated ocean traffic to and from Nicaragua.[13]

The British government, however, challenged the growing American role in the region. British and French policy makers hoped to contain American expansion southward, and the British government was in an advantageous position to take steps to counter American involvement in

13. William O. Scroggs, "William Walker and the Steamship Corporation in Nicaragua," *American Historical Review*, X (1904), 793; "Nicaragua and the Filibusters," 315; Nevins, *Ordeal*, II, 365. Vanderbilt reached an earlier agreement with the Nicaraguan government (1849) granting him the right to construct a canal across Nicaragua, and the 1851 agreement was actually a modification of the earlier contract. See Scroggs, "Walker and the Steamship Corporation," 793.

Central America. By 1849, Britain had a colony in Belize (later British Honduras), claims to the Bay Islands off the coast of Belize, and a protectorate over what was known as the Mosquito Coast (or Kingdom)—the area located between Cape Honduras and the San Juan River, on the eastern shore of what is today Honduras and Nicaragua. In addition, the Costa Rican and Guatemalan governments were pro-British. Frederick Chatfield, the English consul in Central America, was especially active in trying to prevent American inroads. To block American construction of a canal across Nicaragua, Chatfield informed the Nicaraguan government that the canal's proposed eastern terminus, the mouth of the San Juan River, as well as a good portion of that river, lay within the Mosquito territory. He also played a role in the temporary seizure of Tigre Island, which overlooked the Pacific outlet of a proposed Nicaraguan canal route. Ephraim George Squier, American commissioner in the region, took action to thwart British resistance. Squier contested British claims to the San Juan, persuaded Nicaragua and Honduras to affirm the principles of the Monroe Doctrine, and reached agreements with Nicaragua concerning American construction of a canal.

The Clayton-Bulwer Treaty of 1850 between the United States and England temporarily defused the issue. The treaty ruled out American and British colonization in Central America, prohibited exclusive American or British control of an Isthmian canal across Central America, and provided for cooperation between the two countries in the construction of such a canal.

But the relaxation of tension that the treaty afforded proved fleeting. The British asserted that the agreement was prospective rather than retroactive and refused to abandon their past acquisitions. This interpretation was underscored when Britain, in March, 1852, declared that

Ruatan, Bonacca, and four nearby islands had become the
"Colony of the Bay Islands." The Clayton-Bulwer Treaty
became a target of abuse in the United States since it dis-
allowed American expansion into Central America while
permitting a British presence. Democrats had special political incentives for maligning the treaty because it was
the product of a Whig administration. When Franklin
Pierce entered office in 1853, he dedicated his administration to redefining the treaty more explicitly in keeping
with American interests. With the passing of time an
increasing number of leading Americans demanded can-
cellation of the agreement. Abrogation became a major
rallying cry for the "Young American" Democrats. A
state of confrontation evolved between Great Britain and
the United States in Central America. When Captain
George Hollins of the United States Navy bombarded the
British-Mosquito Indian port of Greytown on July 13,
1854, he was in effect serving notice to the British as to
just how bitter Americans had become toward the Clayton-
Bulwer Treaty and British rivalry in the region.

Anglo-American friction in Central America reflected
the generally unsteady relations between the two nations
in the early 1850s, despite the reciprocity treaty of 1854
resolving many Canadian-American problems. British opposition to American expansion was hardly restricted to
Central America. The British interfered in the mid-1850s
with schemes of the Pierce administration to annex Hawaii, as well as Samana Bay in the Dominican Republic.
Britain even interfered with an American commercial
agreement of late 1854 with Ecuador concerning the
guano trade of the Galapagos Islands. It was commonly
believed in the United States that Britain and, to a lesser
extent, France were all that stood in the way of American
acquisition of Cuba. These apprehensions were heightened
when Lord Clarendon talked about British-French cooper-

ation throughout the world in a speech before the House of Lords on January 31, 1854.[14]

In the spring of 1856, controversy surrounding Lord Crampton, the British minister to the United States, increased the friction. According to the Pierce administration, Crampton had recruited Americans for service in the Crimean War, contrary to provisions of United States neutrality laws. The United States government requested Crampton's recall, Britain refused, and Crampton was eventually expelled. Britain then left the post of minister to the United States vacant until Pierce left office. In February, 1856, the Pierce administration, chafed by the presence of a British fleet in American waters, gave considerable thought to going to war with England. For their part, British leaders had cause for complaint with a perceived pro-Russia feeling in the United States after the Crimean War broke out.[15]

Thus, when William Walker thrust himself into Nica-

14. Dexter Perkins, *The Monroe Doctrine, 1826–1867* (Baltimore, 1933), 194–225; Alan Dowty, *The Limits of Isolation: The United States and the Crimean War* (New York, 1971), 34–61, 72–99, 146–48; R. A. Humphreys, *The Diplomatic History of British Honduras, 1638–1901* (New York, 1961), 1–58; Richard Van Alstyne, "British Diplomacy and the Clayton-Bulwer Treaty, 1850–60," *Journal of Modern History*, XI (1939), 149–51, 166–70; Albert D. Kirwan, *John J. Crittenden: The Struggle For the Union* (Lexington, 1962), 271–72; Merze Tate, "Slavery and Racism as Deterrents to the Annexation of Hawaii, 1854–1855," *Journal of Negro History*, XLVII (1962), 1–18; William H. Goetzmann, *When the Eagle Screamed: The Romantic Horizon in American Diplomacy, 1800–1860* (New York, 1966), 78–82. The Mosquito Kingdom also included a "reserved stretch of coast" south of the San Juan River. The total British Mosquito claim came to about eight hundred miles of coastline. See Van Alstyne, "British Diplomacy," 149.

15. Thomas Bailey, *A Diplomatic History of the American People* (6th ed.; New York, 1958), 281. Another incident which contributed to American-British tension occurred in 1856 when a British naval officer stopped and inspected the American steamer *Orizaba* in Nicaraguan waters.

raguan affairs in 1855, he was entering a tense situation. His involvement was prompted by the revolution and civil wars that disrupted Nicaragua. One of the two main Nicaraguan factions, the Democrats (or Constitutionalists), near defeat in 1854, invited Americans to aid their cause. Though funds were scarce, land incentives were generous. Byron Cole, a San Francisco newspaperman who knew Walker and had mining interests in Honduras, visited Nicaragua in 1854 and returned to California with a contract for Walker. The Constitutionalists offered Walker a commission as colonel in their army, monthly pay, and a promise of an extensive grant of land, upon victory, for his services.

The contract not only encouraged Walker's involvement in Nicaragua, but it also cloaked the impending expedition with a semilegal character. General John Wool refrained from clamping down on Walker's preparations, and Walker and fifty-seven other men slipped out of San Francisco Bay aboard the brig *Vesta* shortly after midnight on the morning of May 4, 1855.[16] On June 16 they landed at Realejo in northern Nicaragua and were soon immersed in the Nicaraguan civil war.

The intentions of Walker and his followers at the outset of their adventure merit consideration, since in a little over a year Walker would be posing as a champion of the southern slave system and would describe his expedition as an instrument of the expansion of slavery. Walker had been mildly antislavery; and unlike Quitman's expedition, which was southern in orientation and membership, Walker's Nicaragua enterprise had little sectional character

16. Walker, *War in Nicaragua*, 31–32; New York *Herald*, July 21, 1855; Wheeler, *Reminiscences*, 24; *Blackwood's Magazine*, LXXIX (1856), 320; Scroggs, "Walker and the Steamship Corporation," 794–95. Byron Cole was one of the proprietors of a California newspaper that Walker edited for a while. Wool also may have been lax in enforcing the law because the Legitimists, the Nicaragua faction that Walker would be opposing, were British supported.

or purpose. There is virtually no evidence that the men who left American shores for Nicaragua had anything like the ideological commitment to slavery expansion that motivated some of John Quitman's followers. Walker's *War in Nicaragua* gives no indication that his first recruits were slavery oriented, and the register of Walker's army in Nicaragua, including entries up to March 6, 1857, shows that of the Nicaragua filibusters born in the United States, 347 were born in the North, whereas only 288 were born in the South. A register that lists the occupations of the 314 men who sailed on the steamer *Texas* for Nicaragua in November, 1856, to reinforce Walker, reveals that of the 142 from the slave-holding states, there were only 4 planters, 18 farmers, 2 "gentlemen," and 2 overseers. Even had all these men been involved in the slave system, it is obvious that Walker did not attract the plantation element of the South in large numbers. A list of letters received from the United States in 1856 enquiring about friends and relatives in Nicaragua indicates the same national composition. Of the 62 letters, 37 came from the northern states, 24 from the southern states, and 1 from England.[17] Men came from all over the United States to join Walker, with most departing from San Francisco, New York, and New Orleans.

Love of adventure and desire for the spoils of war gained Walker most of his following. Walker depicted his *Vesta* passengers as men "tired of the humdrum of common life, and ready for a career which might bring them the sweets of adventure or the rewards of fame," words which would have applied to most filibusters of the era. Some undoubtedly were fleeing personal crises back in

17. William Walker Papers, Tulane University Library (Latin American Collection), New Orleans, Folders No. 2, 93, 120. The "South" in these statistics includes all the slaveholding states. There were a large number of Europeans, generally poor, involved in the expedition. The register of Walker's army included 287 Europeans. See Walker Papers, Tulane University Library, Folder No. 120.

the states, such as South Carolinian George Tillman, who
had just killed a gambler. Others were simply capricious:
C. W. Doubleday, mining in California, decided to go to
Nicaragua on a "whim of the moment"; and the fifteen-
year-old son of a large Kentucky landowner ran away and
tried to join Walker because it was "the spirit of the
times." [18]

An account by A. C. Allen, a member of the *Texas* expedition, offers particularly good insights into the rough nature of the men involved. Allen, an officer, described others
on board as gun-hungry, "ugly looking strangers" who
got drunk, pressured him to play poker against his will,
threatened him, and stole his pistol. Allen, however, was
no saint himself. He recounts how he drew his gun on a
sailor who called him a liar and tried to shoot him, "but
my pistol not being cocked, caused a delay," which allowed
others to prevent the murder. Allen also was not overly
alarmed when a fellow officer on a visit to Greytown stag-
gered in the streets waving his revolver, screaming, and
chasing people.[19] Many of the filibusters were unstable, im-
poverished, or degenerate. An employee of a New Orleans
grain merchant wrote his father:

> This is a City in which I would dread being idle, as it is
> a kind of rendezvous for all reckless characters and men
> of desperate fortunes—whose acquaintance I should judge
> it would be hard to shun were a person out of Employ-
> ment—for they are always looking for young men without
> prospects, for various filibustering and piratical expedi-

18. Walker, *War in Nicaragua*, 32; Undated, untitled, anonymous,
typewritten manuscript in Tillman Family Papers, Clemson University Library, Clemson, South Carolina; Doubleday, *Reminiscences*,
2; Asbury Harpending, *The Great Diamond Hoax*, ed. James H.
Wilkins (2nd ed.; Norman, 1958), 5. George Tillman was the older
brother of Ben Tillman, later a famous South Carolina governor and
United States senator.
19. A. C. Allen Diary (photocopy), "The Walker Expedition,"
January 1, 2, 4, 7, 1857, in A. C. Allen Papers, Barker Texas History
Center Archives, University of Texas, Austin.

tions. There are at present numbers of such men in town recruiting for Col. Walker's forces in Nicaragua and they find but little difficulty in procuring young men for their purposes.

A Californian told his brother that Walker deserved a reward because he was "drawing off a class of people from this state that we can afford to part from without shedding a tear." Norfolk, Virginia, people expressed outrage in January, 1858, when the United States Navy deposited 155 of Walker's followers in the city. Claiming that the men's presence created a major welfare crisis, the Richmond *Whig* called for reparations from the federal government and threatened war if such reparations were not forthcoming. The *Whig* complained: "No State in this Union ever before had deliberately let loose within its limits a band of brigands, pirates, and cutthroats." [20]

Many of Walker's soldiers were experienced filibusters. Roberdeau Wheat, one of the men on Allen's *Texas* expedition to reinforce Walker, could even be classified as a professional. He had volunteered for the Mexican War at the age of twenty, fought with López at Cárdenas, helped plan the abortive Quitman movement, and joined revolutionary movements in Mexico. His involvement with Walker would be followed by a stint with Garibaldi in Italy and death in combat for the Confederacy at the battle of Gaines's Mill.[21]

20. J. A. W. Brenan to his father, December 19, 1855, in Miscellaneous Papers, Louisiana State University Department of Archives and Manuscripts, Baton Rouge; Francis Edward Russwurm to James Russwurm, March 11, 1857, in Russwurm Family Papers, Tennessee State Library and Archives, Nashville; Louisville *Daily Courier*, January 4, 6, 8, 1858; Richmond *Whig*, January 7, 1858; A. W. Redding to Stephen Douglas, February 6, 1858, in Douglas Papers; O. T. Watson to John Quitman, January 5, 1858, in Quitman Papers, Harvard University Library.

21. C. R. Wheat to John Quitman, October 11, 1854, in John Quitman Papers, Mississippi Department of Archives and History; John Ford to Hugh McLeod, January 14, 1855, and John Thrasher to Hugh McLeod, January 24, 1855, both in McLeod Papers; Dufour,

Unquestionably some of Walker's recruits were well off, had a fixed purpose in joining him, and did not deserve being typecast as degenerates, villains, or professional adventurers. The son of former United States senator Sidney Breese expressed an interest in joining Walker, apparently with the intention of setting up a law practice in Nicaragua. Land and minerals motivated John Heiss and William Cazneau. Heiss had edited a number of newspapers, including James K. Polk's mouthpiece, the Washington *Union*. Cazneau, a Texas entrepreneur, had been influential in Texas politics and had served as Pierce's special agent to the Dominican Republic.[22] However, most of Walker's cohorts did earn their reputations of being degenerates, villains, and professional adventurers.

Walker's rise to power was swift. An early defeat at Rivas, Nicaragua, was followed by occupation of Virgin Bay, victory at Granada, and control of the transit area. By October, 1855, Walker, his men, and new recruits had so established themselves strategically that General Ponciano Corral, the Legitimist leader, acceded to Walker's call for a compromise end to the civil war. On October 23, Corral came to Granada and agreed to a coalition government, with Don Patricio Rivas, a native Nicaraguan, as

---

Wheat, passim. Wheat was a boyhood friend of William Walker and attended the University of Nashville with Walker's brother James. Like Walker, Wheat had been frustrated in love (his girl did not wait for him during the Mexican War) and profession. He was also extremely hot tempered and suffered suspension from the University of Nashville because of fighting. See Dufour, *Wheat*, 32–34; Gower and Allen (eds.), *Journals of Randal McGavock*, 34–35; Allen Diary, January 17, 1857, in Allen Papers; Scroggs, *Filibusters*, 239.

22. Sidney Breese to Stephen Douglas, March 29, 1856, in Douglas Papers; Ann Stephens to Mirabeau Buonaparte Lamar, January 20, 1858, in Lamar Papers; John Heiss Scrapbook, in Heiss Papers; letter appointing Heiss agent of the North American Chontales Company, dated September 9, 1856, in Heiss Papers; [?] to Guy M. Bryan, October 1, 1857, in Guy M. Bryan Papers, Barker Texas History Center Archives, University of Texas, Austin.

president. Corral and Walker divided the military power: Walker became commander in chief and Corral assumed the position of minister of war. Corral's tenure in office was prematurely terminated when Walker discovered that he was conspiring to rid Nicaragua of American filibusters. Walker manipulated Rivas into having Corral executed for treason (on November 8), thus paving the way for his own ascendancy in Nicaraguan politics.

Simultaneously, Walker made certain that his new stature would not be challenged by rival Americans seeking to take advantage of Nicaragua's weakness. Henry L. Kinney's bid for power was decisively crushed. Kinney was a Texas promoter (one of the founders of Corpus Christi) and a former member of the Texas legislature who had established the Nicaraguan Land and Mining Company, based on a questionable grant from the Mosquito Kingdom. Kinney offered prospective filibusters from 160 to 640 acres of land ("according to location") and a town lot, and attracted approval in influential circles. His preliminary planning actually gained more attention than Walker's in the American press, and his supporters included Joseph Fabens, the American commercial agent in Greytown, President Pierce's private secretary, Sidney Webster, and United States senator from Texas, Thomas Rusk, who purchased five thousand shares of Kinney's stock. Kinney set up a paper government in Greytown in September, 1855, but got no further. Walker, already holding the reins of power in the country, refused an approach by Kinney for an alliance, saying to Kinney's emissaries (one of whom was Fabens) that he would hang the Texan if he ever got his hands on him—a threat so persuasive that both of Kinney's emissaries defected. Walker also saw to it that the Rivas administration voided Kinney's claim. Kinney lingered in Nicaragua for a while. He begged John Quitman for help, promising he would protect southern "institutions" in Nicaragua. He even managed to secure an interview with Walker. But Kinney's quest for an alliance proved fruitless, he suffered arrest for intriguing against Walker, and he returned, defeated, to the United States.[23]

Walker had less success in gaining favor with the United States government. Though Jefferson Davis favored the Walker regime, Pierce had already taken a stand against filibustering, and Marcy and Cushing opposed the expedition in the cabinet. On the very day that Corral was executed, Marcy instructed John H. Wheeler, the United States minister to Nicaragua, that the new government should not be recognized: "It appears to be no more than a violent occupation of power, brought about by an irregular self-organized military force, as yet unsanctioned by the will or acquiescence of the people of Nicaragua." Marcy characterized the government as "temporary" and instructed Wheeler to refrain from all official intercourse with the new rulers. Walker later attributed his ultimate failure to this initial hostility of the Pierce administration. Walker's Central American opponents realized that

23. "A Home in Nicaragua," pamphlet, and microfilm of "Shares of Stock in Nicaragua Land and Mining Company," in William Sidney Thayer Papers, University of Virginia Library, Charlottesville; Certificate dated December, 1854, in Thomas Jefferson Rusk Papers, Barker Texas History Center Archives, University of Texas, Austin; New York *Herald*, December 30, 1854; Clarksville *Standard*, November 10, 1855; Scroggs, *Filibusters*, 93–132; Hortense Warner Ward, "The First State Fair of Texas," *Southwestern Historical Quarterly*, LXX (1967), 163–64; Goetzmann, *When the Eagle Screamed*, 84; Spencer, *Victor and Spoils*, 353–54; Kinney to John Quitman, November 3, 1855, in Quitman Papers, Harvard University Library. Scroggs points out that there were other forces working against Kinney besides Walker's hostility. Secretary of State Marcy opposed Kinney's activities, firing Fabens from his position, United States officials interfered with Kinney's departure, and Kinney's schooner suffered shipwreck on its trip to Nicaragua. See Scroggs, *Filibusters*, 100–106; Marcy to José de Marcoleta (Nicaraguan minister to the United States), May 15, October 10, 1855, in Manning (ed.), *Diplomatic Correspondence*, VI, 68, 73.

the United States government would not intervene in order to protect him.[24]

Wheeler, a North Carolinian, had other ideas. Imbued with an early vision of the "white man's burden," Wheeler viewed Walker as an agent of a superior race that would replace the allegedly syphilis-infected, feeble races of Central America. Wheeler so identified with Walker that he broke codes of diplomatic neutrality and aligned himself with the movement even before Corral and Walker made their temporary peace. The minister tried to convince Marcy that Walker was worth supporting: "I am certain that the influences of Americans from the North will tend to purify their principles and elevate their conduct. With this idea it will prove a blessing if the whole of Central America becomes Americanized by the industrious and interprizing [sic] from the North." Wheeler and Walker dined together, read each other's newspapers, and partied together. And on November 10, before Marcy's instructions arrived, Wheeler recognized the Rivas government.[25]

24. Fuess, *Cushing*, II, 176; John Bassett Moore (ed.), *A Digest of International Law* (8 vols.; Washington, D.C., 1906), I, 140; Walker, *War in Nicaragua*, 107; *Texas State Gazette*, June 13, 1857; John Heiss Scrapbook, in Heiss Papers. Scroggs agreed with Walker's conclusions. Marcy's denunciation of recognition of Walker on the basis that the Rivas government did not have the consent of the Nicaraguan people was "loudly heralded in every quarter of Central America and strengthened the hands of those who were meditating Walker's destruction." See Scroggs, *Filibusters*, 170.

25. Wheeler to Marcy, June 15, 1856, in Manning (ed.), *Diplomatic Correspondence*, VI, 537, 485ff; Edmund Ruffin Diary, February 20, 1857, in Ruffin Papers; John Wheeler Diary, November 4, December 6, 1855, March 24, 1856, in John Wheeler Papers, University of North Carolina Library, Chapel Hill; Baltimore *Sun*, October 4, 1856; Randall O. Hudson, "The Filibuster Minister: The Career of John Hill Wheeler as United States Minister to Nicaragua, 1854–1856," *North Carolina Historical Review*, XLIX (1972), 288–91. Years later, Wheeler would remember Walker in a similar vein: "Doubtless Walker had faults, but he supplanted a government of ignorance, superstition, indolence, imbecility, and treachery. Had he

The State Department reprimanded Wheeler for this action and obstructed the delivery of supplies to Walker. Pierce issued another proclamation on December 8, warning American citizens not to participate in the Nicaraguan venture, and dispatched Commodore Paulding to Nicaragua to keep a watch on affairs. When the disreputable Parker H. French, Rivas' minister to the United States, arrived in Washington, Marcy refused to accept his credentials.[26]

Walker, nevertheless, gradually consolidated his position. The Accessory Transit Company willingly cooperated with Walker because company officials viewed him as a stabilizing influence on the country. In addition, the company had failed to live up to its financial obligations under its transit contract and was in debt to the Nicaraguan government. The free passage to Nicaragua which the

---

succeeded, he would have rivaled the fame of Houston, and added to the area of human liberty and enjoyment. Compare the present condition of Texas and California now with Mexico. There is a destiny in the affairs of nations, as well as of men." See Wheeler, *Reminiscences*, 21.

26. Scroggs, *Filibusters* 126; Fuess, *Cushing*, II, 177; Roy F. Nichols, *Franklin Pierce: Young Hickory of the Granite Hills* (Rev. ed.; Philadelphia, 1958), 460. Carr asserts that Pierce's reluctance to recognize Walker was influenced by the protests of the English, Spanish, and French ministers, the financial interests of men close to Pierce in the rival Kinney expedition, and Parker French's newspaper attack on Marcy. See Carr, *Walker*, 156–61, 179–82.

An adventurer from his youth on, French most recently had been in Sonora, where he lost his right hand and part of his right wrist in a gunfight, had robbed a mail coach in Mexico, and had been in jail; at one point he had even been sentenced to be shot. He had made Walker's acquaintance as a Sacramento publisher and promoter when Walker was in California and had aided Walker's recruiting efforts for Nicaragua. Walker had appointed him his minister of public credit, a position that French used to cheat the Nicaraguan clergy. It may well be that Walker gave French the appointment to the United States as a means of getting him off his hands. See Edward McGowan, *The Strange Eventful History of Parker H. French* (Los Angeles, 1958), 2–11, 30, 36–37, 153–54; Scroggs, *Filibusters*, 165.

company granted to Walker reinforcements proved a boon to the American cause.[27] By the spring of 1856 more than twelve hundred Americans had come to the country, and about six hundred of these enrolled in the Nicaraguan army. In the late fall of 1855, and through most of the winter, Nicaragua enjoyed its first period of peace in many years.[28]

Walker also played on American sentiment against British involvement in Central America to break down United States government antipathy to his progress. He focused his attention on Senator Stephen Douglas, a recognized expansionist and nationalist. Walker wrote Douglas that Britain was supplying arms to his enemies, and Parker French urged Douglas to get the American neutrality laws revoked for Walker's benefit and to punish England "for the course she has pursued and is now pursuing." Walker also sent intercepted correspondence that revealed the British role against him to the United States State Department. Later, one of his first acts after inauguration

27. Scroggs, "Walker and the Steamship Corporation," 796–801. The corporation owed Nicaragua 10 percent of all profits made from its control of the transit route. It had never paid this money, and the money that the company put out to transport recruits to Walker was charged to the outstanding debt. Scroggs also points out that the transit company helped Walker in a more indirect fashion. Because peaceful passengers to California intermingled with the filibusters aboard transit company vessels, it was difficult for United States officials to determine which travelers were filibusters, and government efforts to impair Walker's position by enforcing the neutrality laws were thus hampered. See Scroggs, "Walker and the Steamship Corporation," 801–802.

28. Walker, *War in Nicaragua*, 159, 177; Edmund Ruffin Diary, February 20, 1857, in Ruffin Papers. One of Walker's chief recruiters in the United States was Appleton Oaksmith, a Maine-born, former shipping agent who had become involved in New York Democratic politics. He had also been involved in the Quitman filibuster. See John J. TePaske, "Appleton Oaksmith: Filibustering Agent," *North Carolina Historical Review*, XXXV (1958), 427–47. Walker even made a special effort to encourage scientists to come to the country. See Walker to John Lindsley, November 26, 1855, in Windrow, *Lindsley*, Appendix, 192.

as president of Nicaragua would be to claim the whole British-controlled Mosquito coast for Nicaragua.[29]

Support for Walker in the United States mounted in late 1855 and in 1856, particularly in the South. A correspondent of the Richmond *Dispatch* in New Orleans, the "hotbed of filibustering," observed: "I need not tell you that, in this quarter, there is an ardent desire for the success of Walker, and for the establishment of American institutions in Nicaragua." The New Orleans *Daily Picayune* and the Mobile *Daily Register* both followed Walker's activities closely and called for his recognition. In Congress, Representative Lemuel Evans of Texas urged recognition of the Rivas government to protect transit across the Isthmus: "The public voice demands it. . . . The people demand the retirement of Mr. Secretary Marcy, and the immediate recognition of the present Government of Nicaragua." James Mason, chairman of the Senate Foreign Relations Committee, argued that Nicaragua's government had only undergone a change in personnel, that the Rivas government was the most stable in a long time, and that it should not be discredited because it was brought about by Americans. This southern support for the recognition of Walker was apparent to the New York *Daily Times*, which rebuked it in two editorials.[30] But Walker's sympathizers numbered many northerners also.

The Democratic party gave Walker a ringing endorsement at its national convention at Cincinnati in June,

---

29. Walker to Douglas, March 30, 1856, and French to Douglas, February 14, 1856, both in Douglas Papers; Official Records of the Nicaraguan Legation to the United States, folder for July–September, 1856, Walker to Oaksmith, August 13, 1856, and Oaksmith to Marcy, August 26, 1856, all in Appleton Oaksmith Papers, Duke University Library, Durham, North Carolina.

30. Richmond *Daily Dispatch*, May 13, 1856; New Orleans *Daily Picayune*, December 16, 25, 1855, February 12, March 4, April 30, 1856; Mobile *Daily Register*, May 18, 1856; *Congressional Globe*, 34th Cong., 1st Sess., Appendix, 570–71, 601; New York *Daily Times*, May 6, 10, 1856.

1856. For months the local party organ, the *Enquirer*, had been building a case for Walker, and Walker spokesmen converged on the city during the convention, making the political atmosphere even more cordial. At Masonic Hall one evening, Parker French lectured on Walker, and the *Enquirer* published a timely letter from William Cazneau portraying Walker as a bedrock of American resistance to British aggression. A plank endorsing "American ascendancy in the Gulf of Mexico" won convention approval by a 229 to 33 vote, and the delegates balloted 221 to 38 for a plank which proclaimed: "That, in view of so commanding an interest, the people of the United States can not but sympathize with the efforts which are being made by the people of Central America to regenerate that portion of the continent which covers the passage across the Interoceanic Isthmus." [31]

Pierce finally reversed his position on May 14, shortly before the Democratic convention, by receiving Walker's new minister to the United States, Padre Vigil. A rupture between the Nicaragua Transit Company and the Rivas government, and the necessity for securing interoceanic communication across Nicaragua, necessitated diplomatic intercourse. The president stated in a message to Congress the day after receiving Vigil, that it was United States policy to recognize all governments, without questioning their formation, so long as they were the *de facto* governments and had popular support. Pierce's policy transition was eased by the contrast between Vigil's personality and background and his predecessor's. Vigil, unlike French, was educated, well-respected, and a native Nicaraguan. Pierce, in addition, calculated that recognition of Walker

31. Cincinnati *Enquirer*, April 9, May 3, June 1–7, 1856; *Official Proceedings of the Democratic Convention . . . 1856*, 27–31. Two other men active in the Walker cause who were in Cincinnati were Pierre Soulé and John Quitman. Soulé served in the convention as a delegate; Quitman was an alternate delegate from Mississippi and was never seated.

would pressure the British government into accepting the American interpretation of the Clayton-Bulwer Treaty.[32]

Walker apparently was successful. He had come to Central America as a soldier of fortune, with a small band of men, and now was the "power behind the throne." The United States had recognized his government, and exaggerated reports that the Nicaraguan natives were enraptured with him regularly filtered back to his homeland. People back in the states were already calling him the "grey-eyed man of destiny." Cuban revolutionary Domingo Goicuría joined Walker and raised recruits for him with the understanding that once the American position in Nicaragua stabilized, he would use Nicaragua as a base from which to launch a new Cuba expedition.[33]

At the very time of his apparent triumph, however, Walker was being undermined by a number of developments. The people of Nicaragua had never wholeheartedly embraced his intervention, and his opponents within the country were finding allies. Fears were prevalent in other Central American republics that Walker would conquer them if not opposed early, and Costa Rica commenced hostilities as early as March, 1856. In mid-July, Honduras, Guatemala, and San Salvador would enter into an alliance to overthrow him. More ominously, Walker had provoked Cornelius Vanderbilt—a dangerous man for anyone to contend with. A faction of the Accessory Transit Corpo-

---

32. *Congressional Globe*, 34th Cong., 1st Sess., 1239; Dowty, *Limits of Isolation*, 195–215.

33. John Heiss to Stephen Douglas, August 12, 1856, in Douglas Papers; Clarksville *Standard*, January 19, 1856; Scroggs, *Filibusters*, 217–19; William O. Scroggs, "William Walker's Designs on Cuba," *Mississippi Valley Historical Review*, I (1914), 198–211. Scroggs says that Walker did get along with the Nicaraguan natives fairly well until a group of Texas Ranger reinforcements showed up and did much looting. For one thing, Walker never impressed natives into his service, a practice that was regularly resorted to by other Central American generals. Forty Nicaragua natives stayed with Walker to the bitter end. See Scroggs, *Filibusters*, 301.

ration headed by Charles Morgan and C. K. Garrison had seized power while Vanderbilt was away in Europe. Walker, partly because he was deeply indebted to these men for aiding him during and after the hostilities that brought him to power, sided with them against Vanderbilt. Walker revoked the company's charter, seized its ships and property in Nicaragua, and transferred them to the Morgan group, to which he issued a new charter. Vanderbilt then sided with the allied republics opposing Walker and set up a new Panama line with fast, inexpensive steamers. This line, of course, would compete against the line of his old associates.[34]

Walker's position was further weakened by the United States government's reversion to its earlier antagonism toward filibusters. Padre Vigil's stay in Washington was brief. Snubbed by ministers of other Central American republics, and given a cold reception by American clergymen, the minister departed for Nicaragua only six weeks after his initial reception by Pierce, leaving John Heiss as charge d'affaires to handle Nicaraguan matters in Washington until Rivas could appoint a new minister. But Rivas defected to the allied republics, and Walker appointed the next minister soon after he won the presidency of Nicaragua on June 29, 1856, in a tainted election. Walker's inauguration followed on the evening of July 11 in Granada Plaza below American, French, Nicaraguan, and Cuban flags, and his first champagne toast honored President Pierce. Appleton Oaksmith, Walker's emissary-designate to replace Padre Vigil, also toasted "Uncle Sammy." Their enthusiasm, however, was soon deflated. The British gov-

34. Nevins, *Ordeal*, II, 365; Earl W. Fornell, "Texans and Filibusters in the 1850's," *Southwestern Historical Quarterly*, LIX (1956), 414; Philadelphia *Public Ledger*, September 29, 1856; TePaske, "Appleton Oaksmith," 437. For a full discussion of the Vanderbilt split, see Carr, *Walker*, Chapter 12, and James P. Baughman, *Charles Morgan and the Development of Southern Transportation* (Nashville, 1968), Chapter 4.

ernment was retreating in the Clayton-Bulwer Treaty controversy. Pierce, now a lame-duck president with no motive to appease pro-Walker elements in his party, refused to receive Oaksmith when he arrived in Washington.[35]

Walker's difficulties with the United States were compounded by a parting of the ways with Goicuría. The Cuban, initially a brigadier general in Walker's army, received appointment as Walker's minister to England. To enhance the possibility of Goicuría's achieving British recognition of the filibuster regime, Walker instructed him to stress to the British not only that Walker had no intention of seeking annexation to the United States, but also that he would help prevent the expansion of the United States into the Caribbean. Goicuría, however, went to London by way of New York City, and while there tried to effect a reconciliation between Vanderbilt and Walker. Walker repudiated him harshly for the effort and dismissed him from the army. Goicuría retaliated by publishing the damaging, apparently anti-American correspondence, and caused Walker's popularity in his homeland to decline considerably.[36]

Walker also turned to John Quitman in the hope of a diplomatic breakthrough. The Mississippian, now a United States Representative, accompanied Oaksmith to a private conference with Pierce the night of August 4, 1856, and

35. William Marcy to Oaksmith, September 13, 1856, in Manning (ed.), *Diplomatic Correspondence*, VI, 86; New York *Sun*, August 6, 1856, clipping in John Heiss Scrapbook, Heiss Papers; William O. Scroggs (ed.), "Walker-Heiss Papers: Some Diplomatic Correspondence of the Walker Regime in Nicaragua," *Tennessee Historical Magazine*, I (1915), 334n; TePaske, "Appleton Oaksmith," 438; Carr, *Walker*, 185–92; Dowty, *Limits of Isolation*, 222–27. It took a number of years to work out the controversy over the treaty, but by 1860 the various problems had been resolved. The boundaries of Belize were defined to American satisfaction, Honduras gained the Bay Islands, Nicaragua and Honduras were given sovereignty over the Mosquito Indians, and Greytown became a free port.

36. New York *Daily Times*, November 25, 1856; Scroggs, "Walker's Designs on Cuba," 204–209.

continued pressing Walker's claim to recognition in the days after Oaksmith left for New York to aid recruiting efforts. Quitman had no greater success in getting Pierce to recognize Walker than he had had in getting Pierce to recognize his own enterprise. He apparently came close, however. On August 13 there was a flurry of excitement when Quitman telegraphed Oaksmith to "come on to Washington." But Marcy again refused to receive the minister, and Oaksmith attributed this to some "secret influence" on the president. The "influence" may have been Marcy's inherent conservatism. Oaksmith reported that Marcy treated him "civilly," but expressed opposition to the Walker movement. An effort of Oaksmith's to work out a postal treaty giving the United States the right of "maintaining the transit of the Isthmus in cases of invasion and insurrection" also came to nothing.[37]

Later diplomatic initiatives were left to John Heiss, who had been embroiled in controversy in Washington since his caning (or possible bludgeoning) of the anti-Walker editor of the Washington *Evening Star*. Walker appointed Heiss special commissioner to the United States and Great Britain. Pierce and Marcy were willing to conduct semiofficial negotiations with Heiss, to the irritation of Oaksmith. But nothing of importance emerged from these negotiations.[38]

By the late summer of 1856, therefore, Walker had managed to acquire more than his share of enemies. His politi-

37. Appleton Oaksmith to Walker, September 9, 1856, Appleton Oaksmith to William Marcy, August 26, 1856, and Walker to Appleton Oaksmith, August 13, 1856, all in Oaksmith Papers; "Official Records of the Legation of Nicaragua, July–September, 1856," in Oaksmith Papers; Appleton Oaksmith to John Quitman, September 4, 1856, in Quitman Papers, Harvard University Library.
38. Appleton Oaksmith to Walker, September 9, 1856, in Oaksmith Papers; Augustin (Padre) Vigil to Marcy, June 23, 1856, in Scroggs (ed.), "Walker-Heiss Papers," 334; John Heiss Scrapbook, in Heiss Papers; Walker to John Heiss, June 29, September 30, 1856, in Heiss Papers.

cal blunderings were so disastrous that they could not be offset by the military benefit gained when Charles Frederick Henningsen, Hungarian revolutionary and the author of several books on military strategy, joined Walker that October.[39]

On September 22 Walker made a bold move to regain the political offensive. Defying the flow of history, he reinstituted slavery in Nicaragua. It was a calculated gamble to arouse a new enthusiasm in the southern United States to compensate for his decline in influence elsewhere. To the extent that the filibuster now became the darling of southern slave expansionists, it worked.

Pierre Soulé's intervention into Nicaraguan affairs may have been the decisive influence on Walker. When the politically tarnished Louisianian returned from Spain, he found his old Louisiana rivals, Senators Benjamin and Slidell, involved in the promotion of an Isthmian transit across Tehuantepec in Mexico. Soulé also learned of Walker's intention to liberate Cuba once his position in Nicaragua stabilized. It was only natural for Soulé, who may have known Walker in 1848 when he edited the *Crescent*, to support Walker. By April, 1856, Soulé was publicly urging New Orleans merchants to contribute funds to the Walker cause on the basis that Walker, if successful, would annex Nicaragua to the United States. As head of the Louisiana delegation to the Democratic convention in Cincinnati that June, and as a member of the platform committee, Soulé drafted the expansionist Central American plank that the convention passed so overwhelmingly.[40]

39. Henningsen, at the time living in New York City, had been a close friend of Louis Kossuth, the famous Hungarian patriot, and also had fought in wars in Spain and Russia. His main contribution to Walker was in training the filibuster's artillery. See Carr, *Walker*, 206–13.

40. J. Preston Moore, "Pierre Soulé: Southern Expansionist and Promoter," *Journal of Southern History*, XXI (1955), 207–10; Walker, *War in Nicaragua*, 275n; Carr, *Walker*, 183.

In August, 1856, Soulé's involvement with Walker went beyond mere public support. He arrived in Nicaragua and probably pushed Walker into the reestablishment of slavery. No conclusive evidence exists to prove this, but it appears that Walker accepted Soulé as an agent of southern sentiment and agreed to reinstitute involuntary labor in return for southern support of his "administration." Walker certainly was satisfied with Soulé's visit; the filibuster threw parties in Soulé's honor and later commented: "His fine head and noble air made a deep impression on the people of the country." Soulé, in return, invested in Nicaraguan land and returned to the United States to promote recruiting and bond selling for Walker's benefit—and possibly for his own advancement as he may have invested in the bonds. The very timing of Soulé's visit adds to its significance; soon after his departure that September, Walker issued his slavery decree.[41]

John Wheeler may have joined Soulé in advocating the slavery decree to Walker, and it is even possible that Wheeler rather than Soulé pressured Walker to reestablish slavery. The North Carolinian owned slaves himself, and although he never took credit for originating the decree, he jumped to its defense immediately, urging it upon Secretary of State Marcy on the grounds that only slave labor could develop the cotton, sugar, rice, corn, cocoa, and indigo that Nicaragua's rich soil produced.[42]

Walker used his slavery decree to every possible advantage. Dispatches and letters quickly left Nicaragua bound for the South (particularly to southern newspapers) em-

41. Baltimore *Sun*, October 4, 1856; Walker, *War in Nicaragua*, 238–39; Philadelphia *Public Ledger*, November 25, 1856; Appleton Oaksmith to Walker, August 9, 1856, in Oaksmith Papers; Moore, "Pierre Soulé," 210–17. One of Soulé's contacts was Major Pierre G. T. Beauregard. Beauregard, in a dull customhouse assignment at the time, almost joined Walker.
42. Wheeler to Marcy, September 30, 1856, in Manning (ed.), *Diplomatic Correspondence*, VI, 574.

phasizing how Walker was now fighting the southern battle for slavery expansion. A Virginian with the filibuster wrote to an Alabama paper and implored its readers to send men and money for Walker's cause because Walker had possessed Nicaragua "in the name of the white race, and now offers [it] to you and your slaves, at a time when you have not a friend on the face of the earth." A Kentuckian serving as Walker's "Sub-Secretary of State" wrote Governor Charles Morehead of Kentucky that "gentlemen from the Southern States, wishing to emigrate to this country with their slaves, are invited to come." [43]

The Walker regime also passed a new land law to further entice American emigrants. Two hundred and fifty acres of good land would be given to each single man and an extra hundred acres to each married man with a family. And an ever-increasing number of Walker adherents left Nicaragua for recruiting duties in the South. Walker's brother Norvell set up an office in Nashville. A. J. C. Kewen appeared in Natchez to argue for the aid of "the men of the South." S. A. Lockridge mustered recruits in Texas. It was at this point that William Cazneau contracted with Walker to send one thousand men within a year in return for a considerable land grant. Soulé, Mason Pilcher, and S. R. Slatter sold some $43,000 of Nicaraguan bonds in New Orleans.

A Rhode Islander had urged Stephen Douglas earlier in the year that it would be politically profitable to support Walker because northerners wanted a safe transit across the Isthmus, and "there is no 'nigger' in it, as was in Texas." But now Walker had brought in the "nigger." Ringing southern endorsements of Walker had been in-

43. Tuskegee *Republican*, December 18, 1856; J. L. Richmond to Charles Morehead, October 30, 1856, published in Frankfort (Kentucky) *Commonwealth*, clipping in John Heiss Scrapbook, Heiss Papers. Also see *De Bow's Review*, XXII (1857), 105.

creasing in frequency even before the decree. The influential *De Bow's Review*, for instance, had predicted that Walker's activities would lead to the annexation of all Central America to the United States. After the decree southern enthusiasm for the filibuster leaped. The New Orleans *Daily Delta* commented that Walker had made Nicaragua a "home for Southern men." The Selma *Sentinel* asserted that "no movement on the earth" was as vital to the South as Walker's.[44] Walker's slavery decree, however, came too late; he would be out of Nicaragua in half a year. The full impact of his decree on southern sentiment would become more apparent after his return to the United States the next May.

Walker was now involved in a raging civil war, and his position was already beyond salvaging. A lack of food, ammunition, and clothing, and the absence of experienced subordinate officers, undermined his cause; yet, he remained an optimist to the end, writing a few days before Christmas that the condition of his army was "improving every day" and that his enemies had "failed in their efforts." He thought that Costa Rica was "prostrate and cannot send another man to Nicaragua," that San Salva-

44. *Texas State Gazette*, January 31, February 21, 1857; Natchez *Daily Courier*, January 8, February 7, 18, 1857; John Heiss Scrapbook, in Heiss Papers; B. H. Cheever to Douglas, April 29, 1856, in Douglas Papers; *De Bow's Review*, XXI (1856), 28; Richmond *Daily Dispatch*, September 18, 1856; *Congressional Globe*, 34th Cong., 1st Sess., 2012; Nashville *Union and American*, October 31, 1856; New Orleans *Daily Delta*, quoted in the Aberdeen (Mississippi) *Sunny South*, November 13, 1856; Selma (Alabama) *Sentinel*, December 16, 1856, clipping in John Heiss Scrapbook, Heiss Papers; Fornell, "Texans and Filibusters," 417–24; J. Preston Moore, "Pierre Soulé," 215; Wallace, *Destiny and Glory*, 183; Scroggs, *Filibusters*, 237–38. For an example of the impact of Walker's slavery decree on the South after his return to the United States, see *De Bow's Review*, XXIII (1857), 312, which discusses resolutions proposed to the Knoxville Commercial Convention explicitly endorsing Walker on the basis of his establishment of slavery.

dor and Guatemala were "very much in the same condition," and that Honduras was defeated.[45]

Soon the overwhelmingly superior allied forces and a terrible cholera epidemic decimated Walker's army, while an agent of Cornelius Vanderbilt seized Walker's small navy, cutting off all hope of reinforcement.[46] Walker surrendered to Commander Charles H. Davis of the United States Navy on May 1, 1857, and the pitiful war was over. He soon departed on the U.S.S. *St. Mary's* for the United States, where he arrived later in the month to a hero's welcome. Walker only planned to stay in the United States a short while. He preferred reconquering Nicaragua, and his struggle to return would have important sectional overtones.

45. Walker to Heiss (?), December 22, 1856, in Heiss Papers.
46. The group of men aboard the "Texas," for instance, tried to link up with Walker, without success. They did manage to capture a couple of forts on the San Juan River. Roberdeau Wheat was in this group as was a Colonel Rudler, who would be with Walker on his last Central American expedition a number of years later. See Allen Diary, January 17, 1857, in Allen Papers.

V

William Walker
and the South

A southerner in the nation's capital in 1857 regarded William Walker as the "greatest *lion* of Washington," and large crowds greeted the filibuster following his return to the United States. But Walker, instead of resting content with his newly acquired fame and safe return, immediately began recruiting for another Nicaraguan enterprise. He journeyed from city to city at a frenetic pace, delivering speeches, pleading for money, and begging for recruits. There is little indication that he ever considered anything other than filibustering. But in an intriguing letter in 1858 he hinted of a romantic interest in an unidentified Nashville widow and said that seeing domestic life in Nashville had taken "some of the temper out of my soul." Insisting he was still the lawful president of Nicaragua, he beseeched A. Dudley Mann to persuade the Buchanan administration to recognize no other government in Nicaragua and asserted that his return expedition would comply with the neutrality laws. Walker knew that his presidential pretensions would become absurd as time passed, and this may partly explain his haste to launch a new invasion.[1]

1. W. Grayson Mann to William Trousdale, June 15, 1857, in Trousdale Papers; Gower and Allen (eds.), *Journals of Randal McGavock*, (May 22, July 6, 8, 1857), 416, 421, 422; Walker to Mrs. Tom Smith, March 3, 1858, in Miscellaneous Papers, Tennessee State Library and Archives, Nashville; Walker to A. Dudley Mann, July 16, 1857, in Walker Letters, Personal Papers, Miscellaneous,

To gain southern support, Walker not only maintained that his slavery decree established him as a champion of the institution's expansion, but that the same northern abolitionists who had obstructed southern expansion westward also had retarded his Nicaraguan enterprise. He sarcastically remarked to a New Orleans crowd soon after his return that it was unfortunate that he had been born in a southern state and could not "consider slavery a moral or political wrong." Since emancipation, Central America had gone to ruin. "Americanization" of the area was the only answer, and southerners should help "execute this mission." From a hotel in Mobile, Walker apprised a noisy audience that he was seeking to "extend your institutions." When recommending a cofilibuster to Alexander Stephens for an Arizona political appointment, he cited the man's "unquestionable . . . devotion to Southern interests." Walker assiduously cultivated his proslavery image. He even startled the vocal Virginia secessionist, Edmund Ruffin, a lifelong supporter of slavery, when he said privately that "the pure Indian race" of Nicaragua could properly "be made slaves, in cases of Americans becoming conquerors and masters there." [2]

Walker's most incredible justifications of slavery can be found in *The War in Nicaragua*. He asserts that the slave decree was the nucleus of his policy: "Without such labor as the new decree gave the Americans could have played no other part in Central America than that of the pretorian guard at Rome or of the Janizaries of the East;

Library of Congress; Walker to John Heiss, July 25, 1857, in Heiss Papers; Greensboro *Alabama Beacon*, October 23, 30, 1857; Memphis *Daily Appeal*, September 2, 1857. The neighbor was a leading Nashville socialite.

2. *Texas State Gazette*, June 13, 1857; Mobile *Daily Register*, January 23, 1858; Walker to Alexander Stephens, March 8, 1858, in Alexander Stephens Papers, Library of Congress; Edmund Ruffin Diary, May 14, 1858, in Ruffin Papers; Gower and Allen (eds.), *Journals of Randal McGavock* (July 6, 1857), 421.

and for such degrading service as this they were ill-suited by the habits and traditions of their race." The decree also demonstrated that the Americans of Nicaragua were the "champions" of the southern slave power in the fight for political control of the United States, and it presented the "only means, short of revolution, whereby they can preserve their present social organization." Obviously a slave Central America was far more feasible than a slave Kansas; the South should fight for realities rather than abstractions. The adventurer calls for a slave "empire" throughout tropical America and defends slavery as a "positive good" with logic befitting John Calhoun: "The white man took the negro from his native wastes, and teaching him the arts of life, bestowed on him the ineffable blessings of a true religion." [3]

In November, 1857, Walker slipped out of Mobile Bay with 270 men aboard the steamer *Fashion*. But his second Nicaraguan expedition was short-lived. On the grounds that Walker was violating American neutrality laws, Commodore Hiram Paulding of the United States Navy used marines to block Walker's intended ascent up the San Juan River and trained his ship's cannon on the filibuster camp near Greytown, thus pressuring Walker into surrendering. The filibuster was sent to New York City, where he arrived in late December, 1857. Walker then enjoyed the strange experience of being taken to Washington in the custody of Isaiah Rynders, his Tammany supporter, who happened to be United States marshal in New York. Rynders presented Walker to Secretary of State Lewis Cass, who dismissed Walker from prosecution. Cass had decided that Walker could not be detained legally by the executive department. A trial for violation of the neutrality laws could occur only by means of regular court proceedings. After a few days in Washington, which in-

3. Walker, *War in Nicaragua*, 256–80.

cluded discussions with the ever-sympathetic Alexander Stephens, Walker headed south.[4]

Walker's arrest put President Buchanan in a ticklish position, because the seizure was of doubtful legality. It was highly questionable that the United States could execute its laws on the soil of foreign nations, and as recently as August, 1855, Secretary of State William Marcy had informed the Nicaraguan minister to the United States that although American officials would be vigilant against filibustering, filibusters could not "be pursued and seized while within" a foreign state. Buchanan could hardly avoid taking some stand on Paulding's action, and the United States Senate put him in an uncomfortable position by asking him to deliver all the information he had pertaining to Walker's arrest. Buchanan complied on January 7, 1858, and sent a message regarding the implications of the incident. Paulding, according to the president, had "committed a grave error" by seizing Walker on Nicaraguan soil. However, the error was mitigated by the commodore's unquestionably "patriotic motives" and the Nicaraguan government's failure to complain of infringement on her territorial rights. In fact, Paulding had "relieved" Nicaragua from "a dreaded invasion." Buchanan concluded his message by defending the American neutrality laws.[5]

The initial seizure, and Buchanan's defense of Paulding and refusal to compensate Walker, provoked a political uproar in the South. People crowded into the largest hall in Petersburg, Virginia, to hear Roger Pryor and others denounce Paulding. Announcement of the arrest caused a disturbance at a New Orleans theater. Recent United

4. Scroggs, *Filibusters*, 174, 238, 333–34; *Congressional Globe*, 35th Cong., 1st Sess., 217; Charleston *Mercury*, January 1, 1858.
5. Marcy to José de Marcoleta, August 22, 1855, in Manning (ed.), *Diplomatic Correspondence*, VI, 70; *Congressional Globe*, 35th Cong., 1st Sess., 174, 216–17.

States congressman Percy Walker gave a one-and-a-half-hour speech for Walker in Commercial Hall in Montgomery. Anti-Paulding resolutions were soon introduced in the Texas, Tennessee, Virginia, and Alabama legislatures. The May, 1858, meeting of the Southern Commercial Convention passed resolutions "approving the Walker-Nicaragua procedures and policy, and denouncing the interference by Com. Paulding." A majority of the members of every state present supported the resolutions.[6]

Southern newspapers joined the onslaught. One paper accused Paulding of having been intoxicated when he captured Walker. The southern press generally termed the incident an "outrage" or "usurpation of power" and frequently demanded that the United States restore Walker to power. A constant charge was that Buchanan, in supporting Paulding, revealed that he opposed the expansion of slavery. Whig, Opposition, and Know-Nothing papers, in particular, seized on the issue as a way of politically discrediting the majority Democratic party and establishing themselves as a more reliable proslavery party. *Brownlow's Knoxville Whig* accused Buchanan of wanting to "crush out the expansion of slavery to the South. They know that the movement of Walker is intimately connected with the slave interests of the entire South." The Richmond *Whig* said that Walker had been "furthering the rights of the South in Nicaragua," but that Buchanan opposed any new slave territories. To the Tuskegee *Republican* the "course of the administration towards Gen. William Walker" was "of such a nature, as to kindle the flame of indignation in the breasts of those, who feel an

6. Louisville *Daily Courier*, January 8, 1858; Edmund Ruffin Diary, January 5, May 14, 1858, in Ruffin Papers; *Weekly Raleigh Register*, January 13, 1858; Tuskegee *Republican*, January 28, 1858; Clarksville *Jeffersonian*, January 27, 1858; O. M. Roberts to John Reagan, January 14, 1858, in John Reagan Papers, Texas State Archives and Library, Austin; Galveston *Weekly News*, January 26, 1858; *House Journal of the State of Tennessee, 1857–1858*, 551–52.

interest in the preservation of Southern institutions." [7] Issues in which the southern opposition could pose as a more trustworthy defender of southern rights than the Democrats in the 1850s were few and far between. Thus, they made the most of the Paulding affair.

But the issue transcended mere partisan loyalties in the South. Members of both parties turned out for pro-Walker rallies, and the correspondence of leading southern Democrats at the time reveals that they too were angry over the administration's course. Alexander Stephens, for instance, told his brother that he restrained himself at first from confronting the administration for fear that an attack on Paulding would give northern Democrats an excuse to oppose the South on Kansas. But "when I saw what they were doing I could not keep my mouth closed—You have seen I suppose what I have said [in Congress]—But I kept back my wrath—the reason of their line of policy and opposition to Walker was their hostility to his enterprise because if successful he would introduce African slavery there." Stephens felt that Paulding should have been court-martialed and dismissed from United States service for his action. Stephens' brother, Judge Linton Stephens, as well as Judge Thomas W. Thomas of the superior court of Georgia, agreed with the congressman's stand. A Virginian assured John Quitman that Walker's cause was popular in his neighborhood, and a Jackson, Mississippi, editor predicted to Jefferson Davis that the "friends of the administration will be much disappointed

7. *Brownlow's Knoxville Whig*, February 20, 1858; Richmond *Whig*, December 30, 1857, January 1, 1858; Tuskegee *Republican*, January 7, 1858. For other comments by the southern press (both Whig and Democratic) against Paulding, see Mobile *Daily Register*, December 31, 1857, January 5, 1858; Jackson *Semi-Weekly Mississippian*, January 5, 1858; Natchez *Daily Courier*, December 31, 1857; Charleston *Mercury*, January 1, 1858; Galveston *Weekly News*, February 2, 1858; Memphis *Evening Ledger*, January 21, 1858; Nashville *Daily Union and American*, January 13, 1858; Batesville (Arkansas) *Independent Banner*, January 7, 1859.

if the President does not stamp with emphatic disapproval the recent high-handed act of Commodore Paulding." Edmund Ruffin noted that the arrest of Walker had distracted the South from more important problems by creating a "great sensation" and a "general condemnation." Relying on this widespread bipartisan support, Walker predicted to Irvine Fayssoux, now recruiting for him in New Orleans, that the pressure would prove too much for the president and that Buchanan would reverse his policy.[8]

The southern antagonism toward Paulding even infiltrated administration newspapers. The Corpus Christi *Nueces Valley Weekly*, Clarksville (Texas) *Standard*, and Memphis *Daily Appeal*, expecting Buchanan to repudiate Paulding, spontaneously denounced the Commodore when news of the incident arrived in the South, and later had to clumsily reverse themselves in order to follow the administration line. In early January, the *Standard* called Paulding "grossly ignorant of the extent of his powers," but later pointed out that he "thought he was doing right"; and in February it wholeheartedly supported Buchanan's position.[9]

The halls of Congress witnessed a heated debate on the Walker-Paulding affair. This debate not only revealed the depth of southern support for Walker, but also contributed to sectionalizing the Democratic party on the question of

8. Alexander Stephens to Linton Stephens, January 3, 20, 1858, and Linton Stephens to Alexander Stephens, January 3, 1858, in Stephens Papers, University of North Carolina Library; Thomas W. Thomas to Alexander Stephens, January 3, 1858, in Phillips (ed.), "Correspondence," 430; John Merrit to John A. Quitman, January 28, 1858, in Quitman Papers, Harvard University Library; E. Barksdale to Jefferson Davis, January 8, 1858, in Davis Papers, Library of Congress; Edmund Ruffin Diary, January 5, 1858, in Ruffin Papers; Walker to Irvine Fayssoux, January 5, 9, 1858, in Walker Papers, Tulane University Library.

9. Corpus Christi *Nueces Valley Weekly*, January 2, 23, February 13, 1858; Clarksville *Standard*, January 9, 28, February 27, 1858; Memphis *Daily Appeal*, December 31, 1857, January 22, 1858.

the extension of slavery. And it gave new indications that the Republican party had united against southern attempts to bring Caribbean slave territory within the union.

Buchanan's message defending Paulding spurred an immediate debate in the Senate that lasted intermittently until May. Antislavery Republicans rushed to Buchanan's support in a rare display of bipartisanship. William Seward took the lead on January 7 by praising the president's stand and by denouncing Walker for invading another country: if Walker could invade Nicaragua, then other countries had the right to invade the United States. James Doolittle of Wisconsin upheld Seward's stand and, on January 13, introduced a joint resolution proposing that a medal be given to Commodore Paulding. Doolittle emphasized that his resolution was motivated by antislavery sentiments. Although wanting American borders to extend from the Arctic Ocean to the Isthmus of Darien, he opposed any venture that would extend slavery. Solomon Foot of Vermont also backed Buchanan and even denied that Paulding had made a mistake.[10]

Lower-South senators broke completely with the president. Five "Gulf" senators spoke, four of whom attacked Paulding. Albert Gallatin Brown of Mississippi proved the most vociferous and spoke on a number of occasions. Brown defended Walker as the "de facto" president of Nicaragua, criticized Paulding for not obeying the letter of the law, and asserted that "each individual has the right to go away, and that you have no power to arrest him." Brown attacked Doolittle's "medal" motion and amended it to ask Congress to disavow Paulding's act as a violation of the "territorial sovereignty of a friendly Power." Brown mocked Doolittle:

> Great God! Commodore Paulding, commanding as many, perhaps, as one hundred guns . . . having disposed of them

10. *Congressional Globe*, 35th Cong., 1st Sess., 219–21, 336–60, 378.

at his leisure, with five or six hundred men, captures—what? Walker and a handful of fillibusters [*sic*], who laid down their arms at the very first summons, and made no sort of resistance upon paper or anywhere else, and Congress is called upon to vote a falsehood—that in this there was extraordinary gallantry!...Why, sir, I suppose the next thing will be, if our army should approach Salt Lake, and all the Mormon men should be away, and they should make a desperate charge and capture all the women, they must all have medals for their extraordinary gallantry.

Robert Toombs upheld Walker's legitimacy as president of Nicaragua, and he, Jefferson Davis, and Stephen Mallory of Florida all criticized Paulding's interpretation of the neutrality laws. Davis, for instance, asserted that the United States Navy could only enforce the neutrality laws within American territorial waters.[11] John Slidell, the fifth lower-South senator to speak out on the matter, was too closely tied to Buchanan politically to criticize the administration's handling of the incident; besides, he had little respect for Walker as an individual, which he made clear in his comments. He took the occasion, nevertheless, to make what had by now become, for him, a customary attack on the neutrality laws; he repeated his 1854 suggestion that the president should be given the power to suspend the laws during periods of congressional recess, if he judged it in the public interest. He felt that this might be necessary in the near future to save Mexico, which he believed to be in imminent danger of invasion from Spain.[12]

Upper-South senators differed from their "Gulf" cohorts. John J. Crittenden of Kentucky, James Mason of

11. *Ibid.*, 217–18, 220–22, 360–62, 378, 1538–41, 2209. Although Davis disapproved of Paulding's handling of the situation, he nevertheless mentioned in passing that he was unsympathetic toward filibustering, a position consistent with his earlier policy of suppressing Walker's Mexican movement and his opposition to the Quitman filibuster.

12. *Ibid.*, 461–62.

Virginia, and James Pearce of Maryland all attacked Walker. Mason, as chairman of the Committee on Foreign Relations, reported to the Senate on January 25, concerning Buchanan's message, that the United States had never had a "more striking instance of the wisdom and expediency" of the neutrality laws "in preserving the public peace" than in their use against the "extraordinary attempts which have been made by this man, Walker, as I fear, to bring them into jeopardy." [13]

Only George Pugh and Stephen Douglas, of the northern Democratic senators, commented on this issue, which was obviously dividing their party. Pugh, though opposed to Walker, contested Paulding's right to make an arrest on foreign soil. Douglas attacked filibusters as impeding American expansion, but also asserted that the president could apply the neutrality laws only up to one marine league from the American coast, and defended Walker's right to expatriate himself.[14]

Doolittle's motion and Brown's amendment were never voted on, and the Senate dropped the Paulding question in May as it neared adjournment. Although the debate demonstrated that Walker's support was concentrated among Gulf-state senators, it did not particularly inflame sectional rivalries because slavery was incidental to the legal issues that commanded the Senate's attention. In the House, on the other hand, sectionally oriented speeches dominated the debate; and a vote revealed that William Walker's campaign to become a symbol of slave expansionism had succeeded.

In the House, twelve northern Republicans, seven northern Democrats, eighteen southern Democrats, and two southern Americans expressed opinions about the Walker-Paulding affair between January 4 and May 31, 1858. Every northern Republican and northern Democrat who

13. *Ibid.*, 218, 246, 378, 457.   14. *Ibid.*, 223, 362.

spoke supported Paulding. Of the eighteen southern Democrats, fourteen attacked Paulding. The two southern Americans were divided.[15]

The debate centered on a February 3 majority report of the Committee on Naval Affairs. The committee stated that Paulding's act was unauthorized by his instructions from the Navy Department and called for congressional disapproval. But a minority report stated that Paulding "acted within the spirit of his orders" and deserved the country's approval. The Committee on Foreign Affairs entered the controversy by presenting proposals on May 4, stating that the United States had no right to enter the territory of a friendly country to carry away an individual, but that because President Buchanan agreed with this principle, no congressional action was necessary. On the same day, David Ritchie, a Pennsylvania Republican, suggested a substitute for the committee's report that would have offered congressional thanks to Paulding. William Barksdale of Mississippi countered with a substitute amendment that denounced Paulding's act as "without authority of law" and as meeting with the "condemnation of the House." John Quitman complicated the issue by moving that the part of the president's annual message that concerned the neutrality laws be referred to a select committee of five endowed with power to prepare a bill concerning the neutrality laws.

Most representatives, hoping to avoid inflaming sectional tensions, approached the Walker-Paulding dispute on the basis of whether or not Paulding had a moral or legal right to arrest Walker on foreign soil. Vattel and

15. The Americans were John A. Gilmer of North Carolina and Felix K. Zollicoffer of Tennessee. Gilmer defended Paulding, while Zollicoffer defended Walker's character and denounced Paulding. The four southern Democrats who supported Paulding were John Millson and Charles Faulkner of Virginia, James B. Clay of Kentucky, and Francis Preston Blair, Jr., of Missouri. Blair was a free-soiler. See *ibid.*, 198, 213, 275–76, 284–85, 293, 301.

other authorities on international law were cited frequently. But George Hawkins of Florida, A. R. Wright of Georgia, and Thomas Clingman of North Carolina all defended slavery expansion in the debate. Hawkins stated that American expansion southward was inevitable and warned that northern opposition might provoke a "war of opinion." Wright called Buchanan's position the "political blunder of the nineteenth century" and complained that the president had abandoned the slave states: "Can it be possible that the President was amusing the South with the 'Kansas abstraction,' while *practically* he was using the *power of the Government* to take '*slave labor*' out of Central America and put free labor in? Was he not only giving *territory* to 'free labor' in Kansas, and *principle* to the 'slave power,' but was he doing the same thing in the *tropics*? His antecedents would not lead us to such a conclusion. Facts *seem* to point that way." Clingman, who had originally introduced the pro-Walker report of the Committee on Naval Affairs, included a defense of slavery in his anti-Paulding comments.[16]

This southern defense of Walker and slavery came primarily in May and was instigated by earlier attacks on slavery by northern congressmen. As early as January 7, Eli Thayer, a Massachusetts Republican already famous for his involvement in promoting a free Kansas through northern emigration, said that northern emigration to Central America could effectively exclude slavery in that area and called for the formation of a corporation to encourage such emigrants. Emory Pottle of New York, an-

16. The other southern Democrats who attacked Paulding, though not on a slavery basis, were Alexander Stephens and James Seward of Georgia, Miles Taylor of Louisiana, John Quitman and William Barksdale of Mississippi, Thomas Bocock and William Smith of Virginia, Warren Winslow of North Carolina, Lawrence Keitt of South Carolina, Sydenham Moore of Alabama, and Edward A. Warren of Arkansas. See *ibid.*, 178, 194–95, 197–99, 258, 261, 290–93, 326, 504, 556, 1194, 1972–77; *ibid.*, Appendix, 458–61.

other Republican, attacked Walker's "career of crime." Pottle asked whether "our southern neighbors" had "invited" the United States to "Americanize" their institutions and proclaimed his opposition to any further American expansion that allowed a role for slavery. On January 14, Francis Preston Blair, Jr., a Missouri free-soiler, blamed slavery for causing the whole controversy and asserted that the Walker expedition was part of a slave plot:

> There is a party in this country who go for the extension of slavery; and these predatory incursions against our neighbors are the means by which territory is to be seized, planted with slavery, annexed to this Union, and, in combination with the present slaveholding States, made to dominate this government, and the entire continent; or, failing in the policy of annexation, to unite with the slave States in a southern slave-holding Republic.

Blair attacked Walker's slave decree as a key reason for the uniting of Central Americans against the filibuster. He added that the settlement of free American blacks in Central America would be the best way to solve the filibuster problem, rid the United States of the troublesome free-Negro problem, and aid Central America "in developing the incredible riches of those regions." [17]

Northern Democrats, desiring to sustain the Buchanan administration without offending the South, generally avoided such sectional arguments in their vocal support of Paulding. Thus, Daniel Sickles of New York claimed that Walker's purpose had been to wage war on Nicaragua and cited a Supreme Court decision and international law to prove that so long as Walker's "intent" had been to wage war, he was liable to arrest. Walker had violated the neutrality laws, even though he did not have arms

17. *Ibid.*, 227–29, 277–78, 293–98. The Memphis *Daily Appeal* reported about the time of Thayer's speech that he had petitioned the New York legislature for a charter for an emigration company to purchase a tract of land in Central America for settlement by Americans. See Memphis *Daily Appeal*, May 1, 1858.

on board his ship when he left the United States. According to Sickles, expeditions such as Walker's would hurt American relations and commerce with Central America, and would actually impair the future expansion of the United States. William Groesbeck avowed that it was the duty of the United States government to maintain peace with other nations, and that the sea was no sanctuary for crime. Republicans such as William Kellogg of Illinois noted the split in Democratic ranks and enjoyed their rivals' discomfiture.[18]

The House Committee on the Judiciary smothered the proposed revision of the neutrality laws. And Quitman failed to get either a select committee to consider the question or a direct vote on a bill to repeal the neutrality laws. But questions of censure or approval lingered after the adjournment of Congress in the spring of 1858, and they appeared again the next winter in the second session of the Thirty-fifth Congress.[19]

On January 11, 1859, David Ritchie's year-old resolution offering congressional thanks to Paulding and his officers, and William Barksdale's amendment censuring Paulding, finally came to a vote. The House first rejected Barksdale's amendment by a 128 to 56 vote. Of the votes for Barksdale's amendment, 52 were from the slave states. The 4 free-state votes were all from Democrats. Only 20 southerners voted against the Barksdale amendment; 17 of these were from the upper South. But 25 representatives from the upper South joined the minority in the anti-Paulding vote.[20]

18. *Congressional Globe*, 35th Cong., 1st Sess., 208, 249–52.
19. *Ibid.*, 326–53.
20. *Ibid.*, 2nd Sess., 318. The four northern Democrats were Joseph C. McKibbin and Charles L. Scott of California, and George Pendleton and Clement Vallandigham of Ohio. Scott later served in the Confederate army, and Vallandigham became a notorious dissenter against the Union war effort. For purposes of these statistics, the upper South has been defined as the states of Maryland, Delaware, Missouri, Kentucky, Tennessee, North Carolina, and Virginia.

More significant, however, was the 99 to 85 vote that approved Ritchie's resolution. The 85 opponents of the resolution included only 12 representatives from the nonslaveholding states. All 12 were Democrats. Of the 99 supporters of the resolution, only Blair of Missouri, Henry Davis (an American) of Maryland, and John H. Reagan (a Democrat) of Texas were from the slave states. In addition, there were 25 northern Democrats who supported Ritchie. Thus the northern Republican and American parties were united to a man in favor of Paulding; the southern representatives, Democratic and American, were united almost to a man against Paulding, and the northern Democratic party was split—approximately two-thirds for Paulding and one-third against.[21]

The two votes, together, indicate that anti-Paulding sentiment in the lower South exceeded that in the upper South, but that over half of the upper-South representatives nevertheless supported Walker's position. The votes also suggest that although the American party of the South contained a larger conservative, antiexpansionist wing than the Democratic party, this wing by no means controlled the party members in Congress. Only Henry Winter Davis, of the southern Americans, voted with the North on Ritchie's resolution commending Paulding, and the Americans split almost evenly on Barksdale's amendment censuring Paulding: 8 southern Americans opposed the amendment, 7 supported it.

Southerners in the House refused to let the Paulding matter rest and occasionally referred to the matter in speeches concerning other topics. It is quite clear, from the nature of their comments, that Walker had become a sectional symbol. Thomas Bowie of Maryland complained that American neutrality laws infringed on the South's right to regain its power in the union by expansion: "You cannot, with my consent, allow emigration from the North into

21. *Ibid.*

the Territories of the Union, with the view of making them free States, and thus counteract what has been called the slave power, and yet forbid emigration from the South, even if made for the purpose of producing an equilibrium of political power." William T. Avery, a Tennessee Democrat, flatly stated: "In my judgment, a heavier blow was never struck at southern rights, southern interests, the advancement, the fulfillment of our great American destiny, than when Commodore Paulding perpetrated upon our people his highhanded outrage under the pretext of these same forms of law." [22]

The congressional debate cast the national spotlight on Walker more than ever. He tried to capitalize on the publicity by again crisscrossing the South in an attempt to engage men and money for yet another Nicaraguan venture. The year 1858 might be designated his banner year. Roger Pryor, James Seddon, and other Virginia notables gave him a complimentary dinner at the American Hotel in Richmond; a ten-gun salute and large crowd greeted his arrival at the Mobile wharf; Aberdeen, Mississippi, enthusiasts pledged ten thousand dollars to his cause; the Southern Commercial Convention of 1858 in Montgomery granted him a seat, and twenty delegates attended a special speech by the adventurer; influential Alabamian William Yancey brought Walker home for a party and attended a Montgomery barbecue with him. It all added up to a nineteenth-century version of the banquet circuit. Everywhere people seemed to want to hear him talk.[23]

22. *Ibid.*, 299, 347, 562.
23. Richmond *Whig*, January 16, 1858; Mobile *Daily Register*, January 23, 1858; Gower and Allen (eds.), *Journals of Randal McGavock*, (February 10, 21, September 28, 1858), 455, 457, 489–90; John Berrien Lindsley Diary, February 8, 10, 11, 20, 1858, in Lindsley Family Papers, Tennessee State Library and Archives, Nashville; Louisville *Daily Courier*, May 13, July 15, 1858; Rainwater, *Mississippi*, 73; Edmund Ruffin Diary, January 12, May 14, 15, 17, 18, 1858, in Ruffin Papers. Walker also maintained his New York ties, visiting that city in August and meeting with Pierre Soulé. See Moore, "Pierre Soulé," 222.

Walker persisted in his claim to be the lawful president of Nicaragua, even though Buchanan, in November, 1857, had recognized his former ally, Don Patricio Rivas. Walker exclaimed to John Quitman that he hoped the State Department would not permit itself "to become the dupe of diplomatists who have a 'fatal facility' for deceit and falsehood." [24]

The filibuster finally won a battle with federal authorities in May of that year. Judge John Campbell of the New Orleans Circuit Court, undismayed by the hostile public reaction to his ruling against Quitman years earlier, heard charges against Walker for violating the neutrality laws. Although Campbell was hostile to Walker and his attorney, Pierre Soulé, the jury could not agree on a verdict, and the district attorney dropped the prosecution. According to a codefendant, Walker addressed the court himself, stressing that a southern jury could hardly be expected to restrain men seeking to perpetuate "Southern institutions," and was carried out of the courtroom on the shoulders of spectators after a favorable public reaction to his speech intimidated the jury.[25]

Walker collided with the administration in still another dispute. During January, while in Mobile, Walker made the startling charge that Buchanan had once favored his expedition, but had turned against it in revenge for Pierre Soulé's thwarting of John Slidell, Buchanan's ally, in a Mexican transit scheme. Months later Walker expanded his charge, stating that in mid-October, 1857, he had been informed by his artillery commander Charles Henningsen that Secretary of War John Floyd had intimated to Henningsen privately that despite administration disapproval of filibustering to Nicaragua, Buchanan would wel-

24. Walker to John Quitman, January 19, 1858, in Quitman Papers, Harvard University Library. Rivas never accepted Walker's takeover, declared Walker a traitor, and set up a rival government.
25. Connor, *Campbell*, 100–102; Scroggs, *Filibusters*, 368–69; Moore, "Pierre Soulé," 221; Doubleday, *Reminiscences*, 195–96.

come Walker's intervention in the civil strife then raging in Mexico. The administration suggested that "while in Comonfort's service," Walker and his men "might by some act, such as tearing down the flag of Spain, bring about a war between Mexico and Spain, and Cuba might then be seized by the former power." [26]

Though Floyd and the administration newspaper, the Washington *Union*, denied the accusations, many southerners accepted Walker's remarks at face value. The Mobile meeting that first heard the speech adopted resolutions supporting Walker, and *Brownlow's Knoxville Whig* accepted the charges without hesitation. The authenticity of Walker's remarks has neither been established nor denied by historians. Certainly Buchanan's known interest in Cuba and Mexico gives some credibility to Walker's remarks. In addition, the Buchanan administration was upset about the possibility of Spanish intervention in Mexico. Cass wrote Augustus Dodge to this effect at the very time that Walker said Henningsen had met with Floyd. It is possible that Floyd had merely hinted to Walker that Buchanan would favor an incursion against Mexico. Two years later he would make just this sort of hint in response to a suggestion that Sam Houston and the Texas Rangers should invade Mexico. [27]

Walker's third Central American expedition, which left

26. Mobile *Daily Register*, January 23, 26, 1858; Jackson *Semi-Weekly Mississippian*, July 27, 1858; Carr, *Walker*, 239–40; Scroggs, *Filibusters*, 339.

27. Mobile *Daily Register*, January 26, 1858; *Brownlow's Knoxville Whig*, February 20, 1858; Jackson *Semi-Weekly Mississippian*, July 27, 1858; Cass to Dodge, October 21, 1858, quoted in Alexandria *Gazette*, December 18, 1858; Forbes Britton to Sam Houston, March 3, 1860, in Governors' Letters, Sam Houston. See also Scroggs, *Filibusters*, 340. Scroggs asserts that Walker's charges were probably false since the results of Soulé's opposition to Slidell were not known until after Secretary of State Lewis Cass had called for a strict enforcement of the neutrality laws in a circular letter to federal officers.

Mobile in early December, 1858, departed somewhat from the format that Walker had followed in the past. The Tennessean was not among the filibuster passengers of Captain Henry Maury's schooner *Susan*. Attempting to mask the enterprise as peaceful, his supporters procured a charter from the Alabama legislature in February for a Mobile and Nicaragua Steamship Company to help Americans "emigrate" to Nicaragua for twenty-five dollars per person, and the manifest of the *Susan* listed the seed and agricultural implements being carried, but not the arms and munitions. To enhance the vessel's prospects of avoiding interference by United States officials, Walker sent a vanguard of 120 men under Frank Anderson and C. W. Doubleday, veterans of earlier Walker campaigns, instead of participating himself. Walker planned to arrive on the scene after a foothold was established.[28]

The *Susan* left amidst the usual publicity that surrounded filibuster preparations. The southern expansionist press wished Walker luck in his new endeavor:

> To Nicaragua Walker's bo[u]nd,
>   He scorns your mean frustration,
> Impartial Judges, Northern Spies
>   And Buck's Administration

> Success to Maury and his men,
>   They'll safely cross the water;
> Three cheers for Southern enterprise,
>   Hurrah for Gen. Walker[29]

Walker intended to enter Nicaragua by the back door this time, by having the expedition land first at Honduras and then move to Nicaragua by land, thus escaping the ever-watchful war vessels stationed at Nicaraguan ports.

28. Doubleday, *Reminiscences*, 195; William O. Scroggs, "Alabama and Territorial Expansion Before 1860," *Gulf States Historical Magazine*, II (1903), 172–85; Scroggs, *Filibusters*, 372–73.
29. Mobile *Mercury*, quoted in Tuskegee *Republican*, December 30, 1858; Batesville *Independent Banner*, January 7, 1859.

But the *Susan* crashed on a coral reef about sixty miles from Belize, the filibusters had to live on a small island for a number of days, and a British war sloop courteously returned the men to Mobile, less than a month after the expedition started.

Mobile gave the returnees the now traditional heroes' welcome: crowds turned out for filibuster speeches, Nicaraguan flags were hoisted, and parades were held. However, Walker's support in the South as a whole had noticeably decreased. Fayssoux, in New Orleans, observed that the Crescent City had "little interest" in another expedition. Newspapers that once avidly followed Walker's activities now ignored him. Doubleday had tired of him. Walker converted to Catholicism in 1859, apparently to enhance his position among the Catholic peoples of Central America, but this did little to improve his public image in the generally Protestant United States. The filibuster kept recruiting in places as disparate geographically as New York, San Francisco, and Mobile, but most of his efforts failed.[30]

The "grey-eyed man of destiny" chose the spring of 1860 to launch his pathetic last expedition to the tropics. As part of a *modus vivendi* for Central America worked out between the British government and the Buchanan administration, the British were on the verge of handing the island of Ruatan back to Honduras. Englishmen on the island, upset by the impending change, approached Walker concerning an alliance, and Walker proved receptive. He hoped to secure Ruatan as a base from which to attack the Central American mainland and eventually make good on his claim

30. Doubleday, *Reminiscences*, 196–216; Scroggs, *Filibusters*, 375–76, 381; Walker to Irvine Fayssoux, July 12, August 13, 1859, June 5, 1860, Walker to B. R. Daniels, August 16, 1860, and Fayssoux to Walker, May 24, 1859, all in Walker Papers, Tulane University Library; New York *Herald*, January 19, February 13, 1859; *Daily Ohio State Journal*, February 18, 1859; New Bern *Daily Progress*, April 24, 1859; Washington *Union*, January 6, February 13, 1859; Carr, *Walker*, 255–60.

to the Nicaraguan presidency. Starting in April, small parties of men embarked for Ruatan on fruit schooners, using subterfuges to deceive American officials such as packing their rifles in boxes marked "agricultural implements" and designating their ammunition "Mixed Pickles."

Walker's American support, however, had waned significantly over the last two years. Recruits were hard to locate; one of Fayssoux's last letters to Walker explained that he could only find ten reinforcements in New Orleans. And the British spoiled Walker's strategy by delaying cession of Ruatan. Walker and his ninety-seven men consequently had to alter their plans. From the small island of Cozumel near Ruatan, the filibusters attacked the Honduran fort at Truxillo on the eastern coast, capturing both fort and town on August 6. Walker's tiny force, however, could hardly hope to retain the town against growing numbers of Honduran troops as well as the British warship *Icarus*, which arrived on the scene on August 19. The Americans, spurning an offer of protection by the British flag, struck off into the dense tropical forest, hoping to link up with rebellious troops under former Honduran president, Trinidad Cabañas. A number of skirmishes with native troops followed. Faced with a growing casualty list, Walker surrendered to Captain Norvell Salmon of the British Royal Navy, with the understanding that he would not be given to Honduran officials for trial. Instead, Salmon turned Walker over to local authorities, and a firing squad executed him on September 12.[31]

When Mrs. A. A. Henningsen, the wife of Walker's former artillery commander, heard about Walker's impending execution, she reacted bitterly: "Will the South

31. H. C. Lea, "Walker's Last Campaign in Central America," (1881), in Florida State Library, Jacksonville; Fayssoux to Walker, September 15, 1860, in Walker Papers, Tulane University Library; Memphis *Daily Appeal*, September 8, 1860; Greenville *South Alabamian*, October 6, 1860; Carr, *Walker*, 261–72; Scroggs, *Filibusters*, 382–92.

stand by and permit him to be shot down like a dog? If so, let her renounce forever her reputation for chivalry, valor, policy, or pride! It ought to have been the policy of the South long since to have espoused, fearlessly, the cause of Walker, and to have rendered him all assistance necessary to subjugate Central America. Both policy and philanthropy, united to recommend such a course." [32] Her remarks are indicative of the most important element of the legacy that William Walker bequeathed to the political history of the United States. Despite dwindling support in his later years, he had become a hero of the Caribbean expansion movement. His efforts had contributed to a growing awareness among many southern political leaders, especially in the Gulf states, that American expansion into the Caribbean presented a feasible means of extending slavery within the union.

Like John Quitman, Walker attracted a significant number of followers among prominent southern politicians of both parties. In Alabama, for instance, former governor Winston, William Yancey, Judges Arthur Hopkins and A. B. Meek, and Charles Langdon were all known Walker supporters. Yancey, the most prominent secessionist in the state, made a number of speeches praising Walker. Meek, a Democrat, was the associate editor of the Mobile *Daily Register* and Speaker of the Alabama House of Representatives; and Hopkins, a converted Whig, had a long history of government service that included membership in the state Constitutional Convention of 1819, as well as a career in the state senate, house, and supreme court. Hopkins was also the temporary president of the national Whig Convention of 1844 that nominated Henry Clay for president. Langdon was a Whig and former editor of the Mobile *Advertiser*. Vocal Texan supporters of Walker included E. H.

32. Mrs. A. A. Henningsen to Fayssoux, September 17, 1860, in Walker Papers, Tulane University Library.

Cushing, editor of the Houston *Telegraph,* John Henry Brown, a member of the Texas house, and Judge David Burnet, the former president of the Texas Republic. Other Texans who supported Walker included the editors of the Galveston *Civilian* and Galveston *News,* the director of the Rutersville Military Institute, the mayor of Corpus Christi, a lieutenant governor of Texas, and H. R. Runnels, the governor of Texas as of December, 1857. And although the lower South gave Walker his strongest backing, he attracted upper-South followers too. A North Carolinian, for instance, wanted to contribute two to three thousand dollars. Virginians Roger Pryor and Edward Pollard vocally championed Walker's cause, and Pollard included pro-Walker comments in his justification of slavery, *Black Diamonds.* A number of border congressmen supported Walker in the House debates and votes of 1858–1859.[33]

Many of these people favored Walker primarily because of his proslavery stand. Yet northerners, particularly Republicans, often opposed him for this very reason. The Republican New York *Times* even accused Walker of "laying the basis" for a "Southern Slave Empire." This sectional conflict over Walker increased southern alienation from the union in the late 1850s. An Arkansas paper asserted in late 1860, on the eve of the union's dissolution, that secession could have been averted if Walker had succeeded because the South would have possessed "ample and undisputed outlet for her surplus slave population." The newspaper probably overstated Walker's significance, yet it is

33. Albert Burton Moore, *History of Alabama* (University, 1939), 261–62; Fornell, "Texans and Filibusters," 414–23; Earl Fornell, *The Galveston Era* (Austin, 1961), 215–30; R. Raub to John Quitman, January 18, 1858, in Quitman Papers, Harvard University Library; Pollard, *Black Diamonds,* 111–14. For a letter from a Missourian sympathetic to Walker, see Thomas Harney to Quitman, March 7, 1856, in John Quitman Papers, Mississippi Department of Archives and History. Harney was a delegate to his state's Democratic convention in 1856.

apparent that southern dissatisfaction increased in the late 1850s because of his failure. Southern states' righters could not overlook the antagonism of two northern Democratic administrations toward Walker. Pierce and Buchanan had indicated that southern leaders could not rely on northern Democratic support for southern expansionist aims. And Republican opposition to Walker's slavery decree was even more irritating. Senator Albert Gallatin Brown told a Hazlehurst, Mississippi, crowd in September, 1858, that refusal of the North to acquiesce in slavery expansion southward would be just cause for secession.[34]

Ironically, Walker seems to have had little intention of promoting an empire for the benefit of the southern slavocracy, notwithstanding his public pronouncements. It is apparent that he wanted power for himself in Nicaragua. And it is likely that he desired a Central American empire for his own sake. Walker enticed southern support as a means to his own ends.

Walker's minimum empire would have embraced all of Central America. He confided to Edmund Ruffin that he wanted Central America to be an "American conquest and colony" and he echoed these sentiments in *The War in Nicaragua*. By "American conquest" he meant emigrants from the United States under his direction taking over Central America rather than the annexation of Central America to the United States. His diplomatic instructions to John Heiss in September, 1856, are very revealing. He cautioned Heiss not to pledge "the future action of Nicaragua either towards the neighboring states of Central America or towards the United States" in his attempt to regain American recognition of the Walker regime. To Walker, recogni-

34. New York *Daily Times*, November 25, 1856; Fayetteville *Arkansian*, October 18, 1860; Tuskegee *Republican*, February 25, 1858; Galveston *Weekly News*, February 2, 1858; Nashville *Union and American*, October 31, 1856; Cluskey (ed.), *Speeches of Albert Gallatin Brown*, 588–99.

tion was not worth the price of forfeiting a prospective empire.[35]

Walker's imperialistic aims apparently included Mexico as well as Central America, although he may not have been associated with the well-publicized attempt of two of his subordinates to involve themselves in the Mexican revolution under General Santiago Vidaurri in 1858. In April, 1859, Walker asked Fayssoux to call on Pierre Soulé and question him about the "state of affairs" in Tehuantepec, especially concerning various transit companies, "all without giving Mr. S. any idea that my eyes are directed to the Isthmus." And C. W. Doubleday claimed that Walker, during a walk down a beach on Nicaragua's Pacific coast, had unfolded "plans of empire" in which Walker would conquer Mexico as well as Central America.[36] Walker's long-term intentions toward Cuba are less clear, but he may have had ambitions concerning that country too.

Many southerners who revered Walker for establishing slavery in Nicaragua were, therefore, misguided. The filibuster was his own man, and his end was personal power. His self-transformation into a sectional symbol was a public relations triumph, conducted for the sake of gaining southern support. He was able to play a significant role in the North-South estrangement that led to the Civil War because his performance was so convincing.

35. Edmund Ruffin Diary, May 17, 1859, in Ruffin Papers; Walker to Heiss, September 30, 1856, in Heiss Papers; Walker, *War in Nicaragua*, 256–80.

36. Walker to Fayssoux, April 19, 1859, in Walker Papers, Tulane University Library; Doubleday, *Reminiscences*, 165–66; Guy M. Bryan to Laura Jack, April 3, 1858, and Laura Jack to Guy M. Bryan, May 8, 1858, in Bryan Papers; New York *Herald*, February 4, 1859; Memphis *Daily Appeal*, May 5, 1858; Greensboro *Alabama Beacon*, April 2, 1858; Corpus Christi *Nueces Valley Weekly*, May 1, 1858; Scroggs, *Filibusters*, 369–70. Walker's recruiting agent in the United States, Appleton Oaksmith, encouraged Walker in such imperialistic sentiments. See Oaksmith to Walker, August 9, October 13, 1856, in Oaksmith Papers.

VI

The "Waif"
on the Southern Border

"Permit me to suggest the idea of expressing your views on the subject of annexing Mexico," wrote a Texan to Stephen Douglas in December, 1858. Advocacy of annexation, he continued, would "confer a favor on many Texans, and the South generally." [1] The Texan's views were representative of a large number of people in his part of the country in the 1850s. Through the Treaty of Guadalupe Hidalgo in 1848, the United States gained New Mexico, California, and the Rio Grande boundary for Texas; but expansionists clamored for still more additions at the expense of their southern neighbor. This feeling was so strong in the South, and to a somewhat lesser extent in the North, and there were so many American interventions in Mexico during this period, that it is remarkable the Gadsden Purchase was all the United States could secure from Mexico in the 1850s.

Southerners advocated acquisition of Mexican territory in the 1850s for a number of reasons. One of these was a growing belief that slavery could be reintroduced in Mexico. A North Carolina newspaper argued that once Mexico were taken, the South "might introduce Slavery there to some advantage." *De Bow's Review* envisioned slaves developing the lands of Sonora. John Ford of Texas, a leader in the movement, said that Mexico was the South's guarantee of future slavery expansion. The *Texas State Gazette*

1. [?] from Danville, Texas, to Douglas, December 21, 1858, in Douglas Papers.

commented that the eyes of many southerners were "long-ingly turned" to Mexico's "cotton and sugar lands." A cor-respondent of John Quitman desired the creation of "a chain of slave states from the Atlantic to the Pacific Ocean" through the incorporation of Sonora and southern Cali-fornia.[2] Mexico was simply too visible and accessible a tar-get to be overlooked in an era when southern expansionists were searching throughout the tropics for a place to estab-lish their institution.

Southerners, particularly Texans, were further moti-vated by Mexico's open door policy for runaway slaves. A Texan wrote President Buchanan that the United States should acquire Mexico to end her protection of "absconding slaves." John Ford entreated John Quitman to lead an ex-pedition to eliminate the bothersome problem. "Something must be done for the protection of slave property in this state," Ford complained. "Negroes are running off daily. ... Let the frontier of slavery begin to recede and when or where the wave of recession may be arrested God only knows." [3]

Although there are no exact figures, slaves had taken advantage of Mexican protection ever since Texas inde-pendence, and John Ford estimated that as many as four thousand lived between the Rio Grande and the Sierra Madres in northern Mexico. Throughout the 1850s Texas leaders advocated an extradition treaty with Mexico, but negotiations between the governments bore no fruit. The approaches made by influential Texans to Governor San-

2. New Bern *Daily Progress*, May 3, 1859; *De Bow's Review*, XXI (1856), 480–81; *Texas State Gazette*, October 9, 1858; John Ford to John Quitman, July 2, 1855, and John R. Wells to John Quitman, April 20, 1856, both in John Quitman Papers, Mississippi Department of Archives and History.
3. [?] to James Buchanan, July 29, 1859, in Records of the De-partment of State, Miscellaneous Letters, National Archives; John Ford to John Quitman, July 2, 1855, in John Quitman Papers, Uni-versity of Virginia Library, Charlottesville.

tiago Vidaurri, the ruler of the northern Mexican state of Nuevo León, had no positive results, although Vidaurri was more receptive than the government in Mexico City and consulted United States officials in Washington about the matter. Texans even launched a Mexico filibuster in 1855 under Texas Ranger Captain James Callahan for the purpose of recovering fugitives. Callahan had been commissioned by the governor of Texas to chastise marauding Indians in Bexar and Comal counties in south-central Texas "wherever they may be found"; but he stretched his instructions and invaded Mexico with 111 Texas Rangers. A Mexican-Indian ambush terminated Callahan's advance; but before escaping across the border, he burned the Mexican village of Piedras Negras and confiscated a considerable amount of property, particularly jewelry. Although Callahan's expedition apparently gave some Mexicans second thoughts about aiding runaways, it did not end the difficulty.[4]

Furthermore, Mexico allured southerners, and some northerners, for commercial reasons. Transportation opportunities were particularly inviting. Southern entrepreneur Duff Green, for instance, envisioned a complex railroad system that would have linked Washington with the Pacific Coast via Mexico City, and for years he was embroiled in negotiations with the Mexican and United States

4. Ronnie C. Tyler, "Runaway Slaves and Border Diplomacy," paper delivered at the meeting of the Southern Historical Association Convention at Houston, November 19, 1971, *passim*; Ronnie C. Tyler, "The Callahan Expedition of 1855: Indians or Negroes?," *Southwestern Historical Quarterly*, LXX (1967), 579–82; *Texas State Gazette*, October 9, 1858. Tyler points out that Ford, at about the same time he was approaching Quitman for a Mexico expedition, was acting as an agent for San Antonio and Bastrop slaveholders to negotiate with Vidaurri about the fugitive slave problem; he and another representative of the slave interests had been authorized to offer Vidaurri one thousand armed and mounted soldiers to help Vidaurri establish his independence if he would cooperate with Texans on the issue in the future. Ford deferred his mission when he heard about the Callahan enterprise. See Tyler, "Runaway Slaves," 6.

governments, various state legislatures, and a number of railroad systems.[5]

Mexico's southern neck, the Isthmus of Tehuantepec, attracted additional interest. A road, railway, or canal across the isthmus that could compete with the Central American routes seemed an excellent prospect since it would be further north. James K. Polk's administration had tried to get a right of transit across Tehuantepec included in the Treaty of Guadalupe Hidalgo, and throughout the 1850s southern leaders were involved in enterprises to secure a concession from the Mexican government favorable enough to make the construction of a transit route financially feasible.[6] Foremost among the promoters of a Tehuantepec project were the major figures of Louisiana politics, including John Slidell, Judah P. Benjamin, Emil La Sère, and Pierre Soulé. In the late 1850s, when the agitation for a Tehuantepec transit came to a head, Soulé served as attorney for a group of New York promoters headed by A. G. Sloo; Slidell, Benjamin, and La Sère were involved with competing New Orleans interests. Both the New York promoters and their Louisiana competitors claimed title to a generous land and finance concession, the Garay grant, which the Mexican government had offered in 1842 to a Mexican citizen as incentive for construction of a transit.

The weak condition of Mexican government in the 1850s, especially after the overthrow of Santa Anna in 1855, further encouraged southern hopes of annexation. After Santa Anna went into exile in August, Mexico entered "La Reforma"—a period dominated by Benito Juárez and marked by internal strife between Conservatives and Liberals centering on the Constitution of 1857 and Liberal-supported

5. *Congressional Globe*, 34th Cong., 1st Sess., Appendix, 1296; Fletcher M. Green, "Duff Green: Industrial Promoter," *Journal of Southern History*, II (1936), 34–37.

6. James Fred Rippy, "Diplomacy Regarding the Isthmus of Tehuantepec, 1848–1860," *Mississippi Valley Historical Review*, VI (1919–20), 503–31.

anticlerical and antiarmy laws. Mexico quickly passed through a succession of regimes. Juan Álvarez, the Indian caudillo who had led the resistance to Santa Anna, withdrew from the Mexican presidency in December, 1855. His successor, Ignacio Comonfort, a compromiser, resigned in January, 1858. Three years of civil war followed. Juárez, the Liberal leader, established his own government at Vera Cruz. Power in Mexico City rested briefly with the Conservative spokesman, General Félix Zuloaga, and then with Miguel Miramón. Juárez's armies finally occupied Mexico City in January, 1861. The influence achieved by regional potentates such as Santiago Vidaurri further undermined the Mexican government.

Factionalism within Mexico, particularly in the late 1850s, encouraged American expansionists, particularly southerners, to mouth once again the "manifest destiny" slogans that had served them so well during the Mexican War. "It is *manifest destiny*," exclaimed Representative Thomas Bocock of Virginia, "which will ever make a strong, vigorous, and healthful race overrun and crush out a weak and effete one. Our people *will* go South among the Mexicans and Spaniards, and *will* carry with them the love of our civilization and our liberty." A Texan railed against Mexican Catholicism, Mexico's legislative system, and the important role of the military in her government, and warned Mexico : "Your glorious country must be redeemed, the destiny of America requires it, you must do it yourselves, or we will do it for you." Southerners called Mexico the "sick man" of the Western Hemisphere, fading at a rate comparable to Spain and Turkey.[7]

Expansionists viewed chaos in Mexico as a threat to American security that could be eradicated only by inter-

7. *Congressional Globe*, 34th Cong., 1st Sess., Appendix, 425; *ibid.*, 35th Cong., 1st Sess., 736; *De Bow's Review*, XXI (1856), 352–60; Richmond *Daily Dispatch*, July 25, 1855; Memphis *Daily Avalanche*, January 28, 1860.

vention. A number of incidents in the late 1850s provoked speculation among expansionists that European powers would attempt to take advantage of Mexican disorders and would use outstanding claims against Mexico as an excuse for aggression. In one instance, British and French warships intervened on the Conservative side, forcing satisfaction of debts by threatening to shell Vera Cruz. Rumors of a Spanish invasion of Mexico caused anxiety in the United States, particularly after the Spanish minister of foreign affairs wrote the American minister to Spain in August, 1857, that Spain might have to act to protect Spanish subjects and property in Mexico. The danger of imminent Spanish intervention did not subside until 1859.[8]

American annexation of Mexico would have relieved that danger, and expansionists often invoked the specter of European intervention to buttress their case for annexation, just as they warned of an English and French threat to rally Americans behind annexing Cuba. John Quitman, for example, told the House of Representatives that the United States should seize Mexico because she was a "waif" waiting to be conquered by "some stronger power." An Alabama newspaper called Mexico "a floating wreck, on fire," and argued that the law of "self-preservation" (the same "law" cited by the Ostend Manifesto) required that the United States take over Mexico before England, France, or Spain did so.[9] Such alarmist sentiments were not totally

8. Pedro J. Pidal to Augustus C. Dodge, August 15, 1857, Lewis Cass to Augustus C. Dodge, October 21, 1858, and Augustus C. Dodge to Lewis Cass, November 15, 1858, December 25, 1858, January 5, 1859, all in Manning (ed.), *Diplomatic Correspondence*, XI, 930, 229–30, 956, 962–65. James Fred Rippy mentions that since at least 1844 various American consuls and ministers in Mexico had been warning of European intervention in Mexico, and that these warnings sharply increased in 1856 and after. See Rippy, *United States and Mexico*, 201–208. The threat to shell Vera Cruz arose in early January, 1859.

9. *Congressional Globe*, 34th Cong., 1st Sess., Appendix, 668; Montgomery *Daily Confederation*, March 9, 1860. See also *Congressional Globe*, 34th Cong., 1st Sess., Appendix, 1298.

divorced from reality, as the French establishment of the Maximilian puppet government in Mexico during the American Civil War would prove.

Unredressed American grievances against Mexico constituted yet another foundation for the agitation for intervention. An American in Mexico wrote Congressman Guy Bryan of Texas in 1858 that "to be an 'Americano' is a disgrace and subjects one not only to annoyance, but to the finger of doom, and kicks of the lowest official in the land," which often resulted in prison sentences, the loss of rights, and the confiscation of property. His sentiments were echoed in other complaints that poured into Washington.[10] Such grievances had served as a pretext for a strong American policy in the chain of events preceding the Mexican War, and Americans urging an aggressive stand toward Mexico in the 1850s put the issue to identical use. Sam Houston asserted in his inaugural address as governor of Texas in December, 1859, that since Texas was a "border state," her security depended on "the restoration of order, and the establishment of good government" in Mexico. President Buchanan's second annual message to Congress (December, 1858) painted a panorama of decadence in Mexico, stressed that American claims against Mexico exceeded $10 million, and argued for American intervention.[11]

10. [?] to Guy Bryan, November 10, 1858, in Bryan Papers; Franklin Chase (American consul at Tampico) to Isaac Toucey (secretary of the navy), February 23, 1858, William C. Whiting to James Buchanan, October 15, 1858, and Charles Butterfield to Lewis Cass, December 2, 1858, all in Records of the Department of State, Miscellaneous Letters; Philadelphia *Public Ledger*, January 28, 1859.

11. Amelia W. Williams and Eugene C. Barker (eds.), *The Writings of Sam Houston* (8 vols.; Austin, 1938–43), VII, 383; John Bassett Moore (ed.), *The Works of James Buchanan* (12 vols.; Philadelphia, 1908–11), X, 253–56. See also *Congressional Globe*, 35th Cong., 2nd Sess., 298; Lewis Cass to John Forsyth, July 17, 1857, in John Forsyth Papers, Alabama Department of Archives and History, Montgomery. In Cass's letter the secretary of state

Texans, in particular, expressed worry about the weakness of Mexican government. Conditions on the Texas-Mexico frontier, especially along the Rio Grande, deteriorated throughout the 1850s. The thick chaparral on the banks of the Rio Grande from its mouth to the point at which it joined the San Pedro River provided cover for those who wanted to cross the border for hostile reasons, and the river itself could be forded a good part of the time. Troubles would have plagued the Texas-Mexico frontier had the Mexican government closely supervised the area; the absence of such supervision added to an explosive situation. Throughout the 1850s, Indians crossed the river to find booty and scalps at isolated ranches, farms, and settlements in southern Texas knowing they could recross the river if resistance were encountered.[12]

These intrusions culminated in the Juan Cortina raid on Brownsville, Texas, a border town near the Gulf of Mexico, in late September, 1859. Cortina was a Mexican-American whose mother's ranch above Brownsville straddled both sides of the Rio Grande. On September 28, while most of the town's inhabitants were attending a fiesta across the Rio Grande at Matamoros, Cortina and his followers raided the Brownsville jail, freed the prisoners, and murdered the jailor. After threatening to burn the town, Cortina withdrew to the ranch, issued a proclamation of war against Americans, raised a Mexican flag, and gathered recruits. Over the next few months he continued to trouble the border by organizing various operations in Matamoros; on one occasion he captured a United States mail rider. Far more irritating to Texans than Cortina's actual exploits were

---

urged Forsyth, American minister to Mexico, to use American claims as a lever to force territorial cessions from Mexico.

12. George C. Clendenen, *Blood on the Border: The United States Army and the Mexican Irregulars* (London, 1969), 2, 5–6; James Fred Rippy, "Border Troubles Along the Rio Grande, 1848–1860," *Southwestern Historical Quarterly*, LXX (1967), 91, 98, 100.

the false rumors that swept the state in the waning days of 1859 and in early 1860, such as the report that he had burned Corpus Christi and murdered all its citizens. Throughout this period Mexican authorities conspicuously avoided a confrontation with him.[13]

The Cortina crisis almost provoked a major invasion of Mexico by Governor Sam Houston of Texas. On February 18, 1858, Houston advocated to the United States Senate that the United States establish a protectorate because of Mexican anarchy, but his proposal was laid on the table. Houston then warned that he might take individual action if the United States continued to refuse to forcibly involve itself. When he delivered his inaugural address as governor of Texas in the midst of the Cortina panic, he reiterated his threat. Paternalistically describing Mexicans as "mild, pastoral and gentle people" terrorized by "demagogues and lawless chieftains," he said that if federal authorities could not correct the situation, he might have to exercise his "fullest powers."[14]

Houston nearly carried out his threat in 1860. Besieged by complaints from his constituents of Mexican infringements of the border, Houston wrote to the War Department and sent emissaries to Secretary of War John Floyd to get more troops on the Rio Grande or financial support for a Texas Ranger regiment to police the border. Simulta-

13. Rippy, *United States and Mexico*, 181–83; Clendenen, *Blood on the Border*, 20–38; John Ford to Sam Houston, March 23, 1860, and Angel Navarro to Sam Houston, January 31, 1860, both in Governors' Letters, Sam Houston. Clendenen points out that there had been some twenty indictments against Cortina in the United States for everything from petty theft to murder before the raid, and that the attack may have been provoked by an incident the previous summer when Cortina, as a recently commissioned captain in the Mexican army, had come into Brownsville with some followers. An American marshal arrested one of Cortina's men, and Cortina had rescued his adherent—wounding the marshal in the process—and fled the town. See Clendenen, *Blood on the Border*, 21–22.

14. *Congressional Globe*, 35th Cong., 1st Sess., 716, 735–37, 1679–82, 2630; Williams and Barker (eds.), *Writings of Houston*, VII, 382–83.

neously, he undertook preparations for an invasion of Mexico in the event that federal support was not forthcoming. Houston even contacted Colonel Robert E. Lee, temporary U.S. Army commander of the Department of Texas at San Antonio, for the purpose of engaging him in a leadership role in the filibustering expedition. But Lee declined; he would not involve himself in any such enterprise without federal authorization. Had the invasion occurred, it would probably have been led by Houston himself and would have consisted mainly of a large force of Texas volunteers. How close Houston came to putting the enterprise in motion is unclear, but a Corpus Christi correspondent of Duff Green wrote on February 16, 1860, that he had dined with Houston and felt "he really intends to march into Mexico to punish the enemy if the President omits to order it to be done." Another letter to Green two months later said that "old Sam" was "itching" to begin the invasion. Walter Prescott Webb, in his history of the Texas Rangers, proposes that Houston wanted to get the English bondholders of the Mexican debt to finance the enterprise, and that he planned to employ Texas Rangers mustered to fight Indians, Indian guides, and perhaps even the Indians themselves for a grand move into Mexico.[15]

It is certain that had Houston made a move, Texas citi-

15. Houston to John Floyd, February 13, March 12, 1860, Houston to Ben McCulloch, February 13, 1860, Houston to Forbes Britton, March 29, 1860, Forbes Britton to Houston, March 3, 1860, Ben McCulloch to Houston, March 4, 1860, W. R. Drinkard to Houston, March 14, 1860, Lemuel Evans to Houston, March 19, 1860, and John Ford to Houston, March 25, 1860, all in Governors' Letters, Sam Houston; David Porter to Duff Green, February 16, April 5, 1860, in Duff Green Papers, University of North Carolina Library, Chapel Hill; Walter Prescott Webb, *The Texas Rangers: A Century of Frontier Defense* (2nd ed.; Austin, 1965), 205–15; Carl Coke Rister, *Robert E. Lee in Texas* (Norman, 1946), 102–104. Houston's thoughts of invading Mexico were hardly dampened by the reaction of the Buchanan administration. When asked what the administration would do if Houston invaded Mexico with a volunteer force, Secretary of War Floyd answered that he would clap his hands and "holler Hurrah." See Forbes Britton to Houston, March 3, 1860, in Governors' Letters, Sam Houston.

zens would have rallied to his banner. It was common knowledge throughout the state that the hero of the Texas Revolution was planning to invade Mexico, and Texans were anxious to get another chance to fight their old foes. A Canton supporter wrote Houston: "We are now anxious for you to call us a round [*sic*] you and march into Mexico and take charge of that unhappy country." Another supporter wrote Houston's wife that he hoped the general would take a "trip" to Mexico, "establish a Government" there, and hasten back to run for the presidency in 1860. "A little Filibustering would help Mexico," wrote yet another backer. Former United States representative Lemuel Evans exhorted Houston to launch an invasion for the implausible reason that some of Houston's "lady friends" in Washington were rooting for him to strike a "grand *coup de main*" against Mexico. Houston never completely assimilated the pieces of his plan. The closest the invasion came to realization was the temporary crossing of the border by Ranger forces in late 1859 and early 1860 to engage hostile Mexicans. The Cortina threat gradually receded, the United States government augmented federal forces in the Rio Grande region, and the coming of the American Civil War ended Houston's last hope for an intervention in Mexico. Houston continued pleading for federalized Texas Rangers, however, to the end of his term as governor.[16]

16. Columbus B. Smith to Houston, May 6, 1860, Thomas Carothers to Mrs. Houston, undated, F. G. Nicholson to Houston, March 20, 1860, Lemuel Evans to Houston, March 19, 1860, John Ford to Houston, March 25, 1860, Forbes Britton to Houston, March 3, 1860, and Houston to John Floyd, February 13, November 28, 1860, all in Governors' Letters, Sam Houston; Clendenen, *Blood on the Border*, 34–41. See also Augustus Chapman Allen to Houston, September 19, 1859, Ben McCulloch to Houston, March 4, 1860, Angel Navarro to Houston, January 31, 1860, John Patton, John Stubbe, Charles Ross, and W. W. Lancy to Houston, March 14, 1860, R. E. Rankin, Jr., to Houston, March 24, 1860, Augustus P. Zantzinger to Houston, March 29, 1860, Wily Morgan, Jr., to Houston, March 24, 1860, and T. T. Gammage to Houston, March 1, 1860, all in Governors' Letters, Sam Houston.

Those who proposed intervention on the basis of Mexican persecution of Americans or the destruction of American property naturally found it convenient to ignore Mexico's legitimate grievances. When interventionists argued that the weakness of the Mexican government was the cause of border problems, they often left unmentioned the lack of a sizeable United States law enforcement contingent in the area. In fact, one major reason that Cortina had such staying power on the Texas frontier was that earlier in 1859 United States troops had been withdrawn from the Rio Grande area to fight Comanche and other Plains Indians in northern Texas. When interventionists asserted that Mexicans discriminated against Americans in their midst, they never referred to the persecution of Mexicans in the mining areas of California or the miserable treatment of peaceful Mexican residents in Texas. And when interventionists fulminated against the raids of Juan Cortina and others, they rarely pointed out that American adventurers were engaged in the same activities.[17]

The number of American filibuster raids into Mexico in the 1850s is staggering. The Walker incursion into Lower California and Sonora and the Callahan intervention have been discussed already. Brief mention might be made of the invasion of Sonora in 1851 by Joseph Morehead, a former quarter master general of California with a price on his head for pilfering state funds. From 1850–1855, American merchants and Texas planters gave the Mexican José Carvajal (Carbajal) financial backing and manpower for his scheme to create a new country, the Republic of Sierra Madre, in Tamaulipas in northern Mexico. Carvajal acquired this support by promising to reduce tariff rates on Mexican-American trade and to return fugitive slaves. The

17. Clendenen, *Blood on the Border*, 11–13; William Robert Kenny, "Mexican-American Conflict on the Mining Frontier, 1849–1852," *Journal of the West*, VI (1967), 583–91; Rippy, "Border Troubles," 103–104.

invasion of Sonora in March, 1857, by Henry Crabb, former California state senator and boyhood friend of William Walker, also disturbed the peace of the frontier. Crabb's end was hideous. He and some ninety followers were surrounded soon after crossing the border and surrendered to Mexican authorities on the understanding that they would be allowed to return to the United States. Instead, all were shot except a fourteen-year-old boy. Crabb was decapitated and his head was placed on public display in a large wine-filled vessel to show what kind of reception filibusters could expect in Mexico.[18] These are only some of the expeditions that left American soil for Mexico in the 1850s.

Except for the fact that Callahan wanted to secure slave property in Texas, there is little evidence that filibustering in Mexico was sectionally oriented.[19] But an organization did arise in the South in the years before the Civil War

18. Joe A. Stout, Jr., "Joseph C. Morehead and Manifest Destiny: A Filibuster in Sonora, 1851," *Pacific Historian*, XV (1971), 62–70; Tyler, "Runaway Slaves," 4–5; Rippy, "Border Troubles," 94–97; Rufus Kay Wyllys, "Henry A. Crabb—A Tragedy of the Sonora Frontier," *Pacific Historical Review*, IX (1940), 191; Robert H. Forbes, *Crabb's Filibustering Expedition into Sonora, 1857* (Tucson, 1952), 8–9; Foote, *Reminiscences*, 387. For a sympathetic account of Crabb, see Joe A. Stout, Jr., "Henry A. Crabb: Filibuster or Colonizer?," *American West*, VIII (1971), 4–9. Stout feels that Crabb had been invited into Sonora by Ignacio Pesqueira, who became governor of Sonora by the time Crabb crossed the border, to develop lands and mines. According to Stout, Crabb's steady personality, his lack of secrecy, his success at attracting followers of substance, and the fact that he informed Mexican officials of his intentions all undermine the explanation that his intent was hostile.

19. A correspondent of the New York *Tribune* wrote from Sacramento that Crabb was "positive on this slavery extension question," and Theodore Hittell, in his *History of California*, asserted that Crabb was proslavery in California politics. Hittell, however, presented no evidence to verify his assertion. See the quotation from the New York *Tribune* in "Execution of Colonel Crabb and Associates," *House Executive Documents*, 35th Cong., 1st Sess., No. 64, p. 71; Theodore H. Hittell, *History of California* (4 vols.; San Francisco, 1897), II, 806–807.

with the purpose of extending slavery into Mexico by means of filibustering.

In 1854 or 1855, George Bickley, a disreputable Virginia-born Cincinnati physician and magazine editor, went to Lexington, Kentucky, and formed The Knights of the Golden Circle (or Cross), a secret ritual organization.[20] The name of the organization symbolized its purpose—the creation of a great slave empire. The "Golden Circle" had Cuba at its center, and its circumference included most of the border states, the South, part of Kansas, Mexico, Central America, part of South America, and the West Indies. This goal, supposedly, was symbolized in the Knights' ritual by a crescent surrounded by fifteen stars; the crescent represented the rising southern nation and the fifteen stars the various parts of the empire.[21] Despite grandiose designs, Bickley's main interest was Mexico. The first article of the Knights' constitution made this clear, as did the treasurer in the Knights' initiation ritual when he stated that "the first field of our operations is Mexico," which must be Americanized and southernized.[22]

20. For Bickley's disreputable character, see the comments of Frank Klement in "Carrington and the Golden Circle Legend in Indiana during the Civil War," *Indiana Magazine of History*, LXI (1965), 32. Klement implies that Bickley tried to cheat his wife out of her property and asserts that his main interest in creating the Knights was to build a personal fortune out of ten-dollar membership fees.

Few records exist concerning the Knights, thus much historical study about the Knights has been based on circumstantial evidence and the few contemporary accounts of the Knights that have survived. For different dates of the origins of the Knights, see *An Authentic Exposition of the K. G. C. by a member of the Order* (Indianapolis, 1861), 8; Wallace, *Destiny and Glory*, 141; C. A. Bridges, "The Knights of the Golden Circle: A Filibustering Fantasy," *Southwestern Historical Quarterly*, XLIV (1941), 287.

21. Bridges, "Knights," 288; *Authentic Exposition*, 12.

22. *Authentic Exposition*, 11; J. W. Pomfrey, *A True Disclosure and Exposition of the Golden Circle* (Cincinnati, 1861), 14.

Bickley's public words leave no doubt that Mexico was the organization's objective: "KNIGHTS OF THE GOLDEN CIRCLE, let us be men—Christian and consistent men—energetic Anglo-Americans. Let us move boldly on in our labor of saving Mexico, and of strengthening the South." By "strengthening the South," Bickley meant adding slave states to the union. The leaders of the Knights believed that acquisition of Mexico would sweep into the union twenty-five slave states with fifty senators and sixty or more representatives, thus satisfying southern desires for enough new slave states to achieve sectional equality with the North. Bickley even dared to refer to the Knights as the "only movement ever made in the South to prevent the further agitation of the slavery question." [23] Should the union be broken, Mexican territory would be invaluable to a southern confederacy. Bickley observed:

> Now this truth must be apparent to every thinking man; with Mexico Americanized and *Southernized*, our area of territory would be nearly equal to that of the North, including New Mexico and California. Our population would be equal to her's. Besides we should possess advantages of climate, soil, productions and geographic position of a very marked character. With this addition to either our *system*, the *Union*, or to a Southern Confederacy, we should possess every element of national wealth and power. We shall have in our own hands the Cotton, Tobacco, Sugar, Coffee, Rice, Corn and Tea lands of the continent, and the world's great storehouse of mineral wealth.[24]

The Knights were primarily a Texas organization. Bickley claimed in the spring of 1860 that the Knights were active in almost every state and that there were forty thou-

23. Richmond *Daily Whig*, July 18, 1860; Bridges, "Knights," 290.
24. Bickley to E. H. Cushing (editor of the Houston *Telegraph*), November 15, 1860, in Jimmie Hicks (ed.), "Some Letters Concerning the Knights of the Golden Circle in Texas, 1860–1861," *Southwestern Historical Quarterly*, LXV (1961), 85.

sand members; but Bickley was a notorious liar, and he practically admitted that his organization was primarily Texan in July, 1860, when he begged other southern states to contribute to the cause as his Texan supporters had done. His membership claims should not be taken seriously, and his claim that Texans contributed nearly a half-million dollars to the Knights is absurd. But there were at least thirty-two "castles" of the Knights spread over twenty-seven Texas counties, and newspapers such as the Dallas *Herald* and the Houston *Telegraph* applauded Bickley's activities. How strong the Knights were in other states is problematical, although there was activity in Georgia. An acquaintance of Alexander Stephens reported in March, 1860, that a couple of lectures by the Knights at Atlanta's City Hall were the only events of interest in that city at the time. In April, a Georgia newspaper said that the Knights wanted to raise a regiment in Georgia to fight in Mexico. In Maryland, Bickley set up an expansionist newspaper, the Baltimore *American Cavalier*, to support his cause. Rumor linked political notables throughout the South—including Jefferson Davis, William Yancey, Howell Cobb, John Floyd, John Breckinridge, William Brownlow, and Isham Harris—to the organization at one time or another; but these reports were probably fabrications.[25]

25. Bickley to Lewis Cass, April 13, 1860, in Records of the Department of State, Miscellaneous Letters; *K. G. C.: A Full Exposure of the Southern Traitors; The Knights of the Golden Circle* (Boston, 1860) ; Roy Sylvan Dunn, "The KGC in Texas, 1860–1861," *Southwestern Historical Quarterly*, LXX (1967), 548, 555–56; William H. Bell, "Knights of the Golden Circle: Its Organization and Activities in Texas Prior to the Civil War," (M.A. thesis, Texas College of Arts and Industries, 1965), 5–20; [?] to Alexander Stephens, March 22, 1860, in Stephens Papers, Library of Congress; Macon *Daily Telegraph*, April 2, 1860; Olliger Crenshaw, "The Knights of the Golden Circle," *American Historical Review*, XLVII (1941), 38; Pomfrey, *True Disclosure*, iv; *Authentic Exposition*, 32; David Donald (ed.), *Inside Lincoln's Cabinet: The Civil War Diaries of Salmon P. Chase* (New York, 1954), 125–26; Nashville *Union and*

Bickley made two feeble efforts to get the Knights organized for an actual invasion of Mexico. In early 1860, at the same time that Houston was considering invasion, Bickley summoned his followers to south-central Texas to prepare for hostilities; he claimed that the Knights would not be breaking the American neutrality laws because the Mexican leader Juárez had offered his men land and money to come into Mexico to fight the Conservatives. Leaders of the Texas Knights contacted Houston, informed him of their plans, and entreated him to lead their expedition. A large party of Knights did arrive in the general region, but the effort to get Houston involved backfired. Houston was a moderate on the slavery question and a staunch unionist, whereas the Knights were inclined toward secession. Houston's concern was to establish American rule in northern Mexico and pacify the Rio Grande frontier, whereas the Knights' main goal was to extend slavery. The governor issued a proclamation against the activities of the Knights on March 21, 1860, which dampened Texan enthusiasm for the movement, and the enterprise fell through when Bickley failed to appear on the scene with a force that he had claimed he was raising in New Orleans and other parts of the Deep South. In fact, at the very time Texas members were hastening to the Rio Grande in preparation for the invasion, Bickley was in the Southeast. The Augusta *Daily Constitutionalist* of March 21, 1860, reported his visit to that city. Bickley spoke in Augusta of the need to acquire Cuba and Mexico to help slavery expansion. But this rhetoric did little good for his adherents in Texas; they aban-

---

American, September 16, 1860. For reports of the activity of Knights in Baltimore, see Greenville (Alabama) *Southern Messenger*, April 4, 1860; Montgomery *Daily Confederation*, February 25, 1860. Bickley's exaggerations grew more startling as time passed. In the fall of 1860 he claimed 115,000 members and asserted that within ten days he could get 50,000 men together at any southern point for a move against Mexico. See Dallas *Herald*, November 14, 1860.

doned the Rio Grande region, although some may have delayed their departure to engage in horse stealing.[26]

An open split between Bickley and the Texas Knights resulted from the breakdown in communication. Many Texans, such as Sam Lockridge who had served with Walker, criticized Bickley harshly for overestimating his strength; and in early April a group of Knights met in New Orleans and expelled Bickley. He retaliated by calling for a grand convention of the Knights in Raleigh, North Carolina, for May 7. The convention lasted through May 11 and reinstated Bickley in his position as "President of the American Legion" of the Knights of the Golden Circle.[27]

Bickley's vindication paved the way for a new initiative towards Mexico. He returned to his native Virginia to recruit that summer, and on July 18, in an open letter to fellow Knights published in the Richmond *Daily Whig*, he announced: "I hereby order every member of the order belonging or desiring to belong to our military department, and I respectfully invite all who may wish to join us, to repair to our camp at and near Fort Ewen on the south bank of the Rio Nueces and along the road on the ridge between Prita and Salado Creeks, in ENCINAL County, Texas, by the fifteenth day of September, 1860." [28] The Richmond message was circulated in other southern newspapers.

26. Montgomery *Daily Confederation*, March 15, 1860; I. W. Barrett (?) to Houston, February 20, 1860, and Elkanah Greer to Houston, March 22, 1860, both in Governors' Letters, Sam Houston; photocopy of Ben McCulloch to Houston, April 6, 1860 in Houston Papers, Barker Texas History Center Archives; Williams and Barker (eds.), *Writings of Houston*, VII, 534–35; Bell, "Knights in Texas," 76–92; Augusta *Daily Constitutionalist*, March 21, 1860; Philadelphia *Public Ledger*, April 4, 1860; Macon *Daily Telegraph*, April 2, 7, 1860; Dunn, "KGC," 530–31, 548–50; Bridges, "Knights," 292–93.

27. Philadelphia *Public Ledger*, April 4, 1860; Macon *Daily Telegraph*, April 4, 10, 1860; Dunn, "KGC," 553; Bell, "Knights in Texas," 85–87.

28. Richmond *Daily Whig*, July 18, 1860; Macon *Daily Telegraph*, July 21, 1860.

This time Bickley made it to Texas, arriving on October 10. After setting up headquarters in San Antonio, he traversed the state organizing "castles". Although a few Knights gathered near the Rio Grande, Bickley seems to have had no sincere intention of launching the expedition. He expressed more interest in the presidential canvass and put off all action concerning Mexico until after the election results were known. When Lincoln's victory became apparent, Bickley involved the Knights in secessionist activity, and the Mexican scheme dissipated. Bickley's explanation for abandoning filibustering in favor of secession activity was that it was patriotic for his organization to come to the aid of state governors in the South.[29] It is just as probable, however, that he was unable to put together anything resembling a formidable expedition and immersed himself in the secession movement to divert attention from his failure, which might have raised an outcry for a return of funds donated to the organization.

Soon after Lincoln's election, Bickley left Texas to induce Kentucky and Tennessee to join the secession movement and put his nephew Charles Bickley in charge of the Texas "castles". These "castles" were eventually amalgamated into the Confederate army, but not before they had played a role in promoting Texas secession. Roy Dunn has noted that there were a number of Knights who were radicals in the Texas secession convention, and that the Knights may have suppressed unionist votes during Texas' secession referendum. The Knights helped to force the surrender of the United States garrison at San Antonio, Texas, on February 18, 1861, and destroyed the last union paper in Texas on May 13.[30]

29. Bickley to E. H. Cushing, November 12, 1860, in Hicks (ed.), "Letters Concerning Knights," 83.
30. Bickley to E. H. Cushing, November 15, 1860, *ibid.*, 81–85; Ernest Wallace, *Texas in Turmoil, 1849–1875* (Austin, 1965), 58; Bridges, "Knights," 299–300; Bell, "Knights in Texas," 104–13, 160–85; Dunn, "KGC," 554–72. Dunn points out that local units of the Knights in Texas were noted for secessionist activities such as torchlight parades. Leaders of the Knights, such as Elkanah Greer, spoke

George Bickley was less successful in his promotion of
Kentucky secession; and, after a stay in Virginia, he was
arrested behind Union lines in Indiana in July, 1863, for
spying, although nothing was proved. Imprisonment followed, and Bickley was not released until October, 1865,
months after the Civil War ended. A "broken" man, the
adventurer died in August, 1867.[31]

The widespread clamor in the 1850s for annexation, intervention, and acquisition of transit rights in Mexico was
reflected in national policy. The Whig administrations of
Taylor and Fillmore engaged in negotiations with Mexico
from 1849–1851 with the purpose of securing a transit
treaty. The Pierce administration, responding to southern
pressure for a southern transcontinental railroad route,
concluded the Gadsden Treaty. It provided for Mexican
cession of some fifty-four thousand square miles of land, in
what is today southern Arizona and southern New Mexico,
at a cost of $10 million.

James Buchanan's Mexican policy demonstrated even
more territorial ambition; but it failed. Buchanan's inaugural address revealed that he might be interested in acquiring territory or concessions from Mexico. Praising
American expansion throughout North America, the president declared that the negotiations following the war with
Mexico had illustrated how expansion could be consistent
with national honor. The United States, "unwilling to take
advantage" of Mexico, had purchased acquisitions with a
sum "considered at the time a fair equivalent." The "great
laws of self-preservation" might again necessitate American intervention in Mexican affairs.[32] Throughout his term

out at mass meetings calling for secession. Dunn uses voting statistics to demonstrate that Texas counties which had KGC castles were
more likely to be for secession than counties without castles of
Knights, even when both types of counties had similar social char-
acteristics (such as the number of slaves and Germans per county
being approximately equal). See Dunn, "KGC," 557–59, 561–67.

31. Dunn, "KGC," 572.
32. Moore (ed.), *Works of Buchanan*, X, 113.

in office, Buchanan doggedly pursued the extension of American influence in Mexico. He promoted the schemes of American entrepreneurs to develop a transit across Mexico, tried to acquire Mexican territory, and advocated the establishment of an American protectorate over northern Mexico. Buchanan's role in the Tehuantepec transit negotiations is a classic case of conflict of interest. Early in his administration, his political allies in the Louisiana Tehuantepec Company petitioned him to support their claims to the Garay grant over the claims of A. G. Sloo, and he responded. His decision was almost certainly determined by political loyalties. The president of the Louisiana Tehuantepec Company was Emile La Sère, a strong Buchanan supporter, who had already received the position of disbursing agent for the United States Mint in New Orleans. And two of the president's campaign managers, Senators John Slidell and Judah Benjamin of Louisiana, were deeply involved with the company. Benjamin alone owned $29,000 in company bonds and over $94,000 in stock. Pierre Soulé, attorney for the Sloo interests, was a supporter of Stephen Douglas, Buchanan's rival in the Democratic party. In addition, the influential Robert Toombs of Georgia called on Buchanan in March, 1857, and urged him to send Benjamin to Mexico with an executive endorsement to secure a charter for the Tehuantepec route.[33]

33. A. L. Diket, "Slidell's Right Hand: Emile La Sère," *Louisiana History,* IV (1963), 189–93; Robert D. Meade, *Judah P. Benjamin: Confederate Statesman* (New York, 1943), 74–75, 122–23; Rollin Osterweis, *Judah P. Benjamin: Statesman of the Lost Cause* (New York, 1933), 81, 91; Pierce Butler, *Judah P. Benjamin* (Philadelphia, 1907), 131–33; Robert Toombs to William M. Burwell, March 30, 1857, and Judah Benjamin to William M. Burwell, November 26, 1857, both in William Burwell Papers, Library of Congress; Judah Benjamin to Lewis Cass, 1857 (exact date not given), quoted in Frank B. Woodford, *Lewis Cass: The Last Jeffersonian* (New Brunswick, 1950), 307; Judah Benjamin to Lewis Cass, February 8, 1858, in Records of the Department of State, Miscellaneous Letters.

When Benjamin and La Sère left the United States on August 2, 1857, to try to get the Comonfort government in Mexico to establish their company's claim to the Garay grant, it was with Buchanan's blessing. Secretary of State Cass had already instructed expansionist Alabamian John Forsyth that as American minister to Mexico, he should support the Louisianians rather than the Sloo interests before the Mexican government. Pierre Soulé, however, took the same steamer as Benjamin and La Sère, and won Forsyth's endorsement. Soulé could not win the grant, but his and Forsyth's interference resulted in strict terms being imposed on the Tehuantepec Company. Later, in November, 1858, when the Louisiana Tehuantepec Company was involved in the financing and building of a road across Tehuantepec, the Buchanan administration again came to its aid by granting it the California mail contract for a year.[34]

34. Lewis Cass to John Forsyth, July 17, November 17, 1857, in Forsyth Papers; Moore, "Soulé," 218; Moore (ed.), "Correspondence of Soulé," 71–72; Rippy, *United States and Mexico*, 212–17. Benjamin and La Sère claimed that Forsyth professed support of their mission while in their presence, but undermined their efforts by telling Comonfort in a private conference that the United States no longer backed them, by telling the Mexican Under-Secretary of Foreign Relations that Benjamin and La Sère were only speculators and had no intention of living up to their promises, by praising Soulé's character and asserting that the United States would insist on damages for Sloo if the Louisiana Tehuantepec Company were given the concession, and by supplying information unfavorable to their interests to the Mexican press. See photostat copy of Benjamin and La Sère's account of their mission (no date) in Forsyth Papers; Benjamin to Cass, February 8, 1858, in Records of the Department of State, Miscellaneous Letters.

The company lost the mail contract in 1859 and its financing failed at about the same time. Eventually it fell apart, never coming close to Benjamin's promise to Buchanan that the company would have an Isthmian railroad constructed by the end of the president's "first" term of office, and that the railroad would reduce the New Orleans-San Francisco route to eleven days. See Merle E. Reed, *New Orleans and the Railroads: The Struggle for Commercial Empire, 1830–1860* (Baton Rouge, 1966), 75; Benjamin to Buchanan, November 24, 1858, in Buchanan Papers.

Buchanan's bid to annex Mexican territory was contained in a dispatch that Secretary of State Cass sent Minister Forsyth on the same day that he instructed Forsyth to support the Benjamin-La Sère interests. Cass proposed that Forsyth offer up to $15 million for Lower California, most of Sonora, and Chihuahua north of the thirtieth parallel. Forsyth, however did not follow the directive. Apparently he took seriously statements by President Comonfort that no Mexican territory would be alienated, and he failed to present the offer. Cass was irate; in a dispatch of November 17, 1857, he accused Forsyth of being hypersensitive to Mexican feelings, said that President Buchanan had channels of information to which Forsyth was not privy that encouraged annexationist hopes, denounced the minister for not obeying orders, and criticized Forsyth for "jealousy" and "distrust" that had ruined the hopes of the president concerning the Louisiana Tehuantepec Company. The conflict between the State Department and Forsyth persisted into the next year when Cass rebuked the Alabamian in January for interfering in Mexican politics. Forsyth had tried to get State Department support for a banker's loan of $2.5 million for the Comonfort government so that Comonfort could defeat his rivals. Cass, in lofty hypocritical rhetoric, explained to Forsyth that it was American policy to avoid interfering "with the struggles of contending parties in other nations, in order to give either of them an advantage over the other."

Forsyth did attempt to negotiate cessions with the Mexican government later in 1858, but was unable to achieve anything. At one point he became so flustered that he asked Cass for authority to demand that Mexico cede Sonora and suggested that he be provided a fleet to back up the ultimatum. The Mexican government, now under Zuloaga, requested his recall, and Forsyth departed in October, 1858, bitter toward both Mexicans and the Buchanan administration. In February, 1859, he resigned his commission; and in July of that year he began editing the Mobile

Daily Register, avidly backing the presidential aspirations of Stephen Douglas. [35]

Buchanan's Mexican protectorate scheme clearly illustrates his willingness to intervene in Mexican affairs when he felt conditions were ripe. Buchanan suggested a protectorate in his second annual message to Congress (December, 1858), urging that the United States assume temporary control of northern Chihuahua and Sonora and set up military posts in those regions. But the Senate refused to give him the authorization. Although the Committee on Foreign Relations introduced a bill encompassing Buchanan's recommendation, the Senate rejected a motion to consider the bill. Not a single Republican supported the motion. [36]

Nevertheless, Buchanan continued working on the project. In 1858 he had sent William Churchwell, a former congressman from Tennessee, to Mexico as a special agent to investigate the political climate, and Churchwell had recommended immediate recognition of the Juárez government, which by then controlled a good portion of Mexico. Furthermore, Juárez's foreign minister informed the State Department that the Liberals were willing to negotiate the cession of Lower California in return for American recognition. [37]

In response, Buchanan commissioned Robert McLane of Maryland to recognize the Juárez faction in return for con-

35. Lewis Cass to John Forsyth, July 17, November 17, 1857, January 6, 1858, in Forsyth Papers; Maisel, "Mexican Antipathy Toward the South," 213–18; Rippy, *United States and Mexico*, 214–15; James Morton Callahan, "The Mexican Policy of Southern Leaders Under Buchanan's Administration," *Annual Report of the American Historical Association for the Year 1910* (Washington, D.C., 1912), 138; Ralph Roeder, *Juarez and His Mexico* (New York, 1947), 178–81.

36. Moore (ed.), *Works of Buchanan*, X, 253–56; *United States Senate Journal*, 35th Cong., 2nd Sess., 342.

37. William M. Churchwell to Francis Pickens, October 8, 1859, in Francis Pickens Papers, Duke University Library, Durham, North Carolina; Roeder, *Juarez*, 186; *Daily Ohio State Journal*, February 23, 1859.

cessions in Mexico, and McLane arrived in Vera Cruz on April 1, 1859. On April 5 McLane recognized Juárez and began discussions with Foreign Minister Ocampo on April 7. After many disputes, a "treaty of transit and commerce" was signed on December 14. For $4 million, Juárez granted the United States a transit route across Tehuantepec, as well as the right to intervene in Mexico to protect the lives and property of American citizens. Before he received word of the final treaty, Buchanan submitted his third annual message to Congress and made another plea for a protectorate in Sonora and Chihuahua. Congress, stated Buchanan, should authorize such intervention as well as the use of American naval forces to protect Americans crossing Mexico (as well as Panama and Nicaragua). The president also punctuated his remarks with praise of the Juárez faction, which he viewed as helpless to prevent outrages committed by Conservatives.[38]

Both message and treaty met considerable hostility in the United States Senate in early 1860, primarily from a Republican party ever-watchful of possible concessions to slavery extension, and ever-desirous of defeating the Democratic president. Missouri Republican Edward Bates remarked in his diary that he hoped the "wretched treaty" would be the "last effort" by the administration to establish American dominion over the Gulf of Mexico and the Caribbean Sea. Jacob Collamer of Vermont denounced the protectorate scheme partly because it represented a plan by which "the slaveholding states may come back again to an equal position in the Senate with the free States." Justin S. Morrill agreed and analyzed the protectorate scheme as a southern means of bringing slavery to Mexico in order to "furnish an increased representation of political power in the United States Senate." Massachusetts' Henry Wilson asserted that the president's wish to "march the Army into Mexico" was a response to southern "dreams of empires in

38. Roeder, *Juarez*, 194–96, 200–202, 214; Richardson (comp.), *Messages and Papers of the President*, V, 566–68.

which to plant slavery." And in the House of Representatives, John Perry of Maine stated bluntly: "When they [southerners] talk to us about the acquisition of Mexico, it means the 'EXPANSION and PERPETUATION' of slavery. This is the issue frankly tendered, and it should be as frankly met. . . . The reasons urged by the Democracy and the South *in favor* of the acquisition of Mexico, are the very reasons which compel the people of the free States to *oppose* it." [39]

After a sporadic debate lasting many months, Senate Republicans crushed the treaty on May 31, 1860, by a 27 to 18 vote. The negative votes included 23 from the North, 21 of which were Republican. The 18 supporters of the bill were all Democrats, 14 of them southerners.[40]

The protectorate scheme was not *per se* a southern measure. Its strongest advocates, James Buchanan and Sam Houston, could not with justice be described as slavery expansionists. Nor was the scheme necessarily intended as a prelude to permanent annexations of Mexican territory. But everything in Buchanan's personal history leads to such a conclusion, and Secretary of War John Floyd admitted privately at the time that the administration hoped the McLane-Ocampo Treaty would lead to the acquisition of "a large portion of northern Mexico." The important thing, however, is that many southern expansionists interpreted the protectorate and treaty as a means to annex-

39. Howard K. Beale (ed.), "The Diary of Edward Bates, 1859–1866," *Annual Report of the American Historical Association for the Year 1930* (4 vols.; Washington, D.C., 1931–33), IV, 99 (entry for February 5, 1860) ; *Congressional Globe*, 35th Cong., 2nd Sess., 1183–84; *Congressional Globe*, 36th Cong., 1st Sess., 571, and Appendix, 382.

40. *Senate Executive Journal*, XI, 199; Rippy, *United States and Mexico*, 226. Buchanan continued to support Juárez, despite the treaty's failure. In early 1860, for instance, American naval forces captured two transports of the Miramón conservative government. The transports were taken to New Orleans to be disposed of in a prize court. The court found against the captors and released the ships. Juárez, in return, did grant favorable terms to the Louisiana Tehuantepec Company. See Roeder, *Juarez*, 222, 241–43, 262; Macon *Daily Telegraph*, April 7, 1860.

ation and slavery expansion. The Memphis *Daily Appeal* called a protectorate a "half-way house" to annexation of all Mexico, and the Memphis *Daily Avalanche* applauded the McLane treaty as being "the dawn of brighter, better days for the South," for now new "slave territory" would join the union. Southern expansionists viewed the failure of Buchanan's Mexican policy in the Senate as further proof of Republican hostility to the expansion of slavery southward. One Georgia newspaper reacted to the treaty's failure by saying: "The late McLean [*sic*] treaty with Mexico, gave to this country immense commercial benefits, and also a right of armed transit through Mexican Territory to our Pacific possessions. The Abolitionists rejected it—why? Simply because they feared it would induce and enable Texans to carry their slaves into the Mexican Territory, and thus defeat their object of hemming us in forever." [41]

41. John Floyd to William M. Burwell, April 30 (1860), in Burwell Papers; Memphis *Daily Appeal*, December 16, 1858; Memphis *Daily Avalanche*, January 28, 1860; Macon *Daily Telegraph*, December 10, 1860. Republican opposition to the acquisition of Mexico because of the possibility of establishing slavery there was not new in 1859–1860. The six votes against the Gadsden Purchase of 1854 came from Charles Sumner, Salmon P. Chase, William Pitt Fessenden, Francis Gillette, Ben Wade, and William Seward. All, eventually, became strong Republicans. There are many other examples of Republican hostility to acquisition of Mexico throughout the 1850s. See Charles Sumner's speech before the Republican state convention at Worcester, Massachusetts, in 1854, and another speech in New York City by Sumner the following year. William Seward made a couple of speeches in Detroit treating the same topic. See Charles Sumner (ed.), *The Works of Charles Sumner* (15 vols.; Boston, 1870–83), III, 459–60, IV, 43; George Baker (ed.), *The Works of William H. Seward* (5 vols.; Boston, 1884), IV, 271, 312. New York abolitionist Henry B. Stanton expressed similar sentiments in a speech in late 1860. See New York *Tribune*, November 27, 1860. So did antislavery leader Wendell Phillips in a private letter of 1854. See Wendell Phillips to Elizabeth Pease Nichol, August 7, 1854, quoted in Francis Jackson Garrison and Wendell Phillips Garrison, *William Lloyd Garrison: The Story of His Life Told by His Children* (4 vols.; New York, 1889), III, 411.

VII

The Thirty Million Dollar Cuba Bill

Historians have remembered James Buchanan as a weak president because his administration saw the splintering of his party and the disruption of the union. However, in emphasizing domestic policies that led to both developments, there has been a tendency on the part of historians to neglect or downplay his foreign policies. Buchanan the aspiring expansionist has been lost in the process, and this is unfortunate because expansionism was a dominant theme of his term in office. His imperialistic aims rivaled those of James K. Polk, a president who has been considered strong because he acquired, if ruthlessly, part of Mexico and Oregon to the forty-ninth parallel. That Americans today have such diametrically opposed images of the two presidents may be more a result of circumstance than of their respective competencies. Polk's term in office coincided with the flowering of the "manifest destiny" movement. Although his options were somewhat restricted by sectional differences as to whether slavery would be permitted in new acquisitions, his expansionist intentions were not blocked. When Buchanan was president (1857–1861), sectional conflict over the extension of slavery cast an ever-lengthening shadow on proposals for expansion and shattered Buchanan's imperialistic hopes. Republican party opposition to Buchanan's proposals to expand the American domain southward had as much to do with his failure as did his personal incapacities.

Buchanan's Mexican schemes received attention in the last chapter. But his favored project was the annexation of Cuba. He came into office fresh from his involvement with the Ostend Manifesto and had every intention of following up the initiative for Cuba started by his predecessor Franklin Pierce. The more Buchanan's administration foundered in the Kansas issue, the more important acquisition of the island became to him. By 1859, annexation of Cuba appeared to be the best means of reunifying his party as well as securing renomination in 1860.

Buchanan commenced his initiative for Cuba in December, 1857, by sending Christopher Fallon to Europe. Fallon, a Philadelphian who had business connections with both August Belmont and the Spanish Queen Mother, proceeded under instructions to question Spanish officials as to what offer for Cuba might be acceptable. According to the president the transfer of Cuba to the United States "for a reasonable and fair price would greatly promote the interest of both countries." Fallon found Spanish officials unreceptive, but nevertheless expressed optimism. He claimed in April, 1858, that the only way to gain Cuba, given the hostility of Spanish authorities, would be for Buchanan to send a new minister to Spain with a large sum of money and no ostensible interest in Cuba. The funds could be used clandestinely to purchase the island.[1]

Buchanan accepted Fallon's advice. Word quickly spread in administration circles that the president was looking for a new minister to Spain, and Buchanan soon found eager applicants for the position. Most anxious was August Belmont, who had been a party to Pierce's Cuba enterprise in 1854. Belmont made a blatant appeal for the job in a letter of June, 1858, to John Slidell, his uncle and Buchanan's

1. James Buchanan to Christopher Fallon, December 14, 1857, in Moore (ed.), *Works of Buchanan*, X, 165; Roy Nichols, *The Disruption of American Democracy* (New York, 1948), 228–29. Fallon, Spanish-born, had settled in Philadelphia and had invested much of the Queen Mother's money in Pennsylvania lands.

campaign manager. Belmont informed the Louisianian that the time for action concerning Cuba was "at hand" and claimed that his appointment would be a "popular one." Belmont wanted the letter to fall into Buchanan's hands, which it did, along with Slidell's recommendation. Slidell suggested his cohort Judah Benjamin as an alternative, should Buchanan be reluctant to appoint Belmont.[2]

Buchanan did not want Belmont, even after Benjamin and Senator Stephen Mallory of Florida turned down his offer. In October, 1858, the president paid off a political debt by choosing William Preston of Kentucky, who had been soliciting a federal appointment all year. The former Whig member of the United States House of Representatives and Democratic convert had played an instrumental role in Buchanan's nomination and election in 1856. It had been Preston, at the time a Stephen Douglas supporter, who had moved Buchanan's nomination by acclamation at the Cincinnati convention, and the Kentuckian had then stumped for Buchanan, speaking at such disparate places as Poughkeepsie, New York, Williamsburg, Pennsylvania, and Chicago. Apparently Buchanan felt that Belmont's support was expendable, because his choice of Preston led to Belmont's joining the Douglas wing of the party.[3]

2. Belmont to Slidell, June 5, 1858, and Slidell to Buchanan, August 22, 1858, both in Buchanan Papers.

3. Copy of Buchanan to Benjamin, August 31, 1858, and Benjamin to Buchanan, September 7, 1858, both in Buchanan Papers; William Preston to John White Stevenson, January 23, 1858, in John White Stevenson Papers, Library of Congress; John White Stevenson to Alexander Stephens, October 8, 1858, in Stephens Papers, Library of Congress; Philip Melvin, "Stephen Russell Mallory: Southern Naval Statesman," *Journal of Southern History*, X (1944), 148; Albert Lewis Diket, "John Slidell and the Community He Represented in the Senate, 1853–1861," (Ph.D. dissertation, Louisiana State University, 1958), 1; Cincinnati *Enquirer*, June 5–7, September 27, October 7, 31, 1856; Irving Katz, *August Belmont* (New York, 1968), 59. Katz termed Belmont's interest in Cuba an obsession and stated that a principal reason Buchanan turned Belmont down was because he wanted Slidell to accept the Paris mission and realized congressional antagonists would complain of nepotism if both men received appointments.

Preston told his sister that he accepted the position at great sacrifice: "all hands" agreed that he would have received the Democratic nomination for governor of Kentucky, and he predicted that he would have swept the state with a twenty-thousand-vote majority. Actually he was delighted at having been selected. He firmly believed in the desirability of acquiring Cuba, and his wife longed to see Paris, which could easily be taken in on the trip to Madrid. Preston purchased the house in Louisville that he had been renting, leased it, closed his other affairs, and hastened to Washington—although a stop was made in Philadelphia so that his wife could visit a "milliness" for proper attire. Preston and his wife left for Europe in early 1859. As planned, they visited France, where they left two of their daughters in a convent, and arrived in Madrid in early March.[4]

Administration strategy for Cuba centered on the fluctuating nature of Spanish politics. In an unstable situation, a faction of the Spanish government might need instant funds to attain or retain power. Such funds could be supplied by the United States as a first payment for Cuba. Belmont had suggested this in his letter to Slidell, and Preston and Buchanan advocated the same strategy. Preston felt that the down payment should be at least $20 or $30 million, the higher the better; for if Spain should repudiate a treaty of cession after such a down payment, "the money would in all probability be *squandered and lost so that a recision would be practically impossible* and the United States would have a valid lien on the Island." In fact, Preston believed that the only reason Pierce's acquisition scheme had failed was because Pierre Soulé did not have funds at his disposal at the time of the *Black Warrior*

4. William Preston to his sister (Mrs. Howard Christy), October 8, November 14, December 2, 1858, February 24, March 8, 1859, in Preston Family Papers, Filson Club, Louisville, Kentucky; Louisville *Daily Courier*, October 11, 1858.

incident. Should Spanish politicians prove reluctant to respond to such incentives, there were ways to increase the pressure. Robert Toombs of Georgia told Buchanan that American citizens could purchase the Spanish debt to British subjects, which, though amounting to some $200 million, could possibly be purchased for as little as $34 million. Should Spain default on the debt, the United States could then claim Cuba for payment. Belmont and Fallon suggested certain individuals connected with Paris banking houses who might be willing to extend their aid in such a scheme.[5] There was also a possibility that aid might be forthcoming from the English or French governments. Belmont felt that England would regard American annexation of the island favorably because it would halt the slave trade, and that France would welcome United States acquisition of Cuba because it would restrict Britain's naval superiority. Slidell gave passing consideration to the idea of going to France as American minister because Napoleon III might be persuaded to exercise his influence with the Spanish government. Preston felt that a threat of an American alliance with Russia would be enough to dissuade the English from obstructing annexation of Cuba.[6]

Administration leaders had few illusions about the difficulties Preston would face in Europe. Preston commented that no Spanish ministry ceding Cuba would "live an hour," and that the Spanish people were "bitterly opposed" to a transfer of the island to the United States. Nor were

5. Belmont to Slidell, June 5, 1858, and Christopher Fallon to William Preston, January 6, 1859, both in Buchanan Papers; William Preston to William Preston Johnston, December 12, 1858, and William Preston to Reuben T. Durrett, December 14, 1858, both in Albert Sidney Johnston Papers, Tulane University Library, New Orleans; Robert Toombs to William M. Burwell, March 30, 1857, in Burwell Papers.

6. Belmont to Slidell, June 5, 1858, and Slidell to James Buchanan, May 30, June 14, July 3, 1859, both in Buchanan Papers; Preston to William Preston Johnston, January 14, 1859, in Johnston Papers.

they unaware of the difficulties they would face in getting Congress to approve the money necessary to make the scheme function. Congress might well object to major appropriations for the sake of diplomatic intrigues about which it was only partially informed. Before Preston left, he tried to build a groundwork of public support for congressional appropriations, particularly in his own state. He instructed his nephew: "Threaten rain & wrath to the laggard or irresolute—I must have a big pile of *cash* (not *credits*) at Madrid. . . . Pour hot-shot into any recreant anti Cuban democrats." He urged the editor of the Louisville *Courier* to influence the upcoming Democratic state convention (January 8) "to speak boldly, pointedly, & powerfully for Cuba. It is all important to me. If the Douglas men shirk, refer to his antecedents & taunt them with hypocrisy. . . . If they advance cheer them." But if negotiations in Europe failed, the administration could still choose more forceful means, including the invoking of the Monroe Doctrine and outright seizure.[7] And if Congress proved recalcitrant, Cuban acquisition might be developed into an attractive campaign issue for the 1860 elections.

Buchanan approached Congress cautiously by means of his second annual address (December 6, 1858). He urged the acquisition of Cuba by "honorable negotiation" and requested guidance from Congress on the matter. Although offering no specific legislative recommendation, the president did say that "it may become indispensable to success that I should be entrusted with the means of making an advance to the Spanish Government immediately after the signing of the treaty, without awaiting the ratification of it by the Senate." Buchanan obscured his implicit admis-

7. Preston to William Preston Johnston, December 12, 17, 1858, and Preston to Reuben T. Durrett, December 14, 1858, both in Johnston Papers; Louisville *Daily Courier*, January 10, 1859. Preston also expected considerable interference from Napoleon III. See Preston to William Preston Johnston, December 12, 1858, in Johnston Papers.

sion that Cuba would be acquired in an unseemly diplomatic coup by referring to Thomas Jefferson's purchase of Louisiana.[8]

Congressional expansionists immediately began mapping legislative strategy to meet Buchanan's request. A number of members of both houses began drawing up their personal Cuba bills shortly after Buchanan's message. To achieve consensus on a program and to minimize friction, Slidell called a caucus of Democratic senators and won support for his own bill. In the House, Lawrence Branch of North Carolina took the lead and tried to get the Committee on Foreign Affairs to report a bill encompassing Buchanan's recommendation for funds.[9]

Buchanan's program encountered resistance even before it arrived on the floor of Congress. Part of the resistance came from Republicans who opposed annexation because of Cuban slavery. Every Republican member on the House committee opposed granting the funds.[10] Just as serious was some southern resistance. A number of southern expansionist radicals felt that negotiations would break down as they had in 1854, and that the South would have nothing to show for its effort. The United States government, according to this reasoning, would do better to use force than to negotiate. Representative Reuben Davis of Mississippi, for instance, told the House long before any plan emerged from committee that a bill should be passed "authorizing and requiring" President Buchanan to seize Cuba if the Spanish debt to United States citizens was not paid within six months. Lawrence Keitt of South Carolina called for seizure of Cuba in retaliation for Spanish discrimination

8. Moore (ed.), *Works of Buchanan*, X, 251–52.

9. New Bern *Daily Progress*, February 17, 1859; New York *Herald*, January 17, 1859; Jackson *Semi-Weekly Mississippian*, January 21, 1859; Lawrence Branch to his wife, January 8, 25, 1859, in Mrs. Lawrence O'Bryan Branch Papers, State Archives of North Carolina, Raleigh.

10. *Daily Ohio State Journal*, January 15, 1859.

against American commerce. Lawrence Branch complained that southerners who preferred to take Cuba "by force and robbery" impaired the progress of committee action on a Cuba bill.[11]

Branch finally succeeded in getting his bill out of committee and before the House on January 24. The modified bill authorized the president to conclude a treaty with Spain for the cession of Cuba and appropriated $1 million for this purpose. If Buchanan saw fit, the funds could be used, "in advance of the ratification of the treaty by the Senate." The sum was amended, after the bill's introduction, to $30 million. Branch's report accompanying the bill called for American acquisition of Cuba for commercial advantages, national security, and the redress of grievances against Spain.[12]

However, only sporadic discussion followed the bill's introduction; and except for a few speeches, the House ignored the Cuba problem in the coming months, despite southern demands for action. William Avery of North Carolina made one pro-Cuba speech on January 24. He supported Buchanan's plan on the traditional grounds that annexation would help American commerce, prevent European domination of the Western Hemisphere, and repay the United States for damages done to American citizens by Spain. Seven days later, Reuben Davis renewed his demand to seize Cuba. And on February 2, Miles Taylor of Louisiana introduced a bill authorizing the president to spend up to $120 million, but Republican Elihu Washburne of Illinois objected to submitting the bill to a committee. Finally, on February 9, Davis warned that if Branch's bill were ever brought to a vote, he would amend it to read that

11. *Congressional Globe*, 35th Cong., 2nd Sess., 185, 296–97, 430–31, 453–57; Branch to his wife, January 8, 25, 1859, in Branch Papers.
12. *Congressional Globe*, 35th Cong., 2nd Sess., 553; *ibid.*, Appendix, 96–100.

the United States should "take" Cuba rather than purchase it.[13]

While this sparring was going on, Republicans served notice once again that they would never permit American acquisition of a tropical slave country. On January 24, the day that Branch introduced his bill to the House, Albert Jenkins of Virginia shrewdly maneuvered William Kellogg of Illinois into admitting that the main reason Republicans opposed the bill was unwillingness to add another slave state to the union. Kellogg was in the midst of a speech stating that it was useless to discuss purchase of Cuba because Spain was adamant in its determination to retain the island, when Jenkins interrupted by asking Kellogg if he would "vote to admit Cuba into the Union as a slave state" if Spain were willing to cede the island. Kellogg did not flinch: "I say to him now, and to his friends, that I propose, by all constitutional, legal, and honorable means, to prevent the extension of slavery to the Territories." Similarly, Homer Royce of Vermont warned the South in February that even if Cuba were acquired, it would never be admitted to the union as a slave state. "A large majority of the people" of the country would prevent such an event. Southerners who supported the bill to increase their section's political strength were "laboring under a great delusion." [14] The House never acted on Branch's bill.

Buchanan's suggestions elicited a much stronger response from the Senate. On January 10, John Slidell introduced a bill that would have appropriated $30 million for the president's use. Though worded slightly differently, Slidell's bill contained the same provision as Branch's for the use of the funds as a down payment prior to acceptance of a treaty by the Senate. Opponents of the bill seized on this provision because it seemed to require the Senate to

13. *Ibid.*, 560–63, 703–706, 747. Avery also called for American extension into Mexico and Central America.
14. *Ibid.*, 563; *ibid.*, Appendix, 114.

approve any treaty negotiated for Cuba in order not to squander the money. Not only would this procedure subvert senatorial control over foreign policy, particularly treaty making, but the money appeared to be intended as a bribe to influence certain Spanish politicians to agree to the cession. Buchanan and Preston, of course, were not averse to using the funds as a bribe; and the charges against the provision were not without foundation, although Branch, in his report to the House accompanying the bill, gave as the official reason for the advance payment Buchanan's desire to have funds immediately available should Spain desire to make a treaty ceding the island. Slidell's bill was referred to the Committee on Foreign Relations, of which he was a member.[15]

On behalf of the committee, Slidell submitted the bill to the Senate for consideration on January 24, along with a report justifying American annexation of Cuba. The report affirmed that "the law of our national existence is growth" and cited comments by Thomas Jefferson, John Quincy Adams, Martin Van Buren, Henry Clay, James Buchanan, Edward Everett, and William Marcy as authoritative evidence that the United States' need for the island was a compelling one. There were also the standard rationalizations: the Cubans wanted annexation, Americans would interdict the slave trade, and the island offered great commercial advantages. To make the case airtight, a wealth of statistics was included, and the report even appealed to humanitarians on the grounds that Cuban slaves would supposedly receive better treatment under American masters.[16]

After the report, James Mason of Virginia, chairman of the Committee on Foreign Relations, was the first to speak. Mason challenged the premise that the enlargement of America's boundaries should be basic public policy, but nevertheless endorsed acquisition of Cuba as a "political

15. *Ibid.*, 277.   16. *Ibid.*, Appendix, 90–94

necessity." Then Republican William Seward of New York, also a committee member, delivered a blistering attack on the bill. Seward felt that the bill gave an irresponsible Democratic president a blank check of $30 million, and predicted that Spain would never relinquish the island. He suggested that the Senate postpone discussion of Cuba until its next session and, apparently ruffled by the report's praise of southern slavery, commented angrily: "We who have disputed so earnestly, often so vehemently, year after year, year in and year out, over the question whether the institution of slavery shall be introduced into the Territory of Kansas, are expected by the President, in his simplicity, to allow him to determine for the North and for the South, for the free States and for the slave States, at his own absolute pleasure, the terms and conditions upon which Cuba shall be annexed to the United States, and incorporated into the Union." The senator asserted that the time for annexation of Cuba had not yet come.[17]

The day's debate closed after Toombs and James Bayard of Delaware supported Buchanan and Slidell, and after Republicans Solomon Foot of Vermont and John Hale of New Hampshire backed Seward. Toombs felt that the slavery question should not be considered when the obvious merits of annexation such as trade advantages were discussed, and that the United States should as quickly as possible acquire the "tropical empire" lying at its feet.[18] Hale

17. *Ibid.*, 538–39. Seward and many other Republicans in and out of Congress felt that a treaty arranged under the Branch-Slidell formula would have put them in a position of having to accept Cuba, with slavery, so as not to waste thirty million dollars, or to refuse the island and thus throw away the funds. Seward, at the same time, offered a substitute bill which would have ended discussion on Cuba until Buchanan could report on his negotiations for the island to the next session of Congress.

18. *Ibid.*, 540–41. Toombs suggested that the concept of popular sovereignty should be used to govern the annexation of Cuba. When Cuba was ready to become a state, according to Toombs, it should decide for itself whether or not to institute slavery. Toombs claimed

disagreed, explaining that he was opposed to manifest destiny because it "always travelled South." Hale felt that the Senate's time would be more profitably occupied in discussing the building of a Pacific railroad, which would require the very funds needed to acquire Cuba.[19] It was thus obvious by the end of the first day of debate that northern Republicans and southern Democrats were aligned against each other on the bill, primarily because of Cuba's slavery.

The Senate debated the question of acquisition in earnest from February 9 through February 26, 1859. During that period, and for months thereafter, Cuba was a central, if not the central, issue in American politics. A literary society at Yale debated the question. The General Committee of Tammany Hall and the Young Men's Democratic Union Club of New York City endorsed annexation. State Democratic conventions throughout the North and South applauded Buchanan's program, and county conventions and local meetings echoed the sentiments of the parent state conventions.[20] State legislatures considered Cuba resolutions.[21] Some newspapers even gave Cuba more coverage

---

that he would accept Canada in the union as readily as he would accept Cuba—both countries would benefit his nation's welfare. His plan, obviously, would have ensured Cuba for slavery because of the already well-intrenched slave system on the island.

19. *Ibid.*, 543–44. The usually prosouthern expansionist William Gwin of California agreed with Hale's remarks about the precedence of the railroad bill over Cuba annexation. See *ibid.*, 545.

20. Asa Biggs to "Judge," February 16, 1859, in Asa Biggs Papers, Library of Congress; New Bern *Daily Progress*, February 3, 1859; Charles W. Coit to Stephen Douglas, January 24, 1858 [1859?], in Douglas Papers; M. Diefendorf to Caleb Cushing, February 14, 1859, in Caleb Cushing Papers, Library of Congress; Charleston *Daily Courier*, January 24, 1859; New York *Herald*, February 11, 12, 22, 1859; Louisville *Daily Courier*, January 10, 1859; Richmond *Enquirer*, January 24, 1859; Nashville *Union and American*, March 13, 1859; Memphis *Daily Appeal*, June 5, July 10, 1859; Fayetteville *Arkansian*, June 18, 1859; Covington (Kentucky) *Journal*, June 11, 1859; Macon *Daily Telegraph*, July 11, 1860.

21. *Journal of the North Carolina Senate and Assembly, 1858–1859*, 342; New York *Herald*, January 21, February 28, 1859; Jackson *Semi-Weekly Mississippian*, February 18, 1859.

than the spectacular trial of New York Congressman Daniel Sickles, who had murdered his wife's lover.

The bill's political force lay in its appeal to Democrats as a party measure. But since Cuba had been a bipartisan foreign policy goal, the bill attracted enough general popular support to intimidate some of its Republican opponents. Furthermore, the idea of national progress through territorial expansion attracted members of all parties. Republican Senator Lyman Trumbull argued against a frontal assault on the proposal because expansion was a "trait" of American character. "There is scarcely a farmer," Trumbull explained, "who does not want to extend his providences or own another quarter section, & people as a nation bear very much the same feeling." A leading Republican editor in Chicago wrote that the only way to counter the proposal was to sidetrack the issue: "Now it is dangerous for a Republican to take unqualified ground against the acquisition of Cuba. Nor is it safe to take qualified ground for annexation (The Whigs tried that on Texas) [.] If we go half way we gain no credit for the concession, while we help on a wrong. . . . Now my plan is . . . to bring forward *Reciprocal free trade* as a *substitute*." [22] Southern opponents of annexation faced the same dilemma. [23]

John Slidell gained considerable recognition from his advocacy of the bill, perhaps as much as the president. His name constantly commanded newspaper accounts of affairs in Washington. As one correspondent in the capital ex-

22. Lyman Trumbull to B. C. Cook, January 20, 1859, in Lyman Trumbull Papers, Library of Congress; Joseph Medill to John Gurley, August 15, 1859, in Joseph Medill Papers, Chicago Historical Society.

23. Charleston politician John Cunningham warned South Carolina's James Hammond, one of the few southern Democrats vocally opposed to Slidell's bill, to restrain himself if he wanted the Democratic nomination for the presidency in 1860: "Will not Cuba be made the leading issue? If so, you must be silent. *Your friends are for it.*" See Cunningham to Hammond, April 7, 1859, in James Hammond Papers, Library of Congress.

plained, "The chief and exciting topic of conversation in political circles in this city, is the $30,000,000 asked by Senator Slidell to aid in the purchase of Cuba." Slidell's sudden fame was too much for Lawrence Branch to take. He had expected to gain notice by advocating annexation, but his bill had fallen into political oblivion, and Slidell had stolen the show. Branch jealously described Slidell as a mere manipulator, "one of those public men, whose reputation is made and kept up, by keeping the newspaper correspondents in his pay." [24]

The Senate's consideration of Slidell's bill bared sectional enmities. As in the Cuba debate of 1854, most southern Democratic proponents of the bill avoided citing Cuba's slave institutions when they argued for acquisition. This strategy protected sympathetic northern Democrats from the charge of advocating slavery expansion. But some southerners did succumb to the temptation to defend slavery as a positive good. On February 11, Judah Benjamin claimed that only slaves could cultivate the tropics and spoke of Haiti's "decline" since emancipation. Two weeks later, Stephen Mallory of Florida said that he was "indisposed" to connect slavery with Cuban policy because the question disturbed sectional harmony, but he then went on to claim that America's slaves were far happier than free blacks anywhere. Both Mallory and Benjamin warned that the United States should still be vigilant in respect to the possible "Africanization" of Cuba.[25]

The lure proved irresistible to already eager Republicans. Wisconsin's James R. Doolittle and Vermont's Jacob

24. Branch to his wife, January 25, 1859, in Branch Papers; Memphis *Daily Appeal*, January 29, 1859.
25. *Congressional Globe*, 35th Cong., 2nd Sess., 960–63, 1190, 1328. Slidell, Toombs, Bayard, and Trusten Polk (of Missouri) were the southern Democrats who made full speeches favoring the bill without endorsing slave expansionism per se. See the New Bern *Daily Progress*, February 17, 1859, for comment on how Benjamin's speech aroused sectional controversy.

Collamer attacked the idea of spreading slavery into the tropics, and John Hale denied Benjamin's charge that freedom for Negroes had failed in the West Indies. Hale warned that he was not willing "to extend the boundaries of this country for the express purpose of bringing into this Confederacy territories, islands, and States, whose great and controlling merit . . . is that they are slave States, slave territories, and slave islands." James Dixon of Connecticut expressed similar qualms: "It is to perpetuate slavery in Cuba, that the people of the North are requested now to contribute of their means for this acquisition. . . . Why should we do it?" Wade of Ohio, who felt the Senate's time would be more profitably employed in consideration of the issue of free homesteads for the small farmer, explained simply that the "question will be, shall we give niggers to the niggerless, or land to the landless?" [26]

Republicans also damned Slidell's bill as an insult to Spain, a robbery of the federal treasury, and a political trick to reelect Buchanan in 1860. Some Republicans felt that a standing army and a large navy would be needed for Cuba's defense, and this would reverse America's commitment to a small military. Southern Whig-Americans, who also opposed the bill, repeated the Republican arguments. John Crittenden of Kentucky exclaimed that his "national pride as an American" was revolted by the idea that Cuba was necessary to the country's survival.[27]

Northern Democrats, except for George Pugh of Ohio, avoided the battle, apparently realizing that support of the bill could be twisted into a defense of the extension of slavery. On February 10, Pugh spoke briefly on the slavery question, vowing that he was willing to have Cuba in the union "as the people of Cuba wish." Pugh expressed more

26. *Congressional Globe*, 35th Cong., 2nd Sess., 967, 1134–35, 1181, 1354; *ibid.*, Appendix, 164–65.
27. *Ibid.*, 155–60, 905–907, 1058–61, 1079–80, 1179–88, 1334, 1340–45, 1348–52, 1354, 1386.

concern with the richness of Cuba's soil, its "genial climate," and its natural resources. Moreover, Cuba would provide a market for the meat and breadstuffs of the Northwest.[28]

Given the relative silence of northern Democratic senators on the Slidell bill, the general response of northern Democrats to tropical expansion demands attention. Usually northern Democrats supported Caribbean expansion. Expansionism was intrinsic to Democratic ideology in the decades before the Civil War, and northern Democrats rallied to the tropical movement for nationalistic, racial, economic, and diplomatic reasons. The pro-Cuba resolutions passed by Democratic state and county conventions in the North were a better reflection of party sentiment outside the South than the northern Democrats' refusal to debate Slidell's proposal.

The administrations of James Buchanan and Franklin Pierce gave avid backing to the tropical movement, although both presidents turned against filibustering, which was enough to disillusion many of the more extreme expansionists in the southern Democratic party. And the efforts of both men to gain tropical acquisitions through diplomacy attracted praise from most northern Democratic newspapers. Northern Democratic support for tropical expansion persisted to the very eve of the Civil War. Benjamin Butler of Massachusetts, when presiding over the national Democratic convention at Charleston in 1860, told the delegates that he favored the acquisition of Cuba, and a plank of the platform adopted by the Douglas Democrats to that convention declared that "the Democratic party are in favor of the acquisition of the Island of Cuba

28. *Ibid.*, 934–40. Only three other northern Democratic senators commented on the bill: Gwin of California, who eventually voted for the bill, but initially opposed its consideration, Stephen Douglas of Illinois, and Henry Rice of Minnesota. Douglas and Rice made brief comments saying that the Cuba bill should be passed so that the homestead bill could be taken up. See *ibid.*, 545, 1352.

on such terms as shall be honorable to ourselves and just to Spain." [29]

Few northern Democrats so vocally supported the tropical movement as Stephen Douglas. He backed the Cuba initiatives of 1854 and 1859, defended William Walker in 1856, and as late as December, 1860, suggested a plan to Alexander Stephens that would enable Mexico to enter the union as a slave state if the South agreed not to secede. He made speeches for acquisition and included a plea for Cuba in one of his famous debates with Abraham Lincoln. In 1858 he visited Cuba aboard the *Black Warrior* to demonstrate his interest in the island.[30] Many southern expansionists regarded him as their champion. The Montgomery *Daily Confederation*, for instance, said in early 1860: "Our India lies in the tropics. There will we find inexhaustible sources of wealth and power, which none can wrest from our grasps. The policy which Douglas has the wisdom to conceive, and the energy to execute, if entrusted with authority, would surround the Gulf of Mexico with great and prosperous States, all bound to us by the ties of interest and identity of institutions." At about the same time, Susannah Keitt, wife of Lawrence Keitt, a vocal South Carolina states' rights congressman, explained to her father

29. Richmond *Enquirer*, May 8, 1860; McKee, *Conventions and Platforms*, 109; *Official Proceedings of the Democratic Convention ... 1860*, 45–46. The southern delegates who walked out of the Charleston convention later adopted a more extreme plank on Cuba. See McKee, *Conventions and Platforms*, 111.

30. [?] to John Quitman, July 13, 1854, in John Quitman Papers, Mississippi Department of Archives and History; Douglas to Stephens, December 25, 1860, in Robert W. Johannsen (ed.), *The Letters of Stephen A. Douglas* (Urbana, 1961), 506; Charleston *Daily Courier*, January 22, 1859; Jackson *Semi-Weekly Mississippian*, January 21, 1859; *Weekly Raleigh Register*, January 26, 1859; Memphis *Daily Appeal*, November 30, 1858; *Congressional Globe*, 34th Cong., 1st Sess., 1071–72; "Journal of the Committee of Thirteen," *Senate Reports*, 36th Cong., 2nd Sess., No. 288, pp. 8–9; Paul M. Angle (ed.), *Created Equal?: The Complete Lincoln-Douglas Debates of 1858* (Chicago, 1958), 202–203; Damon Wells, *Stephen Douglas: The Last Years, 1857–1861* (Austin, 1971), 154–56.

that she supported the nomination of Stephen Douglas for the presidency because "he is in favor of taking Cuba." [31] Although most southern Democrats in the late 1850s considered Douglas an "apostate" for his role in defeating the Lecompton Constitution, many others acknowledged his gestures concerning the Caribbean. Douglas' base of support in the South in the late 1850s was stronger than most studies of the sectional controversy have implied.

A similar case could be made for Lewis Cass as a tropical expansionist and also for innumerable other spokesmen of the northern Democratic party. Among the many leaders of the northern Democratic party who spoke out for Cuba and other tropical acquisitions were Caleb Cushing, Theodore Sedgwick, William Bigler, Samuel Cox, and August Belmont. Furthermore, in congressional votes on tropical expansion, when a final decision needed to be made, northern and southern Democrats united behind administration measures.

Nevertheless, support of the extension of the United States into the Caribbean and support of the extension of slavery into the Caribbean were two different things. Northern Democrats were well aware that explicit support of the extension of slavery would have been an untenable political position in most of the North in the 1850s. When the question of tropical expansion became too entwined with the issue of slavery, northern Democrats withdrew, either because of personal preference or because of political necessity. This is why the same northern Democratic party that endorsed William Walker at its national convention of 1856 rebuked him two-and-a-half years later

31. Montgomery *Daily Confederation*, March 21, 1860; Susannah Keitt to her father, Sunday the 25th (probably March 25, 1860), in Keitt Papers. See also Horatio Boxley to Stephen Douglas, May 13, 1856, T. N. Hornsby to Stephen Douglas, February 1, 1859, and Barton Pringle to Stephen Douglas, February 22, 1859, all in Douglas Papers.

in the House of Representatives when they voted for David Ritchie's resolution of thanks to Hiram Paulding for capturing the filibuster. During the intervening period, Walker had turned into a vocal defender of slavery.

Northern Democrats, in fact, went out of their way to make clear that their support of Caribbean expansion related to national policy rather than to southern demands. They even argued that tropical expansion would be a means of containing slavery. Thus, the *New Hampshire Patriot*, in backing Pierce's aggressive Cuba policy and the Kansas-Nebraska principle of popular sovereignty, avowed in 1854: "The whole field must be open to fair, bold, manly competition, without Congressional restraints. We of the North say to you of the South—'Give us a free field and a fair fight for new territory, whether in Cuba or Canada, in Mexico, or the Oregon possessions, and we defy the world.' " Four years later, the *Patriot* again called for the annexation of Cuba because this would retard the slave trade and thus "ameliorate and restrict, rather than extend, slavery." [32] The Washington *Union* expressed similar ideas in response to a speech by Albert Gallatin Brown in Tammany Hall. When Samuel Cox argued in Congress for expansion into Cuba, Mexico, and Central America, he told southerners that he hoped the new states would be free and that the South had no right to equality of power in the union. Similarly, Democratic Senator Milton Latham of California explained to southerners in January, 1861, that his state wanted Sonora and Lower California in order to control the trade and commerce of the Pacific coast, but northern representatives "would never ratify a treaty or vote money to obtain either of those States, if they knew that slavery was to be constitutionally forced

32. *New Hampshire Patriot*, November 22, 1854, September 8, 1858.

upon the people of those states during their territorial conditions." [33]

Once Republicans and southern Democrats had raised the slavery question in connection with Slidell's Cuba bill in 1859, northern Democrats realized that a public stance was politically risky. If they were to agree with their Republican colleagues that slavery extension was an evil, they would invite attack from the southern wing of their party and increase southern disaffection with the Democratic party as an institution. If they were to support slavery extension, they would undermine support in their home districts. Any time a northern Democrat spoke on Cuba, he ran the risk of being interrupted by an embarrassing southern or Republican question as to whether he would be willing to admit Cuba into the union as a slave state. Silence was expedient.

The controversy came to a head on February 25, when Doolittle of Wisconsin spearheaded a Republican effort to try to postpone consideration of Cuba in order to permit action on a homestead bill, which had already passed the House. The effort failed, 24 to 35. The Senate's session was nearing its end, and Republicans could have achieved consideration of the homestead legislation had they permitted a vote on the Cuba bill. But, fearing that the Cuba bill might pass, Republicans preferred to see the issue through, even if this meant sacrificing their homestead bill. The day's debate began in the morning and was still going at 11:30 P.M. Finally, Albert Gallatin Brown made a brief speech supporting annexation of Cuba and moved to table Slidell's bill, announcing that he intended to vote against his own motion to table. This forced a test vote

33. Washington *Union*, March 17, 1859; *Congressional Globe*, 35th Cong., 2nd Sess., 430–35; *Congressional Globe*, 36th Cong., 2nd Sess., 403. See also Charles Clarke to Stephen Douglas, December 15, 1857, in Douglas Papers; Robert Winthrop to William C. Rives, February 9, 1861, in William C. Rives Papers, Library of Congress; Philadelphia *Public Ledger*, March 10, 1855.

because Republicans would naturally vote to table. The weary senators accepted his motion and voted 30 to 18 against tabling, in almost a straight party vote.

The 30 were all Democrats; 1 northern Democrat and 1 southern American joined 16 Republicans in favor of tabling. The Senate adjourned at one o'clock in the morning, after Pugh amended the bill to specify that no money would be withdrawn from the United States Treasury until a treaty of cession was completed and ratified by Spain. The following day, Slidell, realizing that he could not get his bill to a vote, withdrew it from further consideration and gave notice that it would be reintroduced at Congress' next session, at the earliest practicable opportunity.[34] Slidell's temporary retreat failed to satisfy his Republican antagonists, who over the following months made it obvious that an attempt to revive the bill would face their unyielding opposition. Missourian Edward Bates, for instance, warned a New York Whig committee that the president was trying, through Slidell's bill, to appropriate Congress' war and financial powers for himself. New York abolitionist Henry Stanton denounced to a Republican mass meeting a "widespread conspiracy" to extend slavery into Cuba.[35]

Ironically, it would have mattered little had Republicans given Buchanan the leeway he wanted; for Preston was having a difficult time in Spain. His trouble with the Spanish and French languages impaired his effectiveness; he ran out of money and had to send home for an additional $5,000; housing problems plagued him, the heat was depressing, and things did not work out for his daughters in

34. *Congressional Globe*, 35th Cong., 2nd Sess., 1326–63, 1385. The Senate session adjourned on March 10.

35. Beale (ed.), "The Diary of Edward Bates" (entry for April 20, 1859), 6; New York *Daily Tribune*, November 27, 1860. Republican newspapers also attacked the Slidell bill, and Republicans opposed pro-Cuba resolutions in the state legislatures of New York and Maine. See New York *Daily Tribune*, January 17, 1859; New York *Herald*, February 28, 1859.

France. The convent in which he had left them had an order against taking in Protestants that was waived, but the "bigotry" troubled the Prestons, and a second convent was too free for one of his daughters, who apparently was fairly prudish. As early as July, 1859, Preston was complaining about his "infernal life" in Spain, and his wife reported that they were both homesick. In addition, his wife was anxious to return so as to push one of their daughters still in the States into marrying James Guthrie, who had been secretary of the treasury under Pierce.[36]

Moreover, Spanish officials failed to respond to Preston's overtures, and his idea of capitalizing on Spanish factionalism did not work. The Spanish Senate voted unanimously against the cession of Cuba in early January, 1859, and Preston reported to the State Department in March that all parties in Spain considered American interest in purchasing Cuba "a grave offense." The Spanish minister of foreign affairs had warned Preston that such proposals would lead to the "immediate cessation of all communication between the two countries." And no help would be forthcoming from France. Preston predicted a break in the Anglo-French alliance and asserted that Napoleon would do all in his power to keep Spain friendly so as not to repeat the mistake of his uncle in the Peninsular War. England offered the only hope, for if she would align herself against both France and Spain, she would let the United States seize Cuba to deny the French shelter for their ships. Preston suggested that Slidell be sent to London to aid negotiations, but he was not enthusiastic about further proceedings. As early as April 25, 1859, when he told Cass to prepare the Democratic party to seize Cuba if France and England were distracted by war, his correspondence had the ring of desperation. In May he informed

36. William Preston to his sister, undated, February 24, March 8, 1859, January 20, 1860, and Mrs. William Preston to Susan Preston, July 14, 1859, both in Preston Family Papers.

the president that his mission was "useless." Only strong pressure from Buchanan kept Preston at his post until early 1861, when Buchanan's term expired. That Preston nearly drowned on a Marseille to Madrid trip seems somehow symbolic of the futility of his whole mission.[37]

By the time the first session of the Thirty-sixth Congress convened in December, 1859, Buchanan and Slidell were ready to acknowledge defeat. The October and November elections had cost the administration control of the House of Representatives. Now, even in the unlikely event that a Cuba bill passed the Senate, it could never clear Congress as a whole. Any bill coming out of the Senate, moreover, would probably carry George Pugh's last-minute amendment or an amendment attached to the bill by James Mason of Virginia on February 21, 1859, which stated that the United States would receive Cuba only when Spain was agreeable, and that the United States would oppose the transfer of the island to any other country.[38] Either one of these amendments would have crippled plans to use funds to induce a faction in Spain to surrender Cuba. Only

37. Augustus C. Dodge to Lewis Cass, January 5, 1859, and William Preston to Lewis Cass, April 25, 1859, both in Manning (ed.), *Diplomatic Correspondence*, XI, 963–65, 969–71; William Preston to James Buchanan, May 8, 1859, in Buchanan Papers; William Preston to his sister, April 9, 1859, in Johnston Papers; Cincinnati *Enquirer*, October 25, 1860. Preston's discouraging comments about Napoleon actually hurt his chances of getting Slidell to Europe. Slidell was on the verge of accepting an appointment from Buchanan to the French mission when Preston's description of Napoleon arrived in Washington. Slidell quickly retracted his offer to go overseas. See John Slidell to James Buchanan, May 30, June 14, July 3, 1859, and James Buchanan to John Slidell, June 8, 24, 1859, both in Buchanan Papers. Raymond Carr has pointed out that Spanish politics at that time were passing through a relatively stable period under the ministry of Leopold O'Donnell. See Raymond Carr, *Spain, 1808–1939* (Oxford, 1966), 260. This stability must have further undermined Preston's mission. It should also be mentioned that Preston did return to the United States for a time in 1860.

38. *Congressional Globe*, 35th Cong., 2nd Sess., 1179; *Daily Ohio State Journal*, March 3, 1859.

the value of publicity explains why Buchanan and Slidell raised the issue at all. Buchanan reaffirmed his desires in his third annual message, but explained that the initiative for Cuba lay with Congress: without Congress' recognition of the necessity for purchase it would be—"almost impossible to institute negotiations with any reasonable prospect of success." Slidell's token effort came on May 30, 1860, when he reintroduced his bill. He then announced with resignation that a lack of support forced him to withdraw it from the Senate's consideration.[39]

Buchanan's stillborn 1859 bid for Cuba aroused southern anticipations to an extent far greater than most historians have acknowledged, and it was truly one of the major nonevents of the antebellum period. Although a Kentuckian's report to Stephen Douglas in February that "nine tenths of all parties here are for acquiring Cuba at the cannon's mouth" was undoubtedly an exaggeration, the intensity of southern interest in Cuba in 1859 was equal to that of 1854 and may have surpassed it. Vice-President Breckinridge of Kentucky favored annexation in a February speech. When Alexander Stephens retired from Congress, his farewell speech in Augusta, Georgia in July envisioned a slave empire that especially included Cuba: "Already, we are looking out toward Chihuahua, Sonora, and other parts of Mexico. Where are to be our ultimate limits, time alone can determine. But of all these acquisitions, the most important to the whole country is that of Cuba." Stephens asked for repeal of the neutrality laws, claiming that Spain held Cuba by force alone, and talked of the South's "unrestricted right" to expand slavery. Beriah Magoffin, in the midst of a successful campaign for the governorship of Kentucky, advocated the purchase of Cuba in a speech in Harrods-

39. Slidell to Buchanan, May 30, June 14, 1859, in Buchanan Papers; Moore (ed.), *Works of Buchanan*, X, 349–50; *Congressional Globe*, 36th Cong., 1st Sess., 2456.

burg. Governor Wickliffe of Louisiana sent a message to his state's legislature calling for acquisition. Albert Gallatin Brown told Tammany Hall Democrats that Cuba needed to be secured to extend slavery. John J. McRae of Mississippi sent pro-Cuba resolutions to the Southern Commercial Convention of 1859 and informed the Mississippi legislature that "the holy stars which looked down upon the beautiful Queen of the Antilles, veiled in all the splendor of her broad savanahs [*sic*], southern bowers and sugar plantations, that nightly watched the underdeveloped loveliness of her glorious plains, proclaimed that she was ours." [40] Newspapers throughout the South clamored for acquisition. [41]

But southern expansionist hopes for Cuba in 1859 were dashed, as were their hopes for other tropical lands throughout the 1850s. The expansionist response was to lash out at the enemies of acquisition, particularly those congressmen who had stymied Slidell's bill. Preston described himself as sick at heart over how the slavery problem had disrupted the Cuba movement; and he exclaimed: "God grant that the Democracy may crush the reptiles under their heels until they writhe again. I hope after my death, that my children may never feel that any act of mine has ever checked America in her advancement to Empire.

40. T. N. Hornsby to Stephen Douglas, February 1, 1859, in Douglas Papers; Natchez *Daily Courier*, February 15, 1859; Henry Cleveland, *Alexander H. Stephens in Public and Private* (Philadelphia, 1866), 645–46; Covington (Kentucky) *Journal*, March 19, 1859; *Texas Republican*, January 28, 1859; Ranck, *Albert Gallatin Brown*, 168; Memphis *Daily Appeal*, May 17, 1859; Memphis *Daily Avalanche*, December 2, 1859.

41. Louisville *Daily Courier*, October 7, 1858, January 1, 11, 12, 25, February 3, 19, 25, 1859; Memphis *Daily Appeal*, February 23, 1859; Nashville *Union and American*, March 24, 1859; Jackson *Semi-Weekly Mississippian*, February 18, March 1, 1859; *Arkansas State Gazette and Democrat*, March 12, 1859; *Texas State Gazette*, December 17, 1859; Macon *Daily Telegraph*, July 11, 1860. The newspaper arguments for Cuba were generally repetitions of the arguments employed during the 1854 crisis. "Africanization," however, rarely received mention.

...I wish the flag to float in the tropics." [42] Jefferson Davis, who had backed Slidell both in committee and on the Senate floor, excoriated Republicans for their antipathy to Cuban annexation and interpreted their opposition as further evidence of the Republican party's desire to prevent the addition of new slave states to the union. Davis warned: "The end, regret it as we may, the inevitable end of continuance in such hostility between the States must be their separation. This brings me to . . . the importance of the Island of Cuba to the Southern States if formed into a separate confederacy. The Commercial considerations in this would probably be less important . . . but the political necessity would be paramount, and the possession would be indispensable." The Richmond *Enquirer* during the 1860 presidential campaign would criticize "Black Republicans" who allied themselves with England to prevent slave expansion south and who "would refuse Cuba as a boon from Spain." [43] After Slidell's defeat, some slavery expansionists concluded that, given Republican unanimity against expansion, tropical lands might best be acquired outside the union. Others continued to fight for expansion within the union.

Southern leaders in the late 1850s demanded evidence that their institutions would be protected in the face of growing northern predominance in the union. Oregon,

42. William Preston to his sister, April 9, 1859, in Johnston Papers; William Preston to his sister, November 9, 1860, in Preston Family Papers. Preston fought for the Confederacy after his return to the United States in 1861. He is perhaps best remembered today as the man who held the dying body of Albert Sidney Johnston at the battle of Shiloh in the Civil War. Johnston was his brother-in-law.

43. New York *Semi-Weekly Tribune*, September 5, 1859; Richmond *Enquirer*, October 5, 1860; Dunbar Rowland (ed.), *Jefferson Davis, Constitutionalist: His Letters, Papers, and Speeches* (10 vols.; Jackson, 1923), IV, 80. The occasion of Davis' remarks was the meeting of the Mississippi Democratic state convention in Jackson, Mississippi, on July 6, 1859.

admitted into the union in the midst of the Cuba debate, symbolized that predominance, as did the territory of Kansas, which by 1859 was destined to become a free state. Cuban acquisition might have served to reassure the South. Instead, its failure heightened southern irritation with the nature of the union and with the national political system. The Republicans who quashed Slidell's efforts were aware of southern anxieties, but were unwilling to pay the price that Caribbean acquisitions would have entailed, namely, the strengthening of slave institutions within the United States. Nor were they prepared to aid the floundering foreign policies of President Buchanan. Buchanan's failure, both domestically and diplomatically, helped pave the way for Abraham Lincoln's election in 1860.

VIII

The Southern
Anti-Imperialists

~~~~~~

Few students of the antebellum South have underestimated the vitality of the southern Caribbean movement of the 1850s as much as the usually astute Clement Eaton. Eaton, in his *History of the Old South,* asserted that "only a small minority of extremists in the South was behind the movement to acquire Cuba as well as areas of Mexico and Central America." [1] Apparently Eaton did not consider the southern newspapers that endorsed tropical imperialism and the votes of southern congressmen on bills to further that end. Did Eaton intend to categorize such mainstays of the southern Caribbean drive as Alexander Stephens, Robert Toombs, John Slidell, John Winston, and William Preston as "extremists"? Should historians dismiss as irrelevant the activities of thousands of southerners who turned out for filibuster rallies and who frequently either contributed money to, or agreed to service in, filibuster expeditions? Most other histories of the antebellum South have avoided such "extreme" conclusions, but there has been a definite tendency to underplay, and even dismiss, the significance of the Caribbean movement.[2]

1. Clement Eaton, *A History of the Old South* (2nd ed.; New York, 1966), 335.
2. Avery O. Craven, for instance, in *The Growth of Southern Nationalism, 1848–1861* (Baton Rouge, 1953), inexcusably ignores the movement. Too many historians still take their lead from Charles W. Ramsdell's provocative 1929 article, "The Natural Limits of Slavery Expansion," *Mississippi Valley Historical Review,* XVI (1929), 151–71, which asserted that the agitation for Cuba

The movement actually was extended to encompass more than has already been indicated. Although southern expansionists placed emphasis on Cuba, Nicaragua, and Mexico, they also expressed interest in bringing their institutions to other parts of the Western Hemisphere, particularly Brazil. A. Dudley Mann's son, William, suggested to the American minister to Brazil in 1857 that William Walker should consider invading Brazil to save "the fairest portion of God's Creation," which was "rotting away in the hands of a decrepit race." Matthew Fontaine Maury spent a good deal of time publicizing Brazil's potential in the 1850s, although his emphasis was primarily opening up the Amazon River valley to American trade.[3]

A great deal of southern filibustering has not been covered in this work, either because it was too minor to merit serious attention or because information is too scarce. One

never reached significant proportions, that William Walker's movement could not have strengthened the institution in the South, and that southern leaders knew that slavery could not exist in Mexico's "high, table-lands" nor compete with cheap native labor in the "low country." See Damon Wells's discussion of the Lincoln-Douglas debates in *Stephen Douglas: The Last Years*, 107–108, for an excellent illustration of the continued life of the Ramsdell thesis. Wells suggests that Lincoln and Douglas, in arguing about the future expansion of slavery, were "tilting at windmills." On the other hand, a number of studies have come to terms with the southern Caribbean drive and the accompanying sectionalization of "manifest destiny." William Barney's *The Road to Secession* gives considerable attention to the tropics within the context of discussing the South's quest in general for new slave territory. Frederick Merk and Eugene Genovese have both assessed the role of the Caribbean issue in transforming "manifest destiny" into a sectional movement. Numerous other studies have touched on different phases of the Caribbean movement. See Barney, *The Road to Secession, passim*; Eugene Genovese, *The Political Economy of Slavery* (New York, 1965), 244–70; Merk, *Manifest Destiny and Mission*, Chapter IX.

3. W. Grayson Mann to William Trousdale, June 15, 1857, in Trousdale Papers; Matthew Fontaine Maury, "Valley of the Amazon," *De Bow's Review*, XIV (1853), 449–60, 556–67, XV (1853), 36–43; Francis Leigh Williams, *Matthew Fontaine Maury: Scientist of the Sea* (New Brunswick, 1963), 197–201.

of the most intriguing of the minor filibusters is Norris S. Reneau, who abandoned his failing drygoods store in Granada, Mississippi, to plan a Cuba invasion. Reneau claimed that President Buchanan had promised him aid in the form of $10,000 in secret service funds as well as immunity from prosecution by federal officials at New Orleans and Mobile, whence he planned to depart; and he strutted around Memphis and other cities sporting epaulettes, a sash, and a long sword. Although Reneau apparently was a crackpot, he convinced the Memphis *Daily Appeal* to the extent of winning its endorsement, and other newspapers commented on his activities.[4] Although Reneau may simply have been seeking headlines, with no intention of risking his neck in an actual invasion, he serves as yet another illustration of the attraction that Cuba held for southerners in the 1850s. Rumors of similar escapades constantly appeared in the southern press. In apparent seriousness, one Arkansas paper in 1859 carried the unlikely story that ten thousand men who had failed in the Colorado gold country were assembling at Pike's Peak for an assault on Sonora, Durango, and Chihuahua in northern Mexico.[5]

Steadfast opponents of imperialism in the South envied the expansionists' success in winning public support. Texas congressman John Reagan's persistent attacks on William Walker and filibustering, including a suggestion that the Tennessean ought to be hung, almost cost him reelection in 1859. Vile attacks from the Texas press even led Reagan to burn his newspapers so that his wife would not get up-

4. N. S. Reneau to James Buchanan, January 6, May 30, June 13, October 25, 1859, and copy of N. S. Reneau to José de la Concha, October 25, 1858, both in Buchanan Papers; N. S. Reneau to James Buchanan, October 25, 1859, in John Fox Potter Papers, State Historical Society of Wisconsin, Madison; New York *Herald*, February 6, 1859; Memphis *Daily Appeal*, December 29, 1858, January 22, 30, 1859; Memphis *Daily Avalanche*, October 21, 1859; Charleston *Daily Courier*, January 25, 1859.
5. Fayetteville *Arkansian*, June 11, 1859.

set.[6] William Boyce of South Carolina, in an antiexpansionist speech before the House of Representatives, noted that "many at the South" supported "the annexation of Cuba as a southern measure." Expansion opponents often found it prudent to temporize their strictures by informing their audiences that they were not imposing ironclad pledges on themselves. Future developments might make antiexpansionism an untenable position. A favorite technique of antagonists to Caribbean annexations was to invoke the "ripe fruit" concept. One could attack acquisitions as impractical, yet still emerge a moderate expansionist. As Boyce put it: "I do not wish to shackle the ultimate action of the country. When the future rolls round, and Cuba emerges independent from its bosom, when the fruit is ripe, then let this great question be decided under the light of all the surrounding circumstances." An Arkansas paper proclaimed: "And so when we really want Cuba —that is when we can't get along well without it, we'll take it." The Memphis *Daily Appeal*, hostile to William Walker, commented: "If our relations were cordial and friendly with the other American powers . . . they would warmly welcome peaceful emigrants to their territories from the United States, and thus there would soon be formed a nucleus of American enterprise in Mexico and all the states of Central America which would finally result in their annexation to the Union." [7]

It would be a mistake, however, to invert Eaton's position, and declare that public opinion in the South was vir-

6. John H. Reagan to James W. Latimer, October 7, 1858, and James W. Throckmorton to John H. Reagan, September 9, 1859, both in Reagan Papers; Reagan, *Memoirs*, 72–74; *Texas Republican*, April 22, 29, June 10, 24, 1859; Clarksville *Standard*, September 18, 1858. Reagan also criticized proponents of reviving the African slave trade, which provoked part of the enmity against him.
7. *Congressional Globe*, 33rd Cong., 2nd Sess., Appendix, 92–93; Memphis *Daily Appeal*, January 22, 1858; Fayetteville *Arkansian*, March 13, 1859.

tually unanimous. At best, a majority of southerners supported expansion. John Reagan may have been carrying on a lonely crusade in Texas (or so his memoirs asserted), but antiexpansionists were both visible and vocal throughout the rest of the South.

Southerners unaffiliated with the Democratic party dominated the antiexpansionist ranks. Before 1854, southern Whigs railed most often against new acquisitions to the south. In the aftermath of the Whig party's disintegration, many southern members found a political home in the American party, also known as the Know-Nothing party. Often political factions hostile to the regular Democratic party in the South were grouped together under the designation "Opposition." All of these non-Democratic groups continued the Whig tradition of restraint concerning expansion.

This does not mean that southern antiexpansionists were invariably Whig-Americans. Some Democrats opposed imperialism, such as Associate Supreme Court Justice John Campbell, a Pierce appointee, who played an instrumental role in a number of court proceedings against filibusters. Senator James Hammond of South Carolina inveighed against imperialism in a stream of letters and speeches.[8] Other Democrats were recalcitrant on one or more specific issues. Usually reliable expansionists, such as Robert Toombs and John Slidell, were among those who voted against consideration of Sam Houston's Mexican protectorate scheme in 1858. The moderate Virginia Democrat John Letcher, as well as the fire-eating Texas Democrat Louis Wigfall, denounced William Walker as a pirate; Wigfall even said that Paulding deserved a sword for rescuing

8. Hammond to William Gilmore Simms, January 20, 1858, January 21, 1859, April 8, 1860, Hammond to M. C. M. Hammond, December 11, 1858, I. W. Hayne to Hammond, January 24, 1858, and James Gadsden to Hammond, May 20, 1858, all in Hammond Papers; *Congressional Globe*, 35th Cong., 2nd Sess., 1183.

Nicaragua. A number of southern Democratic newspapers either ignored or attacked the Cuba movement.[9]

The shifting composition of Democratic expansionist ranks was caused in part by the entrepreneurial aspect of the Caribbean movement. Many leading Democratic expansionists, such as the Louisiana trio of Slidell, Benjamin, and Soulé, were ambitious men who hoped to reap financial windfalls from their expansionist activities. It is not always easy to pinpoint where the expansionist ideology of these men ended and the prospects for personal profit began. Did Slidell offer to go to Paris to aid Buchanan's Cuba purchase plan out of principle, or because he sought to raise European loans to shore up his sinking Louisiana Tehuantepec Company? Did Duff Green plot in 1857 to reestablish William Walker in power in Nicaragua because he believed in Walker's cause, or because the filibuster promised support for Green's claims to guano deposits on the Swan Islands off the coast of Honduras? A leading agitator for Walker's cause at the Southern Commercial Convention of 1858 was a man named Shepherd from Mobile, whom Edmund Ruffin described as trying to recoup a squandered fortune in cotton speculations. Shepherd advocated making Central America a "slave-holding" conquest, but his enthusiasm for Walker may have stemmed from investment possibilities.[10]

9. *Congressional Globe*, 35th Cong., 1st Sess., 2630; F. N. Boney, *John Letcher of Virginia: The Story of Virginia's Civil War Governor* (University, Alabama, 1966), 72; Clarksville *Standard*, February 27, September 11, 1858; Fayetteville *Arkansian*, March 13, 1859.

10. Joseph Fabens to Duff Green, May 29, June 8, 11, 20, 22, 26, 29, July 15, 16, 1857, and Duff Green to Lewis Cass, May 29, 1857, both in Green Papers; Edmund Ruffin Diary, May 14, 15, 17, 1858, in Ruffin Papers. Some southerners, however, apparently supported Caribbean expansionism *against* their own economic interest. Louisiana sugar planters such as Samuel Walker supported the Caribbean movement, although the acquisition of Cuba would have meant more competition for their crops. Contemporaries at the time expressed surprise at the strong Louisiana support for Cuba. During the Cuba debate of 1859, Senator John Thompson asserted that loss

The entrepreneurial aspect of the Caribbean movement sometimes retarded enthusiasm for new acquisitions. When ideology collided with the profit motive, it was the former that gave way. John Slidell's involvement in transportation schemes for the Isthmus of Tehuantepec best explains why he opposed William Walker's intervention in Nicaragua, even though he had been linked to the Quitman enterprise for Cuba. Transit across Nicaragua posed a competitive threat to the Mexican route. That his arch political rival, Pierre Soulé, had financial ties with Walker makes Slidell's opposition even more explicable. No wonder Slidell told the Senate in 1858 that Walker was a poor soldier, "unfit" for the "mission of regenerating Central America." [11]

While southern Democrats occasionally joined the anti-imperialists, southern Whigs sometimes defied party tradition and supported the imperialists. Some southern Americans voted against Commodore Paulding in the House in January, 1859. The American party state convention in Georgia in 1855 and the Opposition state convention of

---

of the protective tariff against Cuban sugar would undermine the Louisiana sugar crop; and he commented, "The zeal and ability with which the Senators from Louisiana press the acquisition of Cuba have struck me with some surprise." See *Congressional Globe*, 35th Cong., 2nd Sess., 1058.

Northern entrepreneurs, of course, also sought personal gain from the tropical movement. Various northern commercial interests were inextricably connected with William Walker. George Law, the expansionist president of the United States Mail Steamship Company, almost single-handedly forced a war between the United States and Spain over Cuba in 1852 when one of his company's ships, the *Crescent City*, was expelled from Havana by Spanish officials because it was suspected of being tied in with the López filibuster movement. Law believed that the annexation of Cuba would improve the trading position of his firm and that he stood a chance of monopolizing passenger service between the island and the United States once Cuba joined the union. See Leard, "Bonds of Destiny," 149–69.

11. *Congressional Globe*, 35th Cong., 1st Sess., 461–62. Slidell's speech included another attack on the neutrality laws.

Tennessee in 1859 endorsed the annexation of Cuba. Mississippi's Vicksburg *Weekly Whig*, during the *Black Warrior* crisis of 1854, supported any federal action against Cuba, including the suspension of the neutrality laws. A number of the leading filibusters of the era, including Roberdeau Wheat and Henry Crabb, were Whigs. Many financiers and organizers for the filibusters were Whigs: banker Samuel Peters of New Orleans and Judge William Ochiltree of Texas both supported Quitman.[12]

Whiggery, nevertheless, was a key factor in the opposition to imperialism in the 1850s. Whig-American negativism was almost inevitable, given the party's minority status and its "opposition" role from 1853 on. The Pierce and Buchanan administrations inaugurated many of the Caribbean projects of the decade, and Whig-Americans could derive political profit from the spoiler's role. Political considerations led some Whig-Americans to back William Walker in the Paulding dispute, while simultaneously attacking Democratic initiatives concerning Cuba and Mexico.

Motives other than simple political calculations added strength to the Whig-American resistance. The Whig traditions of national consolidation and resistance to presidential power, as well as a strong racist and unionist element in the Whig ideology, significantly influenced Whig-Americans' views of the future of the Caribbean.

The Whig predilection for consolidation of the nation rather than expansion of its boundaries, which had been particularly evident during the discussions of the feasibility of annexing all of Mexico during the Mexican War, never disappeared. A Kentuckian spoke out against the an-

12. New Orleans *Daily Picayune*, July 4, 1855; Robert H. White (ed.), *Messages of the Governors of Tennessee* (7 vols.; Nashville, 1952–67), V, 91; Samuel Walker, "The Diary of a Louisiana Planter," entry for December 19, 1859, in Samuel Walker Papers; John Ford to Hugh McLeod, January 14, 1855, in McLeod Papers.

nexation of Cuba: "I think that at this time we ought to compact and bind together and build up and strengthen what we have. We are young. Let the gristle grow into the bone; let us get our muscles developed." Similarly, Whigs adhered to the principle of antagonism to executive "usurpations," which dated from the very origins of the party during the presidency of Andrew Jackson. Slidell's Cuba bill, which signified to some Whigs a surrender of the Senate's authority over foreign affairs to the president, aroused vehement denunciations. William Rives of Virginia complained that Buchanan's Cuba program and Mexican protectorate proposal were attempts to get the "Representatives of the people to transfer to him the power of peace and war; to give him, in effect, the sole treaty-making power; to place millions of the public money at his discretion; and to invest him with military protectorates over foreign States." The Richmond *Whig* predicted that Slidell's bill would transform Buchanan into a "virtual Dictator." [13] Whig antipathy to the Ostend Manifesto was grounded in part on a conviction that the president attempted to circumvent normal diplomatic channels.

Warnings against precipitant expansion and executive usurpation obscured the nativist and unionist underpinnings of the Whig-American opposition. Millard Fillmore reflected both of these strains in the Whig ideology when he questioned the value of incorporating Cuba into the union in his third annual message to Congress: "It would bring into the Confederacy a population of a different national stock, speaking a different language, and not likely to harmonize with the other members. It would probably affect in a prejudicial manner the industrial interests of

13. *Congressional Globe*, 35th Cong., 2nd Sess., 1062; Tuskegee *Republican*, May 26, 1859; Richmond *Whig*, January 28, 1859. See also J. I. Dozier to Stephen Douglas, February 25, 1859, in Douglas Papers; Greenville (Alabama) *Southern Messenger*, April 27, 1859, March 14, 1860.

the South, and it might revive those conflicts of opinion between the different sections of the country which lately shook the Union to its center." [14]

American party members, in particular, came naturally to a racist rejection of tropical expansion because their party was founded on nativist and anti-Catholic principles. The Catholicism of most Cubans appalled Know-Nothing leaders. John L. O'Sullivan urged a moderate Cuba policy to Secretary of State Marcy in 1855 because Know-Nothings would be "sure to oppose a war policy directed toward the object of bringing in at a stroke a whole population of foreign and Catholic citizens." New Orleans Americans frequently cited Cuba's strong Catholic church as a good reason for rejecting the island. When John Claiborne tried to explain to John Quitman in August, 1855, the sudden loss of grass roots support in Mississippi for Cuba filibustering, he stressed the rise of Know-Nothing intolerance: "Men who twelve months since professed to be enthusiasts for Cuba and you, are now disowning you for laboring to introduce a nation of Catholics and foreigners." [15] In North Carolina in the 1850s, public apathy regarding the annexation of Cuba may well have been related to the fact that the state had the nation's highest percentage of native-born citizens.[16]

Nativist feelings were very apparent when Whig-Americans criticized the Cuba bill of 1859. Arch Unionist-Whig John Bell ironically quoted arch states' rights Democrat John Calhoun on the danger of integrating foreign peoples into the union and exclaimed that "no poet ever

14. Richardson (comp.), *Messages and Papers of the President,* VI, 2701–2702.

15. John L. O'Sullivan to William Marcy, June 1, 1855, in Marcy Papers; Urban, "The Idea of Progress," 147–48; John Claiborne to John Quitman, August 16, 1855, in Quitman Family Papers.

16. George H. Gibson, "Opinion in North Carolina Regarding the Acquisition of Texas and Cuba, 1835–1855," *North Carolina Historical Review,* XXXVII (1960), 198.

fabled a goddess of liberty within the tropics." Anthony Kennedy of Maryland implored the Senate not to annex "foreign races, without sympathy, without congeniality of sentiment, without appreciation of the blessings of freedom." And John Thompson, an American from Kentucky, explained that although he had spent half his life among American Catholics and never knew "better citizens," he still opposed admitting a people who professed a "different religion." [17]

Prospects of annexing Mexico aroused similar apprehensions among southern Whigs. Two of the leading southern Whigs who flirted with the Know-Nothing movement, John Bell and John Crittenden, both attacked James Buchanan's Mexican protectorate scheme on nativist grounds. Crittenden complained that he did not "want to see our American tribe mingled up with that sort of evil communication. I mean evil in a political sense. They do not understand our rights; they do not think as we think." Bell said:

> Five million civilized and half civilized Indians to enjoy the privileges of citizenship in Mexico! How many generations would there be before they could be assimilated, or before they could become no longer a poisonous obstruction in the progress of . . . liberty, either in their own country or as auxiliary to the people of this country in protecting them. . . . When you shall have extended your dominion over the states of Mexico and Central America, you will have added twelve million of a population, for the most part perfectly imbecile.[18]

Southern Know-Nothings had company when they attacked tropical expansion on nativist grounds. Republicans found such arguments useful in their opposition to slavery extension.[19] A minority of antiexpansionist south-

17. *Congressional Globe*, 35th Cong., 2nd Sess., 1344–45, 1351, 1059–60.
18. *Ibid.*, Appendix, 160; *ibid.*, 1344.
19. See, for instance, the speeches of Jacob Collamer of Vermont and John Hale of New Hampshire against Slidell's Cuba bill, *ibid.*, 1181; *ibid.*, Appendix, 164.

ern Democrats also expressed concern over the addition of alien peoples. Even Democrats who usually lined up behind the tropical movement had occasional second thoughts. Edmund Ruffin reflected in his diary that possession of Cuba by the United States might be a mistake because it would be very difficult to Americanize what he considered the worthless Catholics and inferior mulattoes and blacks of the island. William Yancey, in opposing expansion into Mexico at the Alabama secession convention, declared that this would entail bringing into the Confederacy an "ignorant and superstitious and demoralized population." [20] The fear of Catholics and foreigners that pervaded the nation during the antebellum period transcended party lines.

The Whiggish tendency to suppress sectionally disruptive issues also motivated the Whig-American attack on tropical expansion. To Senator John Thompson of Kentucky, the Cuba bill of 1859 caused "agitation on the negro question" when he had hoped that after the Kansas controversy "the country would have some quiet." John Bell thought the Cuba bill was a "public calamity" in that it aroused the slavery issue. And to Anthony Kennedy, Slidell's measure risked involving the "whole civilized world in war" and the disruption of the union.[21] Bell, Thompson, and Kennedy knew well that Republicans would never accept new slave territory without a serious fight; Republicans made this clear during the Cuba debate as they had earlier on countless other issues. Whig-American congressmen feared that such a refusal might incite disunion, as the dispute over territory acquired from Mexico had almost done in 1850.

The tropical expansion movement, moreover, never gained momentum in the upper South to the extent that

20. Edmund Ruffin Diary, March 4, 1859, in Ruffin Papers; William R. Smith (ed.), *The History and Debates of the People of Alabama* (Montgomery, 1861), 200, 236–37, 257; *Texas State Gazette*, February 16, 1861.
21. *Congressional Globe*, 35th Cong., 2nd Sess., 1061, 1342, 1347.

it did in the Gulf states. The relative strength of the anti-expansionist American party in the upper South, as compared to the lower South, partly explains this. Of the twenty-one southern Know-Nothings of the Thirty-fifth Congress (1857–1859), only four came from the Deep South.[22] Furthermore, increased trade from the addition of tropical territory would not profit the border states as much as other slave states that were in the vicinity of the prospective acquisitions. And should a war break out over the question of adding new slave states, the border states stood to suffer the most because the war would be fought primarily on their soil.

It may also be that upper South leaders felt that acquisitions would impair the status of slavery in their own states. Without a reopening of the African slave trade— which border state leaders almost universally opposed and which was practically impossible within the union anyway —new additions might have caused a movement of slaves southward and corresponding scarcity of slaves in the upper South. This theme dominated Anthony Kennedy's Senate speech on the Cuba bill of 1859, though he did not say explicitly that he wanted to preserve slavery. The Maryland Know-Nothing viewed the grain-growing upper South as in ruinous economic competition with the grain-growing Northwest on the one hand and the prosperous cotton states on the other. The demand in the lower South for upper South slaves had drained the upper South of its labor supply, thus lowering land values and raising the cost of labor to prohibitive heights. Cuban acquisition would only put the upper South "into a more unequal contest with the planting States" by removing even more of its labor supply to Cuban sugar lands. John Bell presented similar arguments in the same debate, warning that some southerners

22. Overdyke, *Know-Nothing Party*, 51–56; Alice Tyler, *Freedom's Ferment: Phases of American Social History to 1860* (Minneapolis, 1944), 394–95.

were "apprehensive" that the Cuba bill "would produce a drain of too large a portion of the labor peculiar to the South, and of the capital employed in the southern slave States." [23] Bell's and Kennedy's comments, however, did not typify upper South opposition to expansion. Border politicians generally were happy with the high prices slaves were commanding in the interstate slave trade, and prices would probably have gone higher had the United States annexed tropical lands, particularly in Mexico or Central America.[24]

Even within the lower South, Caribbean expansionism failed to gain universal acceptance. South Carolinians, in particular, denounced the movement. James Hammond's views on the tropics found a popular response, and many influential South Carolinians echoed his feelings, including Robert Barnwell Rhett, I. W. Hayne, James Gadsden, William Gilmore Simms, and Waddy Thompson. Rhett's Charleston *Mercury* frequently attacked such expansion in the late 1850s.[25] Harold Schultz noted that of all the South Carolinians in Congress in 1859, only Lawrence Keitt supported Slidell's Cuba bill; South Carolinians were indifferent or hostile toward imperialistic ventures throughout the Pierce and Buchanan presidencies.[26]

South Carolinians attacked tropical expansion primarily because they felt that continuous attention to demands

23. *Congressional Globe*, 35th Cong., 2nd Sess., 1343, 1347–50. See also Richmond *Enquirer*, February 4, 1859.

24. Robert Royal Russell, *Economic Aspects of Southern Sectionalism, 1840–1861* (Urbana, 1923), 224.

25. Rhett to Hammond, July 26, 1858, Hayne to Hammond, January 24, 1858, Gadsden to Hammond, May 20, 1858, Waddy Thompson to Hammond, August 17, 1858, and Francis Lieber to Hammond, February 14, 1859, all in Hammond Papers; William Gilmore Simms to William Porcher Miles, February 3, 1859, in William Porcher Miles Papers, University of North Carolina Library, Chapel Hill; Charleston *Mercury*, January 1, 14, 1858, January 24, 1859.

26. Harold S. Schultz, *Nationalism and Sectionalism in South Carolina, 1852–1860* (Durham, 1950), 178–79.

for Caribbean territory obscured other, more important, southern grievances. South Carolinians had complaints about economic issues such as the national tariff policy that overshadowed Caribbean expansion as a sectional issue.[27] In addition, by the late 1850s many South Carolina leaders had passed the point of no return concerning the union and felt that tropical annexations were held out as a sop to prevent secession. Simms bluntly asserted that Cuba was delusive bait to tie the South to the union against its best interests, and the *Mercury* agreed. Steve Channing has explained how "the alienation of South Carolina radicals was complete" by 1860, and how they had become "disgusted with the troublesome issue of slavery in the territories." [28] While Gulf state politicians, including many secessionists, were willing to consider Caribbean expansion as a means of improving the southern position within the union, South Carolinians asserted that the union was beyond saving.

John Calhoun's campaign against acquiring all of Mexico during the Mexican War seems to have weighed heavily on South Carolinians a decade later. Gadsden reminded Hammond: "Beware of 'Forbidden fruit' Mr. Calhoun admonished on the Polk expansionists. You could not place a more irritating [sore] on the Body Politic of our Federation than the annexation of Mexico—We have trouble enough with 3 millions of Africans." South Carolina's antiexpansionists might also have inherited the constitutional qualms that Calhoun expressed against territorial expansion during the Mexican War.[29]

---

27. Charleston *Mercury*, February 26, 1859.
28. Simms to Miles, February 3, 1859, in Miles Papers; Charleston *Mercury*, January 24, 1859; Steven A. Channing, *Crisis of Fear: Secession in South Carolina* (New York, 1970), 160, 169.
29. Gadsden to Hammond, May 20, 1858, in Hammond Papers; Merk, *Manifest Destiny and Mission*, 152–53, 204; Harry V. Jaffa, *Crisis of the House Divided* (New York, 1959), 99; Charles M. Wiltse, *John C. Calhoun* (3 vols.; New York, 1944–51), III, 328.

There was, therefore, considerable sentiment in the South in the 1850s against acquiring tropical acquisitions, over and above the northern resistance to the movement already discussed. Had all southerners coalesced behind a Caribbean program, it would unquestionably have been more difficult for northern Republicans to block tropical annexations.

Nevertheless, the movement's strength in the South overshadows the antagonism it aroused. The staying power of the "Caribbean dream," given an unbroken string of diplomatic and filibustering failures in the 1850s, demands acknowledgment. A surprising number of southerners maintained that annexation of tropical lands was a sectional necessity. The issue was to arise one more time, in the secession winter of 1860–1861.

IX

The Secession Crisis

On the afternoon of December 20, 1860, South Carolina delivered its answer to the November election of Abraham Lincoln by voting unanimously to leave the union. There were indications that a number of other states would follow South Carolina's lead. Mississippi, Alabama, Georgia, Florida, Louisiana, and Texas had already slated elections for conventions to consider secession. And throughout the South hatred of Lincoln and his party was intense. Few southerners trusted Lincoln regarding slavery (Republicans were commonly called "Black Republicans"), and fear pervaded the South that Lincoln intended to use the power of the presidency to free the slaves and turn them on their former masters.[1] Southerners waited for the response of Lincoln and other Republican leaders to their growing challenge. Would they advocate force to restore the union;

1. Allan Nevins, *The Emergence of Lincoln* (2 vols.; New York, 1950), II, 321–22; Channing, *Crisis of Fear*, 78–82, 88, 93, 161, 231, 235–39; John Slidell to Samuel Cartwright, December 25, 1860, in Cartwright Family Papers, Louisiana State University Department of Archives and Manuscripts, Baton Rouge; St. Augustine (Florida) *Examiner*, December 22, 1860. For an excellent discussion of the early growth of secessionism in South Carolina and the racial fears underlying the secession movement, see William Freehling, *Prelude to Civil War: The Nullification Controversy in South Carolina, 1816–1836* (New York, 1965), *passim*. Because Governor Sam Houston was a unionist and refused to convene the state legislature, the Texas call for an election for a secession convention was irregular, coming from a group of secession proponents at Austin on December 3.

would they accept the dissolution of the country; or would they use their influence and power to aid the programs of political moderates who were trying to preserve the union by offering concessions to the South?

At the time of South Carolina's secession, unionists were intensifying the search for a peaceful way to forestall dissolution of the republic. They knew that time was running out and that it would be much easier to preserve the union than to reestablish it after the southern states seceded. The unionists proposed numerous compromises that they hoped would settle the various differences that had inflamed North-South relations over the past decades. Although men in all walks of life aspired to resolve the crisis through their own personal compromise plans, moderate hopes already centered on the program introduced into the Thirty-sixth Congress by John J. Crittenden, the old Whig-Constitutional Union senator from Kentucky. Mass meetings in many parts of the country would soon be endorsing the plan, and petitions would flood Washington urging senators and representatives to aid Crittenden's efforts.[2]

Two days prior to South Carolina's withdrawal, Crittenden presented to the Senate a comprehensive program that would possibly stall, or even terminate, the secession movement. His legislation was designed to reassure southerners that despite Lincoln's election, slavery would be safe if their states remained in the union. Crittenden had entertained little hope of saving South Carolina, but trusted that if his legislation passed, the rest of the South would feel secure enough to stay.[3]

2. Stephen Douglas' papers reveal how even common citizens drew up their own personal plans to save the country. See I. A. Wilcox to Douglas, January 12, 1861, and M. D. Bogg to Douglas, December 26, 1860, both in Douglas Papers. For the popularity of Crittenden's program in the North, see Kirwan, *Crittenden*, 401–404. For support of Crittenden's plan in the South, see below, 226–32.

3. Crittenden to Orlando Brown, December 6, 1860, in Orlando Brown Papers, Filson Club; *Congressional Globe*, 36th Cong., 2nd Sess., 112–14.

Crittenden had been Henry Clay's "devoted lieutenant" for over three decades in Congress and in Kentucky politics, and it was only proper that he would now try to save the union as Clay had done in the past. Crittenden's biographer has commented that Crittenden's nationalism was so all-encompassing that long before South Carolina seceded the union had become his "only passion." Though a southerner and the owner of a few slaves, Crittenden had rarely sided with proslavery extremists in his long public career and had expressed hope that the institution might eventually be eradicated. He had even opposed the admission of Kansas as a slave state a couple of years earlier because its constitution had not been democratically adopted —a position politically untenable in much of the South. Now, however, he felt that concessions to slaveowners were necessary to preserve the union, and he was willing to make them.[4]

Crittenden's program consisted of a series of constitutional amendments, as well as some suggested congressional resolutions. Of prime importance was his first amendment, because it sought to solve the critical problem of slavery in the territories. The issue of whether slavery should be permitted to expand into new territories had almost split the union in 1850, when territory was acquired from Mexico, and had provoked guerrilla warfare in Kansas in the 1850s. The Kentuckian's first amendment reinstated the old Missouri Compromise line of 1820. This line, repealed only six years earlier, had permitted an unsteady sectional peace for some thirty years. Now Crittenden wanted to revive it and extend it to the Pacific Ocean. Slavery would be prohibited north of the line and protected

---

4. Kirwan, *Crittenden*, vi, 13, 18, 38, 70–73, 263, 267, 268, 322–30, 344, 401–404. Kirwan does point out, however, that a coolness developed between Clay and Crittenden during Clay's last years because of Crittenden's failure to support Clay for the 1848 Whig presidential nomination. These strained feelings were not relieved until shortly before Clay's death, when the two men were reconciled. See *ibid.*, 284.

south of the line, both in present United States territory and in all territory "hereafter acquired." In this way, North and South would share in the development of the American frontier rather than engage in a dispute over it. The repeal of the line in 1854 had led to conflict in Kansas because it caused the status of slavery to become indeterminate. With slave and free areas carefully marked in advance, confrontations such as that which gave rise to "Bleeding Kansas" should be a thing of the past.

Other amendments prohibited congressional interference with the interstate slave trade, slavery in the southern states, or slavery in the District of Columbia; provided that owners of fugitive slaves that could not be recovered because of "violence or intimidation" be compensated by the United States government; and called for stricter enforcement of the fugitive slave law and more effectual suppression of the African slave trade. Crittenden's last amendment assured the South that the compromise would stay in perpetual effect by forbidding any future amendment of the program or of the proslavery provisions of the original United States Constitution. No mere palliative as past sectional compromises had been, this program would permanently end the national crisis, or so Crittenden hoped.

Crittenden's resolutions reaffirmed the legality of the fugitive slave law, suggested that Congress write laws to punish individuals who helped runaways, called on the federal government to require any states that had personal liberty laws protecting fugitive slaves to repeal those laws, asked for revision of the fugitive slave law of 1850 so that commissioners deciding cases would get equal fees whether they judged the black in question to be free or slave, and asserted that the laws against the African slave trade should be strengthened.[5]

5. *Congressional Globe*, 36th Cong., 2nd Sess., 112–14. The original Missouri Compromise line made an exception of Missouri, which was allowed to enter the union as a slave state though above the

Only the provisions for more vigilance against the African slave trade and equalization of commissioners' fees offered anything to the North. But Crittenden's purpose had not been to assuage northern feelings. He was desperately trying to halt what he called the "madness" possessing the South and begged northerners in Congress to make the "cheap sacrifice" and "little concessions of opinions" that his plan required in order to save the country.[6]

Crittenden directed his plea primarily to Republicans. They held the balance of power in Congress, and their reaction would decide the fate of the Crittenden program. Northern Democrats, who had traditionally been more conciliatory toward the South and slavery, could be expected to give the program substantial support.

Some Republicans agreed with Crittenden that a few concessions to the South to preserve the union might be worthwhile, *if the price was not too high.* In the time between Lincoln's election and inauguration (in March), moderate Republicans voiced irregular support for such

---

line. The proposal to extend the line actually had a long history. It had frequently been suggested before and during the crisis of 1850 by such prominent politicians as Thomas Hart Benton, Sam Houston, James Buchanan, Stephen Douglas, Jefferson Davis, and James K. Polk. And when the Republican party came into being in 1854 in reaction to the Kansas-Nebraska Act, which explicitly repealed the old Missouri line, although most Republicans took the stand that slavery should not be allowed to expand anywhere, some conservative Republicans, particularly in Ohio, merely advocated restoring the Missouri line. See Frederick Merk, *Manifest Destiny and Mission,* 175–77; Chaplain W. Morrison, *Democratic Politics and Sectionalism* (Chapel Hill, 1967), 6, 78, 86–87; Hamilton, *Prologue to Conflict,* 59, 61, 65, 95, 99, 102; Eric Foner, *Free Soil, Free Labor, Free Men: The Ideology of the Republican Party Before the Civil War* (New York, 1970), 128, 194–95.

The equalization of commissioners' fees was a pronorthern reform because the 1850 fugitive slave law gave a higher fee to the commissioner if he decided the black in question was slave rather than free, which was, in effect, a bribe to decide in favor of the slaveowner.

6. *Congressional Globe,* 36th Cong., 2nd Sess., 113–14.

proposals as the repeal of northern personal liberty laws, a constitutional amendment guaranteeing slavery in the slave states, compensation to slave owners for fugitive slaves that could not be recovered, and the admission of New Mexico as a slave state. Some Republicans even endorsed restoration of the Missouri Compromise line—the heart of Crittenden's program. Thurlow Weed, the Republican political boss of New York state, had suggested this very idea in his influential Albany *Evening Journal* on November 24, 1860, well before Crittenden introduced his plan to Congress.[7]

Most Republicans, however, opposed major concessions to slavery, and they were particularly repulsed by Crittenden's plan. From the beginning, their response to the program was inflexibly hostile, and their antagonism doomed Crittenden's high hopes. New York Republicans, for example, gave a cold reception to Weed's suggestion of extending the Missouri Compromise line. The New York *Times* was the only Republican organ in the state that endorsed the idea, and United States Senator Preston King's comment that the plan gave too much to slave interests reflected the feelings of New York party leaders and much of the party rank and file.[8] The response of Republicans at the national level was no more encouraging.

Unionists in both houses of Congress, however, fought for legislation that encompassed Crittenden's plan. In the lower house, on December 5, Alexander Boteler of Vir-

7. Charles Francis Adams Diary, December 29, 1860, in Adams Family Papers, Massachusetts Historical Society; Kenneth M. Stampp, *And the War Came: The North and the Secession Crisis, 1860–1861* (Baton Rouge, 1950), 131, 138, 165–66; David Potter, *Lincoln and His Party in the Secession Crisis* (New Haven, 1942), 71. These Republicans, however, vacillated on such programs, sometimes turning against their own proposals. See Stampp, *And the War Came*, 138.

8. Preston King to John Bigelow, December 3, 1860, quoted in John Bigelow, *Retrospections of an Active Life* (5 vols.; New York, 1909–13), I, 317; Potter, *Lincoln and His Party*, 72–74.

ginia successfully moved that a committee of one member from each state (the Committee of Thirty-Three) be established to try to work out a plan to save the union. Republicans cast every negative vote on the resolution, giving an early indication that they were opposed to compromise. On December 17, when a proposal came before the committee to consider a resolution by Thomas Nelson of Tennessee to restore the Missouri line, every Republican voted against it. The motion failed, even though every other member present, except Henry Winter Davis of Maryland, voted affirmatively. Republicans blocked every other compromise measure suggested in the Committee of Thirty-three.[9]

Lazarus W. Powell of Kentucky began similar action in the Senate, moving on December 6 to establish a Committee of Thirteen to find a way to avert secession. Republican senators delayed its establishment until December 18, the day Crittenden introduced his plan. Two days later Vice-President Breckinridge appointed the committee members, among whom were some of the most prominent men in Congress. The sectionally balanced committee included Crittenden, Stephen Douglas (Lincoln's recent northern Democratic opponent), Jefferson Davis and Robert Toombs (vigorous defenders of southern rights, and future president and secretary of state in the Confederate government, respectively), Robert Hunter (a Virginian who had been frequently heralded as being presidential timber), and William Seward (already earmarked for the State Department by Lincoln and generally regarded as the strong man of the Republican party despite Lincoln's stature as president-elect). It was to this committee that Crittenden's program was referred.

The committee pondered Crittenden's compromise on

9. George Fort Milton, *The Eve of Conflict: Stephen A. Douglas and the Needless War* (New York, 1934), 523; Potter, *Lincoln and His Party*, 100.

December 22, during its first meeting, but under terms imposed on the committee by Jefferson Davis. The Mississippian feared that in voting for compromise he might commit the South to terminate the secession process only to discover that Republicans had no intention of going along with the plan and would block it at a later point in the legislative process. Once the secession movement was stalled, it might prove impossible to reactivate it. He therefore moved that no proposition could be recommended by the committee without the approval of dual majorities of both the Republicans and the other members of the committee.[10] Under these conditions, Crittenden's resolutions met rough going. Northern Democrats Stephen Douglas and William Bigler gave the scheme strong support, but Davis and Toombs announced that they would back the proposals only if the Republicans did likewise. When the four Republicans present rejected the plan in a vote, Toombs and Davis joined them, and the committee dropped the Crittenden Compromise for lack of a dual majority.

That night at a Washington dinner, Crittenden commented that he was much more depressed about chances to save the union than he had been in the past, and that his efforts were finished. He overstated his own pessimism, for he continued to labor for compromise legislation over the next few months. But the Committee of Thirteen was stymied, and after a few days of fruitless debate it gave up. On December 31 it reported to the Senate that it could not agree on a plan of conciliation.[11]

10. "Journal of the Committee of Thirteen," 5; Potter, *Lincoln and His Party*, 171–72. Davis knew that even if Republicans could not block compromise in Congress, they might still be able to do so in northern state legislatures when the amendments would be referred to the states.
11. "Journal of the Committee of Thirteen," 1, 5; Charleston *Mercury*, December 25, 1860; New York *Daily Tribune*, December 24, 1860; Charles Francis Adams Diary, December 22, 1860, in Adams Family Papers; Potter, *Lincoln and His Party*, 171–72; Kirwan, *Crittenden*, 391–421.

Republican congressmen had voted against Crittenden's proposal, and their opposition would not diminish in the months ahead. When moderates continued to fight for the proposal in both houses of Congress in the new year, Republicans stood firm. To end the movement in the Senate, Republican Daniel Clark of New Hampshire offered a substitute for the Crittenden measures declaring that "the provisions of the Constitution are ample for the preservation of the Union." It passed 25 to 23. All affirmative votes came from the free states.[12] In the House of Representatives, Republican Elihu B. Washburne of Illinois blocked a vote on the Crittenden plan on January 21.[13]

Crittenden's followers still refused to admit defeat. The Virginia legislature invited all the states to send representatives to a "Peace Conference" in Washington in February. The invitation specifically stated that the Crittenden resolutions "constitute the basis of such an adjustment of the unhappy controversy which now divides the States of this confederacy." [14] Although none of the states that had already seceded sent delegates, twenty-one states did join the conference.

The convention met in a large concert hall attached to Willard's Hotel and struggled throughout February to reach a sectional accommodation that could be reported to Congress. It did not fail for lack of distinguished members. Former president John Tyler presided over the convention. State Supreme Court Justice Thomas Ruffin of North Carolina was in attendance, as was future treasury secretary and Chief Justice of the Supreme Court Salmon Chase of Ohio.

12. *Congressional Globe*, 36th Cong., 2nd Sess., 409; Milton, *Eve of Conflict*, 532.
13. *Congressional Globe*, 36th Cong., 2nd Sess., 498.
14. L. E. Chittenden (ed.), *Debates and Proceedings in the Secret Sessions of the Conference Convention* (New York, 1864), 10. For a detailed description of the conference, see Robert G. Gunderson, "William C. Rives and the 'Old Gentlemen's Convention,' " *Journal of Southern History*, XXII (1956), 459–76.

Once again Republican leaders opposed compromise plans, particularly Crittenden's, claiming that they did not want to cripple Lincoln's freedom to deal with secession by committing him to a program before his inauguration. Chase bluntly told the convention that the Ohio legislature had resolved that it was too early to discuss a solution, that the convention ought to be postponed until after Lincoln's inauguration, and that the Crittenden Compromise was unacceptable to Ohio. An Indiana Republican delegate wrote to his governor from the conference: "We have thus far done all in our power to procrastinate, and shall continue to do so, in order to remain in session until after the 4th of March. For after the inauguration we shall have an honest fearless man at the helm, and will soon know whether the honest masses of the People desire to preserve and perpetuate our Government." [15]

Despite Republican intransigence, the conference passed a watered-down version of Crittenden's plan on February 26. The new version stated that the Missouri Compromise line should be extended to include only present United States territories, and that new territories could be acquired only with the consent of dual majorities of both northern and southern senators. This meant that any new slave states would probably have to come from present territory in the West. Given the history of northern opposition to new slavery acquisitions, it was unlikely that a majority of northern senators would support expansion into areas promised in advance to slavery.

The modification did little to facilitate reconciliation. The peace conference reported its plan to Congress on February 27, and the Senate rejected it in the early morning hours of the day of Lincoln's inauguration. Then the

15. Chittenden (ed.), *Debates*, 54; Godlove S. Orth to Oliver P. Morton, February 21, 1861, in Kenneth M. Stampp (ed.), "Letters from the Washington Peace Conference of 1861," *Journal of Southern History*, IX (1943), 402; Gunderson, "Old Gentlemen's Convention," 468.

Senate voted on the original Crittenden plan and defeated it by a 20 to 19 vote. Not one Republican supported the plan. Though it was too late in the session for the plan to pass the House of Representatives even had the Senate approved it, the rejection marked the end of unionist efforts to resolve the secession problem through legislation. Soon the guns of the Confederate States of America, founded in Montgomery during that same interval, would open on Fort Sumter and the Civil War would begin.[16]

The Republican decision to frustrate compromise efforts was one of the most significant political decisions in American history. Although it would be unreasonable to assert that had Republicans supported compromise they would *definitely* have ended the secession movement and prevented the Civil War, such a result was quite possible given the wide support that Crittenden's plan attracted. The Republican motivation for opposing Crittenden's plan is, therefore, of prime importance. Why didn't Republicans promote conciliation and save Abraham Lincoln from the terrible burden of having to decide whether to allow secession or fight a civil war to restore the union?

Although Republicans explained at the Washington peace conference that they did not want to tie Lincoln's hands, the answer lies much deeper. All the prosouthern aspects of the compromise disturbed Republicans; but their ire was raised in particular by the territorial provisions. The Republican party's strength was contained in its antislavery wing, which was held together by opposition to *any* expansion of slavery. Crittenden's first amendment countenanced the extension of slavery, however fair the division of territory would prove to be. Had Republicans abandoned

16. *Congressional Globe*, 36th Cong., 2nd Sess., 1261, 1331–33, 1405; Kirwan, *Crittenden*, 400, 409–11; Potter, *Lincoln and His Party*, 302. The House also voted on the original Crittenden Compromise on February 27 and defeated it by a 113–80 vote. Republicans in the lower house, as in the Senate, voted unanimously against the measure.

their opposition to slave expansion in 1860, they would have committed political suicide. Such a concession to the South would have constituted a repudiation of their own platform, "an admission that southern complaints were valid," and a confession that Lincoln's election as president warranted secession.[17] The result could only have been Republican disintegration. Republican voters by the thousands cautioned their congressmen and leaders not to compromise with the South and agitated at home against conciliation, as when Pittsburgh Republicans broke up a unionist meeting by turning off the gas, smashing seats, and yelling "God d——n John J. Crittenden and his compromise!" Republicans in Washington read the message correctly.[18] Many Republicans, moreover, underestimated southern willingness to secede and to go to war to preserve the Confederacy.[19] Such beliefs led naturally to the conclusion that concessions were unnecessary to maintain the union.

Republicans opposed Crittenden's territorial plan because they expected that the United States would soon acquire new territories in the tropics—particularly the lands bordering on the Gulf of Mexico and the Caribbean Sea and the islands in that region, especially Cuba. Crittenden's "hereafter clause" meant that these lands would be promised in advance to slavery. Republicans believed that if the federal government refused to purchase or conquer such lands in the future, southern filibusters like Quitman

17. Stampp, *And the War Came*, 148–54.
18. *Ibid.*, 141–46; Macon *Daily Telegraph*, January 31, 1861. A correspondent of Illinois Republican Lyman Trumbull (a United States senator) wrote, for example: "I have written this letter, to give you the views of Republicans in this section, and in my judgment of the State of Illinois. No compromise based on those resolutions [the Crittenden plan] will be satisfactory to our people, and they will not only be unsatisfactory but a perfect storm of indignation will salute every man in the northwest who votes for or sanctions such a measure on his return home." See A. W. Metcalf to Trumbull, February 11, 1861, in Trumbull Papers.
19. Potter, *Lincoln and His Party*, 234–35.

or Walker would independently conquer the tropics and seek admission to the union. Not only would agreeing to such expansion alienate Republican voters and possibly destroy the party, but if enough new slave states were admitted to the union, the South might regain a balance of power in the Senate. Certainly such spreading of slavery would make its eradication increasingly unlikely.

The possibility of expansion into the tropics bothered Republicans far more than the fact that Crittenden's plan promised territory in the American Southwest to slavery. For one thing, slavery had already entered the Southwest. Brigham Young called slavery a "divine institution" and Utah's Mormon leaders permitted slavery. As recently as February, 1859, New Mexico's territorial government had passed a code protecting slavery. Crittenden's plan merely recognized the status quo in the Southwest and actually would have eliminated slavery in Utah and that part of New Mexico above the Missouri Compromise line. This is why some Republicans expressed a willingness to accept Crittenden's program if it were modified to refer only to the present territories in the American West, a change that the peace conference accepted. Furthermore, the aridness of soil in the American Southwest and the limited number of slaves in that region—Utah had only twenty-nine in 1860—encouraged Republicans to believe that even if slavery was protected in the Southwest by congressional legislation, it would never flourish. This confidence enabled Republicans in Congress to agree to bills organizing the territories of Colorado, Nevada, and Dakota without prohibitions against slavery at the very time that they were attacking Crittenden.[20]

20. Memphis *Daily Appeal*, March 5, 1859; Charles Francis Adams Diary, December 25, 1860, in Adams Family Papers; *Population of the United States in 1860*, U.S. Eighth Census (Washington, D.C., 1864), 557, 575; A. S. Fiske to John Crittenden, January 21, 1861, and J. P. Ogden to Crittenden, January 19, 1861, both in John Crittenden Papers, Library of Congress; Charles Desmond Hart, "Why Lincoln Said 'No': Congressional Attitudes toward

Mexico, Central and South America, and the Caribbean presented an entirely different problem. Lincoln abhorred Crittenden's plan because it would allow slavery to expand into these areas, and his views were reflected by Republicans in Congress, as well as by the lower echelons of the party. Lincoln rebuked Thurlow Weed for his support of Crittenden's plan because "the Missouri line extended . . . would lose us every thing we gained by the election; that filibustering for all South of us, and making slave states of it, would follow." To Republican Congressman James Hale of Pennsylvania, Lincoln exclaimed that the Crittenden Compromise would mean the end of the Republican party and of the government. He was convinced that the South "will repeat the experiment ad libitum. A year will not pass, till we shall have to take Cuba as a condition upon which they will stay in the Union. . . . There is, in my judgment, but one compromise which would really settle the slavery question, and that would be a prohibition against acquiring any more territory." [21] Lincoln sent similar letters to other important Republicans and made his position clear well before the Committee of Thirteen met to con-

---

Slavery Expansion, 1860–1861," *Social Science Quarterly*, IL (1968), 737–41; Dennis Lythgoe, "Negro Slavery in Utah," *Utah Historical Quarterly*, XXXIX (1971), 40–54; Loomis Morton Ganaway, *New Mexico and the Sectional Controversy, 1846–1861* (Albuquerque, 1944), 60–71; Robert W. Larson, *New Mexico's Quest For Statehood, 1846–1912* (Albuquerque, 1968), 62–65; Hamilton, *Prologue to Conflict*, 174–76. The willingness of Republicans to allow slavery in the Southwest, however, should not be overstated. Only some Republicans were willing to countenance the concession, and Charles Francis Adams, the Republican who sponsored the idea of allowing New Mexico's entrance into the union as a slave state, had reason to regret it because his constituents wrote him angrily protesting what "they deem a sacrifice to the Slave interests, on my part." See Charles Francis Adams Diary, January 1, 1861, in Adams Family Papers.

21. Lincoln to Weed, December 17, 1860, and Lincoln to Hale, January 11, 1861, both in Roy P. Basler (ed.), *The Collected Works of Abraham Lincoln* (8 vols.; New Brunswick, 1953–55), IV, 154, 172.

sider Crittenden's plan. He had a profound effect on the leaders of his party. As Charles Francis Adams explained at the time, "The declarations coming almost openly from Mr. Lincoln have had the effect of perfectly consolidating the Republicans." There are indications that William Seward might have supported the plan, but did not dare to cross Lincoln because he would have forfeited his coming appointment as secretary of state. Seward's close ties to Thurlow Weed, who originally had proposed the extension of the Missouri line, encourages this hypothesis, as does the fact that rumors circulated at the time that Seward would support Crittenden. Seward, moreover, played a conciliatory role toward the South throughout the secession winter.[22]

Other influential Republicans repeated Lincoln's fears almost verbatim. August Belmont informed Stephen Douglas, who had been laboring for compromise as strenuously as Crittenden: "I am told by Republican leaders that they will not vote for Crittenden's amendments, because they will not accept the Missouri line for future acquisitions of Territory. They say this would be holding out a premium for filibustering against Mexico & Cuba, in order to make new slave states." James Grimes of Iowa, one of the Republicans on the Committee of Thirteen, expressed a belief that the Crittenden plan "would disclose itself to be the very reverse of a measure of peace. Raids would at once begin upon the provinces of Mexico; war would ensue; the annexation of Sonora, Chihuahua, Cohahuila, Nuevo Leon, Tamaulipas, and other provinces would follow; they would

22. Lincoln to Lyman Trumbull, December 10, 1860, Lincoln to Elihu Washburne, December 13, 1860, Lincoln to John Defrees, December 18, 1860, and Lincoln to William Seward, February 1, 1861, all *ibid.*, 149, 151, 155, 183; Charles Francis Adams Diary, December 22, 1860, in Adams Family Papers; Kirwan, *Crittenden*, 370, 380–82; Potter, *Lincoln and His Party*, 161. Lincoln also told Duff Green, who came to Springfield as an envoy from President Buchanan, that he could not support the Crittenden Compromise because it would lead to an attempted annexation of Mexico. See Milton, *Eve of Conflict*, 527.

be converted, at the instant of their acquisition from free into slave Territories, and ultimately be admitted into the Union as slave States. Much as I love peace . . . I am not prepared to pay this price for it." [23] Representative Roscoe Conkling of New York predicted that the "hereafter clause" would "amount to a perpetual covenant of war against every people, tribe, and State owning a foot of land between here and Terra del Fuego. It would make the Government the armed missionary of slavery . . . for purposes of land-stealing and slave-planting, we should be launched upon a shoreless and starless sea of war and filibustering." Horace Greeley, a key Republican editor, later explained that his objection to the plan was based on a belief that it would have tempted southerners to filibuster in Mexico, Central America, Cuba and Haiti: "Her Sam Houstons, William Walkers and Bickleys would have plotted at home and plundered abroad, in the character of apostles, laboring to readjust the disturbed equilibrium of the Union." And one could cite numerous other examples to show how prevalent this fear was throughout Republican ranks. [24] To most Republicans it was obnoxious to even consider slavery's extension into

23. August Belmont to Stephen Douglas, December 31, 1860, in Douglas Papers; James W. Grimes to Samuel J. Kirkwood, January 28, 1861, quoted in William Salter, *The Life of James W. Grimes* (New York, 1876), 133.
24. *Congressional Globe*, 36th Cong., 2nd Sess., 651; Horace Greeley, *The American Conflict: A History of the Great Rebellion in the United States of America, 1860–'64* (2 vols.; Hartford, 1864–66), I, 378; Newark *Daily Advertiser*, January 22, 1861, Howard C. Perkins (ed.), *Northern Editorials on Secession* (2 vols.; New York, 1942), I, 254; Cassius Clay to Joseph S. Rollins, January 8, 1861, in Cassius Clay Papers, Filson Club; W. J. Gregg to Lyman Trumbull, February 6, 1861, in Trumbull Papers. Crittenden received a number of letters from northern sympathizers explaining that Republicans opposed his plan because of the incentive that it held out for the expansion of slavery into the Caribbean. See J. P. Ogden to Crittenden, January 19, 1861, Joseph Lea to Crittenden, February 9, 1861, and John Van Buren to Crittenden, February 14, 1861, all in Crittenden Papers, Library of Congress.

the vast area of the tropics, and they killed Crittenden's plan with no hesitation.

The Republican rationale for opposing the "hereafter clause" appears so strange today that it leads to a suspicion that the fear of Caribbean slavery expansion was spurious and that Republicans opposed reconciliation for trivial or malicious reasons. Crittenden, whom Republicans denounced for encouraging Caribbean expansion, had been (except during his early days as a "hawk" in the War of 1812) a vocal anti-imperialist. During the Mexican War he had opposed large acquisitions as the price of peace, and in the 1850s he had attacked filibustering and other schemes to expand southward.[25] At the least it is ironical that a committed antiexpansionist would take the lead in encouraging the very type of expansion he had always opposed, especially if he anticipated that such expansion would be on a large scale. Furthermore, the Republican opposition seems unnecessary in light of the southern failure to annex territory in the Caribbean during the 1850s. After all, southern expansionists had not even been able to bring Slidell's Cuba bill to a vote in 1859. Those in favor of compromise did charge that Republican fears of Caribbean expansion were unrealistic, and some historians have reiterated the accusation. Although few modern historians would agree with Charles Ramsdell's claim that slavery had reached its natural geographical limits by the time of the Civil War, Allan Nevins did say in *The Emergence of Lincoln* that "Republicans could have afforded to swallow the Crittenden Compromise—for the possibilities of slavery expansion were near their end." [26]

Crittenden, in fact, did not believe that his plan would lead to the Caribbean expansion of slavery. The senator not only expressed a willingness to discard the "hereafter

25. *Congressional Globe*, 35th Cong., 1st Sess., 218; *ibid.*, 2nd Sess., Appendix, 155–60; Kirwan, *Crittenden*, 194–95.
26. Joseph Lea to John Crittenden, February 9, 1861, in Crittenden Papers, Library of Congress; Nevins, *Emergence of Lincoln*, II, 403–404; Ramsdell, "Natural Limits of Slavery Expansion," 151–71.

clause" when he became aware of the extent of Republican antipathy to it, but also felt that the ultimate result of the clause would be to completely forestall territorial expansion because North and South would cancel out each other's expansionist drives.[27]

Crittenden's minimizing of the danger of Caribbean slavery expansion, however, did nothing to relieve the sincere anxieties of Republicans. To Republicans, southerners had come close enough in the 1850s to achieving their goal. That Caribbean desires had not been fulfilled in the past was no guarantee that they would not be fulfilled in the future. Republicans remembered the filibustering expeditions, the Cuba bills, the Ostend Manifesto, and similar evidence of southern designs on the tropics and shuddered. Furthermore, Republicans realized that the idea of Caribbean expansion had strong support in the North, particularly in the Democratic party. Presidents Pierce and Buchanan had both been willing to accept the peaceful acquisition of Caribbean slave territory. Republicans had no stranglehold on the presidency, and with Crittenden's "hereafter clause" in effect, a future Democratic administration might further southern plans in the tropics. Senator Henry Wilson of Massachusetts had said earlier in the year that "dreams of empire" motivated southern leaders; and Republicans, when they vetoed the "hereafter clause," ensured that these dreams would never be fulfilled, at least within the union.[28] The Republican assumption that passage of Crittenden's program would severely endanger the antislavery movement was legitimate, however profound the consequences of that judgment proved to be.

One crucial question concerning Crittenden's plan requires consideration at this point. Did the Republican re-

27. Crittenden to Larz Anderson, copy in the hand of Mrs. Coleman, March 20, 1861, in John Crittenden Papers, Duke University Library, Durham, North Carolina.
28. *Congressional Globe*, 36th Cong., 1st Sess., 571.

jection of the plan really make a difference? Just because the plan was popularly endorsed in many places does not necessarily mean that the southern states would have accepted it and remained in the union. The decision to secede had not been arrived at overnight. Some southern grievances dated back to the very founding of the republic, and secession had been an option commonly discussed in the South for decades. Momentous decisions, so carefully arrived at, are not likely to be reversed for light cause.

Certainly southern fire-eaters such as William Yancey of Alabama, Robert Rhett of South Carolina, Edmund Ruffin of Virginia, Albert Gallatin Brown of Mississippi, and Louis Wigfall of Texas—men who had long agitated for secession—had no use for Crittenden's compromise. Ruffin, for instance, commented even before the Committee of Thirteen was established that he hoped none of the various compromise plans would be successful. A Florida newspaper declared: "We do not want Compromises. We do not want or intend to treat with Black Republicans and abolitionists, until we know that we are free and independent of them." The influential Richmond *Enquirer* denounced the Crittenden proposal as involving "the submission of Southern men, the subjection of Southern States." The *Enquirer* maintained that since the North had not proven true to the original Constitution, there was no reason to expect that it would adhere to the Crittenden amendments if passed. Secessionist Governor Claiborne Fox Jackson of Missouri claimed in his inaugural address that a congressional compromise would "postpone and aggravate the evil, and will utterly fail to reach the disease." The Mississippi commissioner to the Virginia convention considering secession stated: "We ask no compromise and we want none." Such sentiments became stronger once the Confederacy was established. Former secretary of the treasury Howell Cobb of Georgia explained: "There is no compromise that the seceded States would accept. There is not a single member of our Congress in favor of reconstruction upon any terms." [29]

In addition to those southerners who were opposed to *any* compromise, there were others who objected to specific aspects of the Crittenden program, particularly the "hereafter clause." This clause repulsed southern antiexpansionists who felt that it would encourage imperialism. Unionist Reverdy Johnson of Maryland told fellow southerners at the Washington Peace Conference that they should drop the clause and only try to secure the right to extend slavery in the Southwest, because the United States had more than enough territory to sustain its people. A Kentuckian exhorted Crittenden to forget the "hereafter clause" because the "extraordinary thurst [*sic*] for the extension of the 'area of freedom' " caused him "many misgivings for the perpetuity of our institutions." [30] To many southern secessionist expansionists, on the other hand, the "hereafter clause" was a delusive trick that would entice the South to remain in the union but did not guarantee that new lands would ever be acquired for slavery. William Gilmore Simms, for instance, urged a southern congressman to block compromise because the expansion of slavery into Mexico would be better accomplished after secession.[31] James Hammond of South Carolina felt that the Crittenden Compromise was simply irrelevant be-

---

29. Edmund Ruffin Diary, December 17, 1860, in Ruffin Papers; St. Augustine *Examiner*, December 22, 1860; Richmond *Enquirer*, January 22, 29, 1861; *The Messages and Proclamations of the Governors of the State of Missouri* (Columbia, 1922), III, 336; Reese (ed.), *Proceedings of the Virginia State Convention*, I, 56; Howell Cobb to A. R. Wright, February 18, 1861, in Stephens Papers, Library of Congress.

30. Chittenden (ed.), *Debates*, 84–85; Theodore P. Dudley to Crittenden, January 24, 1861, in Crittenden Papers, Library of Congress.

31. William Gilmore Simms to William Porcher Miles, February 22, 1861, in Miles Papers.

cause it merely settled the slavery problem but said nothing of "Taxation & Expenditure"! [32]

However, historians of the secession crisis have concluded that unconditional opponents of the Crittenden plan were in a minority in most of the South from December, 1860, to January, 1861, and would have had trouble securing secession in their states without a boost from the Republican rejection of the proposal. Kenneth Stampp explains that the "only slavery compromise that had an outside chance of satisfying Southerners was Crittenden's. ... It was his plan that congressmen from the upper South demanded when they denounced the others; unquestionably it would have been acceptable to most of the people in the slave states that had not seceded. It was at least conceivable that its passage would have started a reaction against secession leaders in the Deep South and thus prepared the way for eventual reunion." [33]

Studies of individual states confirm Stampp's observations concerning the upper South. The best analysis of Virginia in this period stresses the hopes of many Virginians that the Crittenden Compromise could save the union. Crittenden's plan was "heartily approved in all sections of the state." When the plan failed to win Republican support, the secessionist position in the state was strengthened. Secessionists asserted that Republican opposition proved the

32. James Hammond to [?], January 18, 1861, in Hammond Papers.

33. Stampp, *And the War Came*, 166. Other studies of the secession crisis as a whole substantiate Stampp's findings for the upper South. David Potter commented that Republican hostility to the Crittenden Compromise and other territorial plans was "probably the chief stimulus to secession in the Border states." Albert Kirwan, Crittenden's biographer, agrees. See Potter, *Lincoln and His Party*, 289; Kirwan, *Crittenden*, 366–421. Potter stresses that the Crittenden Compromise was a symbol of territorial settlement. While it was not necessarily the *only* way out of the crisis, it was the program that most of the South united on; Republican failure to offer any substitute for it angered southerners of the border states as much as the initial Republican hostility to the Crittenden plan itself.

"impossibility of redress and the inevitability of the Union's disruption." Accounts of secessionism in North Carolina and Tennessee have reached virtually the same conclusion.[34] Study of the letters and speeches of leaders of the upper South from December, 1860, to March, 1861, as well as analysis of the Washington Peace Conference, reinforces these findings. The Crittenden Compromise had overwhelming support in the upper South.

Governor Isham Harris of Tennessee told his state legislature that Crittenden's compromise line would secure southern rights. Vice-President John Breckinridge felt that Kentucky would not be safe "under any settlement less thorough than this proposed by Mr. Crittenden." Virginia's secession convention approved a resolution of thanks to Crittenden by a 107 to 16 vote and turned down an amendment to the resolution which would have specified that the vote of thanks did not indicate approval of his plan. Virginia's John Brockenbrough informed the Washington Peace Conference that Virginia "and her southern sisters" would accept and abide by the Crittenden resolutions. Daniel Barringer announced that North Carolina's legislature had instructed him that the Crittenden Compromise would be carried "almost with unanimity" in North Carolina if adopted by the conference. Kentucky's legislature passed a resolution accepting the plan even before the Peace Conference began, and its representative, James B. Clay, announced: "We want the CRITTENDEN

34. Henry T. Shanks, *The Secession Movement in Virginia, 1847–1861* (Richmond, 1934), 133, 128; Joseph Carlyle Sitterson, *The Secession Movement in North Carolina* (Chapel Hill, 1939), 202; J. Milton Henry, "The Revolution in Tennessee, February, 1861, to June, 1861," *Tennessee Historical Quarterly*, XVIII (1959), 101; Mary R. Campbell, *The Attitude of Tennesseans Toward the Union, 1847–1861* (New York, 1961), 137, 161–62, 166; Mary R. Campbell, "The Significance of the Unionist Victory in the Election of February 9, 1861, in Tennessee," *East Tennessee Historical Society's Publication*, No. 14 (1942), 20.

resolutions. . . . Almost the entire South, with Virginia . . . in the advance, tells you that these resolutions will be an acceptable measure of pacification." [35]

Upper South leaders, in advocating Crittenden's program, often announced that it was the "hereafter clause" that made his package attractive. Breckinridge, for instance, called the provision vital to prevent "incessant anti-slavery agitation" in the future. "The Southern States," said the former states' rights candidate for the presidency, "cannot afford to be shut off from all possibility of expansion towards the tropics by the hostile action of the Federal Government." James Mason told the Senate that the Crittenden Compromise would be "of no value" without the "hereafter clause." James Seddon of Virginia stated to the Washington Peace Conference that Virginia "insists on the provision for future territory." [36]

It is paradoxical that the upper South, which had only given moderate support to the Caribbean movement during the 1850s, was so insistent on the "hereafter clause" as the price of maintaining the union. Mason, for instance, had attached a crippling amendment to Slidell's Cuba bill. Yet at the Washington Peace Conference, Virginia and North Carolina were so intent on emerging from the gathering with an endorsement of the "hereafter clause" that they

35. *Senate Journal of the Extra Session of the Thirty-Third General Assembly of the State of Tennessee, 1861*, 13–14; John C. Breckinridge to Beriah Magoffin (governor of Kentucky), printed in Macon *Daily Telegraph*, January 16, 1861; Reese (ed.), *Proceedings of the Virginia State Convention*, I, 545–48; Chittenden (ed.), *Debates*, 62–63, 280, 295, 321. See also I. P. Hall to John Crittenden, January 8, 1861, and Benjamin I. Darneille to John Crittenden, January 10, 1861, both in Crittenden Papers, Library of Congress. The Kentucky legislature passed its resolutions on January 25.

36. John C. Breckinridge to Beriah Magoffin, printed in Macon *Daily Telegraph*, January 16, 1861; *Congressional Globe*, 36th Cong., 2nd Sess., 403; Chittenden (ed.), *Debates*, 92–93. See also the remarks of Senator Lazarus Powell of Kentucky and former president John Tyler of Virginia in favor of the "hereafter clause" in *Congressional Globe*, 36th Cong., 2nd Sess., 403; Reese (ed.), *Proceedings of the Virginia State Convention*, I, 647. See also Nashville *Daily Union and American*, April 14, 1861.

voted with six northern states in opposing the conference's peace plan after it had eliminated the provision. The Virginia and North Carolina delegates were willing to risk total failure of the conference rather than accept defeat on the "hereafter clause." In addition, delegates from Maryland and Delaware explained that the only reason they voted for the modified program was that they knew they could not pass the preferred "hereafter clause." [37] And three times as many senators from the upper South voted for Crittenden's original plan as for the modified Peace Conference version when the Senate considered both proposals in March, 1861.[38]

The paradox is resolved when the staunch unionism of the section is considered. Economic ties to the North and Northwest aside, the border states knew that their geographical position made it likely that if a civil war broke out between North and South, they would suffer. Desiring to avert war at all costs, border-state leaders looked upon the Crittenden clause as the only feasible means of attracting the Gulf states—which had been far more expansionist in the 1850s—back into the union. A number of Deep South secessionists proclaimed that the South could achieve a tropical empire in a separate Confederacy. The "hereafter clause" was an answer to this challenge. Daniel Barringer put the issue squarely to the Washington Peace Conference: "In my opinion you will never get back the seceded States, without . . . some hope of the acquisition of future territory. They know that when slavery is gathered into a *cul-de-sac*, and surrounded by a wall of free States, it is destroyed. Slavery must have expansion. It must expand by the acquisition of territory which now we do not own." [39]

Barringer's analysis of the secession movement appears to have been correct. An offer of federal protection for slavery expansion, which the "hereafter clause" amounted

37. Chittenden (ed.), *Debates,* 421, 441.
38. *Senate Journal,* 36th Cong., 2nd Sess., 386–87.
39. Chittenden (ed.), *Debates,* 340.

to, might have been an extreme enough measure to block the secession movement in the Gulf states.

Robert Toombs and Jefferson Davis, the two leading Deep South senators, gave indications that passage of Crittenden's plan might have aborted the secession process. On the surface, these determined states' rights advocates were secessionists when Congress convened in December, 1860, after Lincoln's election. Early in December Toombs had advocated withdrawal from the union in a speech to the Georgia legislature. On December 13, Toombs and Davis joined with twenty-eight other southern congressmen in a public telegram to the South stating that "all hope for relief in the Union is exhausted." And in the Committee of Thirteen both men joined with Republicans in voting against Crittenden's compromise.[40]

But neither senator excluded the possibility of compromise if Republicans were willing to cooperate. Davis, a lukewarm secessionist at best, urged as late as January 4, 1861, that Mississippi delay secession until after Lincoln's inauguration. Toombs, though one of the South's most ardent fire-eaters, faced considerable opposition from unionist Alexander Stephens for control of Georgia. Stephens had a large popular following. To push Georgia into secession, Toombs had to prove that Republicans would not compromise with the South. Had Republicans accepted Crittenden's plan, Toombs might have had to embrace the compromise to retain statewide political power.[41]

40. Macon *Daily Telegraph*, December 4, 17, 1860; New Orleans *Daily Delta*, December 15, 1860; *New Hampshire Patriot*, December 19, 1860.

41. Strode, *Jefferson Davis*, 362–63, 373; Ranck, *Albert Gallatin Brown*, 202; Jefferson Davis to John J. Pettus, January 4, 1861, in Davis Papers, Mississippi Department of Archives and History; New Orleans *Daily Delta*, December 30, 1860; J. Henly Smith to Alexander Stephens, December 20, 1860, in Stephens Papers, Library of Congress. Strode asserts that Davis, feeling the South was unprepared militarily, held out against secession as long as he felt that there was a chance to reach a settlement with the North.

The evidence is overwhelming that both Davis and Toombs would have accepted the Crittenden Compromise had Republicans backed it. Toombs announced to the Senate on January 7, 1861, that he would have accepted the Crittenden proposals and that he would still accept them. No Republican rose to debate the point. Toombs also told Crittenden privately that though he preferred secession or a more strongly pro-South compromise, he would accept the Kentuckian's plan because Georgia approved it. Stephen Douglas confirmed Toombs's public assertion in a March 2 speech, and both Douglas and George Pugh informed the Senate that Jefferson Davis also had favored the plan. Douglas declared that Davis, "when on the committee of thirteen, was ready, at all times, to compromise on the Crittenden proposition." [42]

The "hereafter clause" seems to have been mainly responsible for their willingness to accept the proposals. Toombs told the Senate in his January speech that the plan would have enabled northerners to control the "whole continent to the north pole" and southerners to control the whole continent "to the South pole." [43]

Whether a sufficient number of lower South leaders would have disavowed secession in return for Republican adherence to the Crittenden plan so that the union could have been preserved is one of those questions that can never be answered with certainty. Unquestionably the "hereafter clause," in conjunction with Crittenden's proposals regarding personal liberty laws and the security of the slave system in the southern states, would have gone far toward meeting southern complaints. The compromise also would have kept the upper South in the union, which in turn might have had an impact on the Deep South. A Con-

42. *Congressional Globe*, 36th Cong., 2nd Sess., 270, 1390–91; Samuel S. Cox, *Union-Disunion-Reunion: Three Decades of Federal Legislation* (Providence, 1885), 77.
43. *Congressional Globe*, 36th Cong., 2nd Sess., 270.

federacy without Virginia and the other states of the upper South that eventually seceded would have been in a very weak position militarily. Former vice-president John Breckinridge claimed in Congress on March 26, 1861, that the Crittenden plan would have prevented the secession of every state except South Carolina if it had been adopted early enough in December, 1860.[44]

In 1860–1861, secession was far more than a mere reaction to Lincoln's election. It resulted from the gradual alienation of much of the Deep South from both the northern Democratic party and the union. Whether southerners such as John Slidell, Robert Toombs, and Judah P. Benjamin would have supported secession as they did in 1860 had the Cuba bill been passed in 1859, or Caribbean extension been achieved through other means, can never be known. But the collapse of all attempts to extend slavery into the tropics unquestionably reminded some southern leaders of their section's growing inferiority and reinforced already existing secessionist tendencies. Benjamin had urged Secretary of State Cass in 1857 to favor southern expansion into Lower California, saying, "Let your policy be directed to affording the South legitimate expansion and she will forget all about Kansas, as unworthy of a struggle, whilst her individual energies can be bent on her development in regions where our future is plainly marked out for us." [45] The Buchanan administration had committed its resources in an attempt to meet such demands, but no substantive results came from the effort. By 1861, many southern leaders were beyond relying on the good intentions of northern Democrats.

Southern expansionists recognized, furthermore, that

44. *Ibid.*, Special Session of the Senate, 1507.
45. Benjamin to Lewis Cass, 1857 (exact date not given), quoted in Woodford, *Cass*, 307; Fayetteville *Arkansian*, October 18, 1860. See also manuscript in John Henry Brown's hand dated 1860, in John Henry Brown Papers.

the responsibility for Buchanan's failure to get Congress to act rested with the Republican party and its opposition to slavery expansion. Republican intractability culminated in the destruction of Crittenden's program because it would have permitted the spread of the institution southward. To southern leaders, opposition grounded on such motives was intolerable because it testified to the ultimate aim of the North to abolish slavery in the South. Eugene Genovese points out correctly that slaveholders looked on their control of slaves as a "source of power, pride, and prestige, a duty and a responsibility," and that because many southerners regarded slavery as a positive good by the 1850s, they could not accept restrictions on its expansion: "To agree to containment meant to agree that slavery constituted an evil, however necessary for the benefit of the savage Africans." [46] Similar feelings sparked the resurgence of the movement to revive the African slave trade in the Deep South in the 1850s. Slave-trade advocates were "aggressively avowing their belief in the rightness of slavery." Federal laws banning the trade were a "stigma" and a "brand upon slavery." [47]

It is no accident that many Caribbean expansionists were also slave-trade advocates. Pierre Soulé, John McRae, C. A. L. Lamar, and James De Bow were some of the southern leaders who joined both camps. Associate Supreme Court Justice John Campbell wrote former president Pierce in December, 1860, that individuals who had been active in the Quitman and Walker movements were behind the slave-trade agitations. Campbell's observation seems to have been particularly true in the case of Texas, where leading Texas champions of William Walker, such as John Henry Brown, E. H. Cushing, Hardin Runnels, A. P. Wiley, and Francis Lubbock, strongly endorsed reopening the

46. Genovese, *Political Economy of Slavery*, 250, 270.
47. Ronald T. Takaki, *A Pro-Slavery Crusade: The Agitation to Reopen the African Slave Trade* (New York, 1971), 21, 70.

slave trade. Texans, faced with the rising cost of slaves ($1,200 to $1,500 in the Texas market), wanted to establish "independent slave-holding states, first in Cuba and more definitely later in Central America, which could be used as local trading stations for a traffic in African slaves." Debates at the Alabama secession convention reveal a similar connection. When Alabamians delineated a tropical confederacy, they called simultaneously for the reopening of the trade. John Morgan, for instance, denounced a proposed ordinance specifically banning the trade because he wanted to "leave it to the generations that may occupy the Gulf of Mexico" to decide how many slaves they might need.[48] It should be noted, however, that although there was a link between the Caribbean and slave-trade movements, each existed independently of the other.[49]

48. John A. Campbell to Franklin Pierce, December 29, 1860, in Franklin Pierce Papers, Library of Congress; Smith (ed.), *History and Debates*, 200, 257; Fornell, "Texans and Filibusters," 411, 414–20; Fornell, *Galveston Era*, 215–19, 224. Antiexpansion delegates at the Alabama convention appear to have been against the slave trade. See a speech of William R. Smith, in Smith (ed.), *History and Debates*, 200–206.

49. Ronald Takaki has pointed out that a number of the leading Caribbeanists, such as Albert G. Brown, John Slidell, Robert Toombs, and Lawrence Keitt, were antitrade. See Takaki, *Pro-Slavery Crusade*, 104, 166, 173, 177. Fornell has noted a number of exceptions in Texas. See Fornell, *Galveston Era*, 225. In addition it seems unlikely that slave-trade proponents would desire Cuba for the purpose of facilitating African operations. Cuba, under Spanish rule, and despite British pressure, remained a vital center for the trade in the 1850s. American acquisition could not have enhanced its possibilities as a trade base. It might have led to more serious attempts by the American Navy to suppress the trade. Northern Democrats, in fact, frequently argued for annexing Cuba on the very basis that such action would speed the trade's end. It should also be mentioned that Takaki has stressed that the African slave trade movement had secessionist underpinnings. See Takaki, *Pro-Slavery Crusade*, 27–31. The weight of the argument in this study has been that the Caribbean movement was unionist in essence. Certainly expansionist spokesmen such as Alexander Stephens and John Slidell saw tropical extension of slavery as a means of working within the national political system.

Caribbean expansionism in the 1850s was a positive affirmation of the southern way of life as well as an attempt to guarantee "southern rights" within the union. But by 1860, southerners had lost confidence in their ability to preserve that way of life as part of the United States. The failure of the Caribbean movement paralleled other southern disappointments in national politics, and the rejection of Crittenden's "hereafter clause" marked one of the final blows to southern unionism.

The essence of the Caribbean movement lay in the hope of its fervent exponents that through tropical expansion the South could maintain a viable political position within the union. A minority of the Caribbean expansionists, however, were secessionists. Although there was no formal plan to achieve tropical expansion after secession, the issue was used as a propaganda tool during the debate over withdrawal from the union.

At the time of the Crittenden controversy, many disunionists were informing the southern public that a seceded South, free from vacillating northern Democrats and hostile Republicans, could extend slavery into the tropics and create one of the greatest empires in the history of mankind. Further efforts to extend slavery within the union, they claimed, would prove futile. Republican power in the Senate would preclude the peaceful acquisition of tropical lands. And northern Democrats would never cooperate with expansionist schemes to add territory through war and filibustering—the only feasible means to extend southward. Certainly Buchanan and Pierce had proved unwilling to endorse such tactics. Alabama firebrand William Samford expressed the disillusionment of southern radicals with the northern Democratic party when he wrote in October, 1858: "Indefinite ideas of Southern advantage to result from Mr. Buchanan's election . . . preoccupied the Southern mind before its inauguration—Kansas, Cuba, South America all loomed up as inviting Southern *expan-*

sionism. . . . The dream has been sadly disregarded." [50] Withdrawal from the union, however, offered the South an alternative to forfeiting expansionist hopes and accepting a permanent subordinate status.

Jefferson Davis had hinted of an imperial destiny beyond the union in his Jackson, Mississippi, speech on Cuba in 1859, and in the late 1850s other southern spokesmen embraced the vision. Samford ran for governor of Alabama in 1859 as an independent Southern Rights candidate and advocated the formation of a new country that would extend from the upper South through Mexico, Cuba, and South America. Virginia disunionist Edmund Ruffin remarked in his diary that "abolition influence" had obstructed the drive into the Caribbean and that slave expansion into the West Indies awaited secession. The Vicksburg *Weekly Sun* blamed Republicans for the failure of tropical expansion and urged secession so that the South might "extend her institutions over Mexico, Cuba, San Domingo and other West India Islands and California, and thereby become the most powerful Republic that ever the sun shone upon." [51]

When news of Lincoln's election reached the South, secessionists played on the widespread southern interest in Caribbean expansion as a means of persuading the undecided (and perhaps, of bolstering their own self-confidence) that withdrawal from the union would bring prosperity and greatness. Georgia state senator Philemon Tracy, in a Macon speech, cited Lincoln's opposition to new slave states and warned: "In the Union you can not have

50. William F. Samford to Clement C. Clay, October 20, 1858, in Clement C. Clay Papers, Duke University, Durham, North Carolina.
51. William F. Samford Scrapbooks, in William F. Samford Papers, Alabama Department of Archives and History, Montgomery; Edmund Ruffin Diary, April 20, 1858, in Ruffin Papers; Vicksburg *Weekly Sun*, October 29, 1860, quoted in Rainwater, *Mississippi*, 75. See also Charleston *Mercury*, January 24, 1859; speech of Spencer Adams in Mobile *Daily Mercury*, February 18, 1860, in Samford Papers; Samuel Walker, "The Diary of a Louisiana Planter," entry for December 19, 1859, in Samuel Walker Papers.

an inch of new territory. Out of it, Mexico and Central America invite us. Like ripe fruit, they will fall at our feet almost without need to shake the tree." The Natchez *Free Trader* spoke of a vast slave confederacy with "thousands of Southern sails" whitening the Gulf of Mexico and making it a "Southern lake." Former United States senator Matthias Ward told Texans in a public letter that land would be acquired from Mexico after independence. A book review in the Charleston *Mercury* spoke of acquiring Chihuahua and "all the Gulf country" once the South shook itself free of "the Puritans—and the devil!" The congregation of St. Peter's Episcopal Church in Charleston heard Rector William Prentiss tell them that God willed that they should leave the union and establish a slave empire in the tropics. The Augusta *Daily Constitutionalist* envisioned post-secession slavery as spreading "South to Brazil and from her till stopped by snow." But it was probably the Memphis *Daily Appeal* that conceived the most spectacular slavery utopia. Soon a slave "empire" would arise, extending from "San Diego, on the Pacific ocean, thence southward along the shore line of Mexico and Central America, *at low tide*, to the Isthmus of Panama; thence South—still South!—along the western shore line of New Granada and Ecuador, to where the southern boundary of the latter strikes the ocean; thence east over the Andes to the head springs of the Amazon; thence down the mightiest of 'inland seas,' through the teeming bosom of the broadest and richest delta in the world, to the Atlantic Ocean." With "good luck," Cuba, Jamaica, and "all the other islands of the Gulf" would be included.[52]

Delegates to state secession conventions invoked similar

52. Macon *Daily Telegraph*, November 27, 1860; Natchez *Free Trader*, November 24, 1860, quoted in Rainwater, *Mississippi*, 75–76; Charleston *Mercury*, December 7, 1860; *Texas State Gazette*, February 16, 1861; Augusta *Daily Constitutionalist*, December 4, 1860; Memphis *Daily Appeal*, December 30, 1860; H. Shelton Smith, *In His Image, But ... Racism in Southern Religion, 1780–1910* (Durham, 1972), 172.

images. At the Alabama gathering, James Dowdell said that a seceded South would acquire Central America for slavery, and John Morgan predicted that the South would occupy the Gulf of Mexico and rule over the "Islands of the adjacent seas." The representatives from already seceded Louisiana to the Texas secession convention urged Texans to join Louisiana in the Confederacy because the two states should cooperate in protecting their extended Gulf coast and in acquiring "the entire control of the Gulf of Mexico in due time." In a public letter, William T. Avery of Tennessee told his constituents to join the Confederacy because in the union, Tennessee would be "cut off forever" from the "peaceful spread of empire." [53]

The Caribbean euphoria persisted into the early days of the Confederacy. An Alabamian wrote to Alexander Stephens of a Confederacy including Mexico "as early as possible," as well as "Brazil, New Granada, and all other Slave states on this continent." [54] A Georgia newspaper asserted that expansion into Central America was the "birthright" of the new nation:

> This is destiny, and God grant that it may be accomplished without drawing the sword. But it must be accomplished, because Providence designs the spreading out of African slavery into regions congenial and suitable to its prosperity. Such regions are presented in Nicaragua, Honduras, Chihuahua, Tamaulipas in which our omnipotent staples will flourish beneath the plastic hand of black labor. When these golden visions become realities, when we shall feed the nations, as well as supply their looms and spindles, with raw material, then will the wisdom and prescience of the founders of our new Government be vindicated—then will the proudest nations of the earth come to woo and worship at the shrine of our imperial confederacy.[55]

53. Smith (ed.), *History and Debates*, 200, 236–37, 257; *Texas State Gazette*, February 16, 1861.
54. C. W. H. Haish (?) to Alexander Stephens, February 14, 1861, in Stephens Papers, Library of Congress.
55. Macon *Daily Telegraph*, February 28, 1861.

The question arises as to whether these dreams of empire were only flights of rhetoric for propaganda purposes. Did such visions have an influence on the secession movement? Did secessionists sincerely believe that withdrawal would pave the way for a slave empire in the tropics? If so, did such beliefs actually affect their actions? If Republican politicians of the time are to be believed, tropical expansion motivated many southern disunionists. Republicans frequently opposed Caribbean expansion in the 1850s on the very basis that the South sought new slave territory in the union so as to strengthen her hand if she wanted to secede, and in 1860 they felt that their bad dreams were coming true.[56]

Orris Ferry, a Connecticut representative, explained secession this way to Congress: "Let but the ties which bind the States to the Federal government be broken, and the leaders of the rebellion see glittering before them the prizes of a slaveholding empire, which, grasping Cuba with one hand, and Mexico with the other, shall distribute titles, fame and fortune, to the foremost in the strife. Such, in my opinion, is the real origin of the present revolt, and such are the motives which inspire its leaders." The New York *Tribune* asserted that the South believed that only the union impeded acquisition of a great empire in "Mexico, Central America, Cuba, and perhaps Hayti."[57]

Even before Abraham Lincoln's inauguration in March, 1861, Republicans professed to see indications that southerners had activated their Caribbean programs. George Boutwell of Massachusetts told his fellow delegates to the Washington Peace Conference that the seven seceded Gulf

56. See for instance speeches by Senator Jacob Collamer of Vermont (February 21, 1859) and Representative John J. Perry of Maine (May 29, 1860), in *Congressional Globe*, 35th Cong., 2nd Sess., 1188; *ibid.*, 36th Cong., 1st Sess., Appendix, 382. See also New York *Daily Times*, October 21, 1856.
57. *Congressional Globe*, 36th Cong., 2nd Sess., 552; New York *Tribune*, December 3, 1860.

states were "already looking to Mexico" and "all her neighbors." David Field of New York predicted at the same gathering that the Confederacy planned to enter a "new career of conquest." [58]

Blaming secession on a conspiracy of tropical expansionists was, of course, good politics. The Republican image of southern secessionists as greedy land-hungry rebels helped arouse the northern public against the Confederacy just as attacks against the Mexican War as a slave conspiracy had incited northern anger fifteen years earlier. Moreover, this tactic offered a facile means of dismissing the very constitutional issues that Confederate leaders emphasized to justify their withdrawal from the union.

If, in fact, Republican leaders did employ such arguments for mere propaganda effect, their private correspondence should have been devoid of such pronouncements. But this is not the case. To Francis Blair, Sr., the "programme of this grand Southern Republic" was "the subjection of the Northern States to their policy as well as Mexico and the Tropics." He told his son that the vision that beckoned Robert Rhett's followers was *Empire across this continent to the Pacific, and down through Mexico to the other side of the great Gulf and over the Isles of the sea &c &c.*" Charles Francis Adams enlisted Henry Adams' aid for union diplomacy by arguing: "The Southern confederacy will be aggressive and more slaves and more cotton will be the cry. In spite of England the slave-trade will flourish and their system will spread over Mexico and Central America." [59]

---

58. Chittenden (ed.), *Debates*, 101, 168.
59. Francis P. Blair, Sr. (?) to Francis P. Blair, Jr. (?), November 22, 1860, in Blair Family Papers, Library of Congress; Charles Francis Adams to Henry Adams, August 25, 1861, in Worthington Chauncey Ford (ed.), *A Cycle of Adams Letters, 1861–1865* (Boston, 1920), I, 36. Charles Adams wanted Henry Adams to support the union politically in his book reviews concerning the cotton question.

The fact that unionists who were not Republican party leaders felt the same way offers more convincing proof. David Campbell, a former Virginia governor, wrote in 1857 about how radicals in the South were pushing for a separate confederacy including Cuba, Central America, and Mexico. Moderate John Reagan of Texas, soon to be postmaster general of the Confederacy, claimed in a public letter in May, 1859, that the "revolutionary" leaders of the South believed filibustering and the slave trade to be the two "issues upon which they can most successfully . . . break up the Government and organize a Southern Confederacy." [60]

During the secession winter, many other observers reached similar conclusions. John Campbell felt that for many southerners there was a natural progression from involvement with filibustering to secessionism. A correspondent of Stephen Douglas spoke of a disunionist "dream of a slave republic" that would include Mexico. When a Kentuckian applauded a compromise plan that did not provide for future territory, he claimed that the whole crisis could be traced in "great measure" to the desire of secessionists for the expansion of slavery into future territory.[61] Even English economist John Stuart Mill called for patience with Lincoln's policy toward slavery because the South wanted to plant its peculiar institution in Mexico and Spanish America: "Shall we submit to see fire and sword carried over Cuba and Porto Rico, and Hayti and Liberia conquered and brought back to slavery?" [62]

60. David Campbell to William B. Campbell (former governor of Tennessee), June 30, 1857, in David Campbell Papers, Duke University, Durham, North Carolina; Alexandria *Gazette*, May 12, 1859.
61. John A. Campbell to Franklin Pierce, December 29, 1860, in Pierce Papers; John Dovan to Stephen Douglas, December 13, 1860, in Douglas Papers; Theodore P. Dudley to John Crittenden, January 24, 1861, in Crittenden Papers, Library of Congress.
62. Frank Freidel (ed.), *Union Pamphlets of the Civil War, 1861–1865* (Cambridge, Mass., 1967), I, 340–42. Other hostile interpretations of tropical expansion as the motivation to secession can be

Although it is tempting to conclude from such statements that secession emanated from a dream of Caribbean empire, this would be absurd. Strong secession feelings dated at least to the nullification crisis of 1828–1833. David Potter explains that "the threat of secession became a standard minority weapon" after the Mexican War.[63] Disunionist sentiment certainly antedated the Caribbean movement of the middle and late 1850s.

Also prohibiting such a dramatic conclusion is the fact that not all Caribbean expansionists were secessionists (nor were all secessionists Caribbean expansionists). To give but one example, Alexander Stephens, a leading expansionist throughout the prewar decade, was one of the major holdouts against disunion in the Gulf states in late 1860. Although secessionists discussed tropical expansion as a positive result of withdrawal from the union, they devoted far more attention to grievances with the federal government over such issues as the fugitive slave laws, Republican unwillingness to permit slavery in the West, and John Brown's raid.

Nevertheless, it would be inappropriate to dismiss Caribbean expansionism as irrelevant to the secession movement. Tropical expansion was more than an exercise in propaganda. If southern empire held a subordinate position in secessionist rhetoric, it may be partly because southerners were desperately trying to justify their actions on constitu-

---

seen in a pamphlet by John Motley and a book by John Abbott. See Freidel (ed.), *Union Pamphlets*, I, 51; John S. C. Abbott, *South and North* (New York, 1860), 313–14, 336–37. Not all northern opinion was as hostile to secessionist designs on the tropics. The Democratic New York *Herald* stated that with secession the cotton states could "carry out the favorite idea of many Southern statesmen by the absorption of Mexico, and eventually of Cuba and Central America. . . . The prospect—by no means a visionary one—gives us a view of one of the most remarkable republics that the world has ever seen. She might rival Rome in its palmy days." See New York *Herald*, November 17, 1860.

63. Potter, *Lincoln and His Party*, 1.

tional grounds. Only in this way could they sway the South, persuade the North not to resort to force, and influence European thought. The expansion of slavery into the Caribbean might have precluded further expansion of the North as well as have interfered with northern commerce. Talking about the matter would certainly have inflamed sectional tensions and would not have helped to put the question of secession on a constitutional plane. And one could just as easily assert that the idea of Caribbean expansion outside the union made secession palatable to expansionist unionists like Stephens, as argue that Stephens' tardiness in joining the secession movement proves that the idea had little influence on the withdrawal of the South.

In summation, the secessionist call for a tropical confederacy was the culmination of the sectionalization of manifest destiny before the Civil War. The nationalistic impetus of the manifest destiny movement of the 1840s survived in weakened form into the 1850s: questions of national security, particularly relating to assumed British and French threats, still provided a major cause for American concern with the Caribbean region; commercial interests throughout the nation still saw great advantage in tropical annexations; northerners and southerners still believed that it was the nation's mission to uplift supposedly inferior races inhabiting equatorial climes. But when southern secessionists called for a tropical empire, they thoroughly shed the nationalistic overtones of manifest destiny. Sectional destiny had supplanted American destiny.

Southerners, however, lacked the means to accomplish expansion into the tropics on their own; for the Confederacy was organized on the basis of tremendous miscalculation. Many secessionists believed that Lincoln would not dare oppose secession by war, and that if he did, the South had the means to resist. Lincoln, however, decided to force the issue, and soon the South was engaged in a fight for survival. As total war began to grip the North American continent that spring of 1861, southern leaders found themselves with no resources to spare for tropical expansion. In addition, Confederate leaders felt that their cause depended on European aid, and slavery imperialism could hardly have attracted the sympathy of England and France. Both of these nations had long since abolished slavery, and neither was particularly favorable to American expansion in the Caribbean. As dream and reality met, the South's grandiose vision of empire dissolved in the blood of war.

X

The Waning of
the Caribbean Impulse

Given William Yancey's support of William Walker in the late 1850s, he would appear to be an illogical spokesman for anti-imperialism during the secession winter of 1860–1861. But, disturbed by talk at the Alabama secession convention of future prospects for the South in the tropics, he urged restraint: "Our only outlet for expansion must be through Mexico—and I throw it out as a suggestion—that it is, at least, doubtful whether we should wish expansion in that direction. . . . Upon one point I have no doubt, and that is, that we should never extend our borders by aggression and conquest." [1] Yancey was expressing what would quickly become Confederate policy in respect to the Caribbean; and within a few months after the Deep South states left the union, talk of acquiring Cuba, Mexico, Nicaragua, and other lands became exceedingly rare. But during the few days when southern leaders believed they could achieve a bloodless withdrawal, they fell prey to many visions, one of which was the dream of a Caribbean empire.

Southern leaders foresaw boom times following secession: freedom from the prevailing tariff structure and northern dominance in Congress would pave the way to economic growth, direct trade with Europe, and general prosperity. The North would not dare intercede against an independent South because it was too dependent on the cot-

1. Smith (ed.), *History and Debates*, 251.

ton trade. Even if the unlikely happened, and war came, Britain would rescue the South because her industry relied on southern cotton, and she could not afford to see her trade with the South disrupted by hostilities.[2] For a while, events seemed to bear out these optimistic forecasts. President Buchanan offered but slight resistance to secession, some prominent Republicans and northern Democrats urged that the South be permitted to depart in peace, and as late as January the Republican party opposed a force bill to suppress secession.[3]

So long as faith in "King Cotton" blinded southerners to the precarious status of their new nation, expectations of tropical acquisitions were not unreasonable. Article IV, Section 3 of the Confederate Constitution reflected expansionist currents in the new nation by stating that the Confederacy could acquire "new territory," and that in such territory "the institution of negro slavery, as it now exists in the Confederate States, shall be recognized and protected by Congress and by the Territorial government." [4]

2. Russell, *Economic Aspects of Southern Sectionalism*, 184–87, 237; Frank Lawrence Owsley, *King Cotton Diplomacy: Foreign Relations of the Confederate States of America* (Chicago, 1931), 16–17; E. Merton Coulter, *The Confederate States of America, 1861–1865* (Baton Rouge, 1950), 184–85; Potter, *Lincoln and His Party*, 52–54; Stampp, *And the War Came*, 54–55. For a good example of such reasoning, see Governor Joseph Brown's message of November 7, 1860, to the Georgia legislature, in *Journal of the House of Representatives of the State of Georgia, 1860*, 49.

3. Potter, *Lincoln and His Party*, 52–54; Nichols, *American Democracy*, 477; Stampp, *And the War Came*, 54–55. Buchanan's annual message to Congress, on December 3, 1860, stated that although secession was unconstitutional, the president could not prevent it, and the responsibility for action lay with Congress.

4. James D. Richardson (ed.), *Messages and Papers of the Confederacy* (2 vols.; Nashville, 1905), I, 51. Eugene Genovese has hypothesized that had independence been achieved, Confederate expansionism concerning the West Indies would have reached significant proportions, and that war with European powers would have been a likely result. See Eugene Genovese, *The World the Slaveholders Made: Two Essays in Interpretation* (New York, 1969), 228.

Although this provision reflected southern hopes that territory in the American Southwest would join the Confederacy, it also opened the way to Caribbean expansion. A number of Caribbean expansionists, such as Judah P. Benjamin, Robert Toombs, and Stephen Mallory, took positions in President Jefferson Davis' cabinet. Had the Confederacy ever firmly established itself, it might have become a power in the tropics.

Confederate leaders regained their sense of proportion, however, once they perceived the likelihood of war with the North. Projects that would drain resources from the war effort were rejected. The expenditure of large sums of money to purchase Caribbean countries, and the use of southern manpower to conquer tropical lands, were unthinkable in a struggle for survival. The dream of a Caribbean empire became one of the first casualties of the Civil War.

Although fears that aggressive activities in the Caribbean might involve the Confederacy in a two-front war unquestionably retarded the tropical impulse, southern leaders were primarily motivated by a hope that European countries would intervene and guarantee Confederate independence. Though England and France never recognized the Confederacy nor allied themselves with it, they did recognize the Confederacy's belligerency in May, 1861. Both nations came very close to intervening in the war, and England permitted the building of cruisers for the Confederate navy on its soil.

To encourage European nations to help their cause, Confederate officials from the beginning proclaimed peaceful intentions toward foreign countries. Vice-President Stephens, for instance, said in Montgomery early in 1861: "Our policy should be marked by a desire to preserve and maintain peace with all other states and people. If this cannot be done, let not the fault lie at our door." Similarly, Robert Toombs, Confederate secretary of state, stressed to his commissioners in Europe that the main tenet of Confederate foreign policy was "peace and commerce." [5]

Southern leaders concluded that European aid might depend in part on success in reassuring England, France, and Spain that the day of aggressive designs on Caribbean countries had passed. Spain would never help the Confederacy while she felt her ownership of Cuba threatened; England and France would be repulsed by designs to expand slavery into areas where it had been eliminated. Both countries, moreover, had important trade interests in the Caribbean area, and France entertained imperialistic ambitions in respect to Mexico. Conflict with these countries could only harm southern interests. It was from such considerations that the New Orleans *Delta* announced: "Spain has nothing to fear from the South. The Spanish authority in Cuba, so long as it rests upon the basis of institutions similar to our own, cannot be to us an object of jealousy or hostility." [6] A disclaimer of territorial designs would serve a secondary purpose in that it might help to win the friendship and cooperation of republics to the south. Southern leadership in American expansionism in the 1850s had been duly noted by peoples throughout Central and South America and the Caribbean; there was a prevalent fear in those countries that separation from the North was the initial step in a southern imperialistic scheme. In May, 1861, Matias Romero, Mexican minister to Washington, said: "It is believed that the South wishes to acquire Mexican territory for the purpose of introducing the institution of slavery. Mexico will never consent that any human being shall be reduced to slavery in its territory." [7] Lincoln's

5. Macon *Daily Telegraph*, February 12, 1861; Toombs to William Yancey, Pierre Rost, and A. Dudley Mann, March 16, 1861, in Richardson (ed.), *Messages and Papers of the Confederacy*, II, 7; Coulter, *Confederate States*, 183.

6. New Orleans *Delta*, quoted in Dallas *Herald*, March 27, 1861. See also George Fitzhugh, "Cuba: The March of Empire and the Course of Trade," *De Bow's Review*, XXX (1861), 30–42.

7. Matias Romero to William Seward, May 4, 1861, quoted in Maisel, "Mexican Antipathy Toward the South," 226.

ministers to Latin-American republics encouraged this fear in an attempt to discredit the Confederate cause.[8] Once the fighting started, Confederate leaders acted swiftly to guarantee European countries that the era of southern aggression toward the tropics had ended. In July, 1861, Secretary Toombs instructed Charles Helm, Confederate agent to the West Indies: "If you should discover that any apprehension exists in the minds of the people of a design on the part of this government to attempt the acquisition of that island in any manner, whether by purchase or otherwise, you will leave no efforts untried to remove such erroneous belief. It is the policy of the Government of the Confederate States that Cuba shall continue to be a colonial possession of Spain." When Robert Hunter assumed Toombs's office, he reaffirmed these instructions in a dispatch to the three Confederate commissioners to Europe. And expansionist Judah Benjamin, who succeeded Hunter, went so far as to suggest to Paris-based diplomat John Slidell that he work out a tripartite treaty with England and France guaranteeing Spanish ownership of Cuba—the very proposal that, when it was made by England and France in 1852 to the United States, aroused a vehement denunciation from Whig Secretary of State Edward Everett.[9] Such a doctrine would have been anathema to the Caribbean expansionists of the 1850s of both North and South! It marked a radical change for Benjamin, and can be explained only as the result of the pressure of war.

8. Nathan L. Ferris, "The Relations of the United States with South America During the American Civil War," *Hispanic American Historical Review*, XXI (1941), 52–54; Maisel, "Mexican Antipathy Toward the South," 246–49.

9. Toombs to Helm, July 22, 1861, Hunter to William Yancey, Pierre Rost, and A. Dudley Mann, April 24, 1861, and Benjamin to Slidell, May 9, 1863, all in Richardson (ed.), *Messages and Papers of the Confederacy*, II, 47, 74, 284. Ronald Takaki has suggested that similar tactical motivations were behind the decision of Confederate leaders to refrain from reviving the African slave trade. Southern politicians who believed in the justice of reopening the trade sacrificed their principles for the good of the Confederacy. See Takaki, *A Pro-Slavery Crusade*, 231–43.

Confederate representatives in Europe followed their instructions. When the Spanish secretary of foreign affairs told Confederate commissioner Pierre Rost that he had heard from William Seward (Lincoln's secretary of state) that the South planned to conquer Cuba, Rost retorted that Seward's accusations were "disingenuous and untrue" because it was really the North that craved Cuba, "for the profits of commerce." [10]

Confederate envoys to Mexico conveyed similar messages. Through much of the war, Mexico provided a vital break in the Union blockade. Ammunition and other war necessities reached southern forces via the port of Matamoros, and southern cotton was transported to world markets through northern Mexico. A persistent danger that unionist elements in Texas might combine with Mexican forces in a hostile campaign against the South enhanced Mexico's significance. As Frank Owsley explains, "Mexico was from most angles the most vital foreign problem with which the Confederacy had to grapple." [11] The strategic importance of a Mexico friendly to the Confederacy explains why, even before the shelling of Fort Sumter, former Caribbean expansionists urged a nonaggression policy. John Ford, who was appointed by the Texas secession convention to command Texan forces on the Rio Grande, informed the convention's military committee in February, 1861, that he had already assured a Mexican military commander of the Confederacy's peaceful intentions; and in March he wrote the committee: "We must not embroil ourselves with Mexico." Former consul in Vera Cruz John Pickett, who had served in the López expeditions a decade earlier, and who was to become the Confederate representative to the Juárez government, wrote John Forsyth that the main concern of southern diplomacy toward Mexico

10. Pierre Rost to Robert Hunter, March 21, 1862, in Richardson (ed.), *Messages and Papers of the Confederacy*, II, 204.
11. Owsley, *King Cotton Diplomacy*, 88–89.

should be to obtain commercial rights, resolve the fugitive slave controversy, and counterbalance northern influence.[12]

Secretary of State Toombs instructed Pickett to reach an accommodation with Juárez on the lines of his letter to Forsyth. Pickett, however, never succeeded in persuading Juárez of the Confederacy's friendship. Thomas Corwin, Union minister to Mexico, outmaneuvered Pickett, and the latter was discredited in Juárez's eyes. Pickett was so incautious that he even incurred a thirty-day stay in jail for engaging in a brawl. The Confederate government requested his return in late 1861 and did not even bother to replace him, so complete had been his failure.[13]

Confederate leaders had more success dealing with Santiago Vidaurri, now governor of Nuevo León and Coahuila in northern Mexico. Vidaurri, who was independent of Juárez, and who later linked himself with the Maximilian puppet government that Napoleon III established in Mexico in 1863, adopted a permissive policy towards trade with the Confederacy. Juan Quintero, a Mexican resident, was the special Confederate agent to Vidaurri, and he proved a far more able diplomat than Pickett. Relations reached a high point in June, 1861, when Viduarri, fearing that Juárez might pressure him out of power, proposed the annexation of northern Mexico to the Confederacy. Jefferson Davis declined the proposition. Annexation might have provoked war with Juárez. It certainly would have offended many of the people of northern Mexico, given the rise of anti-Americanism south of the Rio Grande in re-

12. John Ford to J. C. Robertson, February 25, 1861, John Ford to the Committee on Public Safety, March 13, 1861, Ernest William Winkler (ed.), *Journal of the Secession Convention of Texas, 1861* (Austin, 1912), 329, 332; John Pickett to John Forsyth, March 13, 1861, John T. Pickett Papers, Library of Congress.

13. James Fred Rippy, "Mexican Projects of the Confederates," *Southwestern Historical Quarterly,* XXII (1919), 293; Owsley, *King Cotton Diplomacy,* 92–118.

cent decades. And Davis must have realized that Vidaurri's quasi-independent status within the Mexican republic portended a stormy relationship with the Confederacy should annexation occur.[14]

Even more remarkable than abstention from Caribbean imperialism was the willingness of Confederate leaders to condone European infringements of the Monroe Doctrine. Throughout the 1850s, southern expansionists had used the spectre of European intervention in Cuba, Mexico, and Central America to justify annexation as a preventive measure. Monroe's noncolonization principle had been constantly invoked by expansionist congressmen and newspapers. Now it was suddenly discarded. Edmund Ruffin, who in the late 1850s had envisioned southern ownership of all the West Indies after secession, in April, 1861 applauded newspaper rumors that France and Spain were going to intervene in Haiti and the Dominican Republic. Ruffin hoped that such involvement might help distract the North from the secession problem. When Napoleon III set up the Maximilian regime, Confederate leaders deemed it vital to assure him that they would not intervene, and that they even approved of what he was doing. John Slidell told Napoleon in an interview that while "there could be no doubt of the bitterness of the Northern people at the success of his arms in Mexico," the South sympathized with the French.[15]

There was also a negative reason for the slackening of southern interest in the tropics. Southern Caribbean expansionists in the 1850s had looked upon acquisitions as a

14. Ronnie C. Tyler, "Santiago Vidaurri and the Confederacy," *The Americas,* XXVI (1969), 66–76; Owsley, *King Cotton Diplomacy,* 122–44.

15. Edmund Ruffin Diary, April 4, 1861, in Ruffin Papers; John Slidell, Memorandum of Interview with Napoleon III, June 18, 1863, and John Slidell to Louis Thouvenal, July 21, 1862, both in Richardson (ed.), *Messages and Papers of the Confederacy,* II, 516, 282–83; Owsley, *King Cotton Diplomacy,* 538–44.

means of satisfying an urgent need to attain a balance of power in the union. Had tropical countries been annexed, it is probable that very few of the vocal expansionists would have actually migrated with their slaves. (The number of southern slaveholders who settled in Kansas certainly was limited.) But increased representation in Congress was of great importance. Once the South withdrew from the union, this note of urgency passed. Sectional greed replaced sectional need as the main motivation for tropical expansionism, and it was a far weaker inducement. The New Orleans *Delta*, hithertofore abrasively expansionist, expressed the passing of urgency in early 1861: "If there was a time when political interests, perhaps temporary political necessities caused the South to desire the acquisition of Cuba, as a slave State ... that time has passed away, together with the necessities and the desires which characterized it." Confederate Secretary of State Robert Hunter expressed the same understanding when he told the Confederate commissioners to Europe: "If a party was found in these States during their connection with the former Union who desired the acquisition of Cuba, it was for the purpose of establishing something like a balance of power in a Government from whose dominant majority they feared oppression and injury. Standing as they now do separated from that Union, they are relieved from all such fears, and can no longer be influenced by such inducements." [16]

Abstention from imperialism, however, by no means implied that the dream of empire had died. Rather, it was sus-

16. New Orleans *Delta*, quoted in Dallas *Herald*, March 27, 1861; Robert Hunter to William Yancey, Pierre Rost, and A. Dudley Mann, April 24, 1861, in Richardson (ed.), *Messages and Papers of the Confederacy*, II, 74. This theme was repeated in other wartime diplomatic correspondence. See Robert Toombs to Charles J. Helm, July 22, 1861, Pierre Rost to Robert Hunter, March 21, 1862, and John Slidell to Louis Thouvenal, July 21, 1862, all in Richardson (ed.), *Messages and Papers of the Confederacy*, 47, 204, 282–83.

pended. Southern victory in the Civil War probably would have led to its resurrection. John Pickett, for instance, was still a believer. Even in his letter to Forsyth he commented about Mexico that sooner or later some "great power should assume the right to intervene in the domestic affairs of that country. . . . I do not deem it necessary to do more than allude in this hasty note to the immense advantages to accrue to the Confederate States in the future from the boundless agricultural and mineral resources of Mexico, as well as the possession of the invaluable inter-oceanic transit of the Isthmus of Tehuantepec. Southward is our destiny." Pickett's expansionism, in fact, partly accounts for the collapse of his mission to Juárez. Imperialistic convictions found their way into his dispatches to the Confederate State Department, and, unfortunately for the Confederacy, the Mexican government frequently intercepted his messages. His comment that Mexicans discovered fighting for the North would quickly find themselves "employed as cotton pickers or hoeing corn" must have particularly warmed Mexican hearts. Pickett vacated his post hoping that the Confederacy would one day divide Mexico with an intervening European power.[17]

John Ford's sudden conservatism also merits cautious acceptance at best. A close reading of his dispatches to Texas military authorities reveals that expansionism may yet have been lurking beneath the surface. In complaining about a Confederate order removing artillery from the Rio Grande area, Ford commented: "It is not in keeping with our true interests to make war upon Mexico *now* and it *may* not be hereafter, yet that is not proof of the Mexican idea of the proper line of conduct for that nation to pursue. She may make the war, and I have no doubt she will if she deems success at all possible." James Reily, a prominent Confed-

17. Pickett to Forsyth, March 13, 1861, in Pickett Papers; Owsley, *King Cotton Diplomacy*, 95–108; Maisel, "Mexican Antipathy Toward the South," 265–80.

erate army official, wrote Postmaster General John Reagan in 1862 that Chihuahua sympathized with the Confederacy, and that the area would "improve by being under the Confederate flag." "We must have Sonora and Chihuahua," he added. "With Sonora and Chihuahua we gain Southern California, and by a railroad to Guaymas render our State of Texas the great highway of nations." [18]

In a sense the southern dream of a tropical slave empire survived even after the Confederate defeat. Following Lee's surrender, thousands of Confederates streamed into tropical countries, particularly Mexico and Brazil. They left the country for a number of reasons: many had lost their property in the Civil War and hoped for a fresh start in a new land; bitterness against the "Yankees," who now would control both federal and state government, was rampant, and many could not bear the thought of living in the new union; emancipation aroused racial fears; some Confederate officials and army officers expected severe punishment; and service in Maximilian's army was an incentive for the militarily inclined.

Fortunately for these people, circumstances made them particularly welcome in Brazil and Mexico. Both the Brazilian government and the Maximilian regime in Mexico desired Confederate immigrants, although Maximilian would not permit the Confederates to fight as a unified body under him. In fact, southerners were encouraged by special incentives. Brazilian bands greeted southern land agents with "Dixie," and the Brazilian government offered land at very cheap rates, provided long-term loans for the voyage to Latin America, supplied temporary food and housing for migrants, and exempted them from military service. Maximilian, hoping that a Confederate influx might help forestall the Juárist partisans opposed to him, offered similar

18. Ford to Committee on Public Safety, March 20, 1861 (my italics), in Winkler (ed.), *Journal of the Secession Convention*, 403; Reily's comment quoted in Rippy, "Mexican Projects," 294.

inducements. Within months, many southerners were part of the mainstream of life in tropical countries. Thomas Reynolds, once governor of Missouri, served as a railroad superintendent for Maximilian. Henry Allen, former governor of Louisiana, edited the Mexican *Times*, a paper subsidized by Maximilian to encourage immigration. Confederate purchasing agent Colin J. McRae became involved in merchant affairs in Spanish Honduras.[19]

Most of the Confederate exiles, however, gravitated to rural colonies primarily devoted to farming. Extensive plantations devoted to the production of corn, cotton, sugar, and watermelons, arose in the São Paulo province of Brazil. The Confederate colony of Carlota was formed some seventy miles to the west of Vera Cruz on land that Juárez had confiscated from the Mexican church. Confederate General Jo Shelby promoted a colony in the Tuxpan area on the eastern coast of Mexico, north of Vera Cruz.

Few of the southerners who made their way to these and other colonies harbored illusions that they could ever truly recreate the life of the Old South in their newly adopted

19. See Andrew F. Rolle, *The Lost Cause: The Confederate Exodus to Mexico* (Norman, 1965); Lawrence F. Hill, "Confederate Exiles to Brazil," *Hispanic American Historical Review*, VII (1927), 192–210; Carl Coke Rister, "Carlota, A Confederate Colony in Mexico," *Journal of Southern History*, XI (1945), 33–50; Blanche Henry Clark Weaver, "Confederate Emigration to Brazil," *Journal of Southern History*, XXVII (1961), 33–53; Alfred J. and Kathryn A. Hanna, "The Immigration Movement of the Empire as Seen Through the Mexican Press," *Hispanic American Historical Review*, XXVII (1947), 220–46. Napoleon III of France also encouraged former United States senator William Gwin of California in a plan to develop the silver mines of Sonora. Nothing came of the enterprise, however. This was partly due to the unexpected intransigence of Maximilian. Pierre Soulé was connected, for a while, with Gwin's efforts. See Hallie M. McPherson, "The Plan of William McKendree Gwin for a Colony in North Mexico, 1863–1865," *Pacific Historical Review*, II (1933), 357–86; Rolle, *The Lost Cause*, 62–65. For a full discussion of Napoleon III's intervention in Mexico, see Alfred J. and Kathryn A. Hanna, *Napoleon III and Mexico: American Triumph Over Monarchy* (Chapel Hill, 1971).

countries; yet some of the planners envisioned the establishment of societies based on slave labor, or a close substitute for slave labor. Maximilian's land decree of September 5, 1865, permitted Confederate immigrants to bring former slaves with them as servants. Article 6 of the decree included fifteen regulations specifically referring to "persons of color" and restricting such servants within a system of peonage for not less than five, or more than ten, years, unless the employer agreed to a change; runaways were to be returned to their owners. Matthew Fontaine Maury, the famous Virginia oceanographer who became Maximilian's commissioner of immigration, hinted of the reestablishment of slavery in Mexico in some of his letters. Brazil still legally allowed slavery, and the institution's presence was attractive to southerners. When Frank McMullen and William Bowen of Texas promoted land in Brazil, they advertised that only southerners with proslavery sentiments would be allowed to colonize on their property.[20] To further entice settlement, land agents like Maury pictured the regions involved in dream language reminiscent of the rhetoric the Caribbean imperialists resorted to in the 1850s: the various colonies, situated in a land of milk and honey, were waiting to be developed by clever and ambitious American settlers and entrepreneurs.[21]

The Confederate colonies, however, constituted a desperate foothold in the tropics rather than a realization of the once vibrant dream of a slave empire. Although a southern youth who traveled to Brazil after the war remembered that many fellow Confederates left for Brazil out of "love of slavery," few blacks accompanied their former masters on the flight southward. Confederate planters in exile us-

20. Rolle, *The Lost Cause*, 135–39, 183–84; Hill, "Confederate Exiles," 203–204; Rister, "Carlota," 43; Hanna and Hanna, "Immigration Movement of the Empire," 238–42; Robert E. Shalope, "Race, Class, Slavery, and the Antebellum Southern Mind," *Journal of Southern History*, XXXVII (1971), 572.
21. Rolle, *The Lost Cause*, 138–39; Rister, "Carlota," 46.

ually did their own work or used native labor. And the colonies were generally pitiful and short lived. Carlota, for instance, never became the beautiful city envisioned by its planners. Rather, it evolved into a town of "ugly half-built blocks" with "crumbling adobe offices" and "shabby clapboard rooming houses." [22] Isolation, disease, floods, pillaging, homesickness, language problems, high prices, poor job opportunities, and a host of other misfortunes took their toll of the expatriates. Within months of their arrival in Brazil, disillusioned southerners swamped American consuls with appeals for aid in returning to the United States. Since the Juárists soon came to power, the Confederate identification with Maximilian ensured a precipitant death for the Mexican settlements. A decisive attack eliminated Carlota even before Maximilian's execution. Some of the exiles, despite the many hardships, remained in their adopted countries. But many wandered from land to land, or returned, often pathetically, to the United States. [23] The first shots on Fort Sumter had necessitated a suppression of the southern dream of a Caribbean empire. The failure of the Confederate colonies brought that dream to an end.

22. Thomas Tolson Gordon, "Reminiscences," typescript, Barker Texas History Center Archives, University of Texas, Austin; Rister, "Carlota," 43; Rolle, *The Lost Cause*, 92.
23. Rolle, *The Lost Cause, passim*; Rister, "Carlota," 38, 47–50; Hill, "Confederate Exiles," 197–99, 208–209; Weaver, "Confederate Emigration," 47–49. The Confederate migration probably totalled from eight to ten thousand persons, of whom about half went to Mexico. The emigrants included people of all classes, but the number of well-known southerners who fled to the tropics is impressive. Besides those whose names were mentioned in the above text, the southern migrants to Mexico included William Preston of Kentucky, former governors Pendleton Murrah of Texas, Thomas Moore of Kentucky, Generals Edmund Kirby-Smith, Hamilton Bee, John Magruder, Sterling Price, and James Slaughter, and former Arkansas congressman Thomas Hindman. Judah Benjamin fled to Cuba and then to England.

Bibliography

~~~~~~

PRIMARY SOURCES

A. PUBLIC DOCUMENTS

"Abolition of Slavery in Cuba." *House Miscellaneous Documents,* 33rd Cong., 1st Sess., No. 79.

Congressional Globe, 1854–61.

"Correspondence Between the Late Secretary of War and General Wool." *House Executive Documents,* 35th Cong., 1st Sess., No. 88.

Documents of the First Session of the Fourth Legislature of the State of Louisiana, 1858.

"Execution of Colonel Crabb and Associates." *House Executive Documents,* 35th Cong., 1st Sess., No. 64.

House Journal of the State of Tennessee, 1857–1858.

"Journal of the Committee of Thirteen." *Senate Reports,* 36th Cong., 2nd Sess., No. 288.

Journal of the Proceedings of the House of Representatives of the State of Florida, 1856.

Journal of the House of Representatives of the State of Georgia, 1860.

Journal of the North Carolina Senate and Assembly, 1858–1859.

Journal of the House of Representatives of the State of South Carolina, 1854.

The Messages and Proclamations of the Governors of the State of Missouri. Vol. III. Columbia, 1922.

"The Ostend Conference." *House Executive Documents,* 33rd Cong., 2nd Sess., No. 93.

Population of the United States in 1860 (U.S. Eighth Census). Washington, D.C., 1864.

Senate Journal of the Extra Session of the Thirty-third General Assembly of the State of Tennessee, 1861.

United States Senate Journal, 1854–61.

B. MANUSCRIPTS

Alabama Department of Archives and History
John Forsyth Papers.
Colin J. McRae Papers.
Benjamin Perry Papers.
William F. Samford Papers.
Barker Texas History Center Archives
A. C. Allen Papers.
John Henry Brown Papers.
Guy M. Bryan Papers.
Edward Burleson, Jr., Papers.
Sam Houston Papers.
Thomas Jefferson Rusk Papers.
Chicago Historical Society
Joseph Medill Papers.
Clemson University Library
Tillman Family Papers.
Duke University Library
David Campbell Papers.
Clement C. Clay Papers.
John Crittenden Papers.
Lawrence Keitt Papers.
Appleton Oaksmith Papers.
Francis Pickens Papers.
Filson Club
Orlando Brown Papers.
Cassius Clay Papers.
Preston Family Papers.
Harvard University Library
John Quitman Papers.
Historical Society of Pennsylvania
James Buchanan Papers.
Library of Congress
Asa Biggs Papers.
Blair Family Papers.
William Burwell Papers.
John Crittenden Papers.
Caleb Cushing Papers.
Jefferson Davis Papers.
James Hammond Papers.
William Marcy Papers.

Personal Papers, Miscellaneous.
John T. Pickett Papers.
Franklin Pierce Papers.
William C. Rives Papers.
Edmund Ruffin Papers.
Alexander Stephens Papers.
John White Stevenson Papers.
Lyman Trumbull Papers.
William Walker Papers.
Louisiana State University Department of Archives and Manuscripts
    Cartwright Family Papers.
    James Foster Papers.
    Miscellaneous Papers.
    John Quitman Papers.
    Southern Filibusters Collection.
Massachusetts Historical Society
    Adams Family Papers.
Mississippi Department of Archives and History
    J. F. H. Claiborne Papers.
    Jefferson Davis Papers.
    John Quitman Papers.
    Quitman Family Papers.
National Archives
    Records of the Department of State, Miscellaneous Letters.
State Archives of North Carolina
    Mrs. Lawrence O'Bryan Branch Papers.
State Historical Society of Wisconsin
    John Fox Potter Papers.
Tennessee State Library and Archives
    John Brenizer Papers.
    John Heiss Papers.
    Lindsley Family Papers.
    Miscellaneous Papers.
    Russwurm Family Papers.
    William Trousdale Papers.
Texas State Archives and Library
    Governors' Letters, Sam Houston.
    Mirabeau Buonaparte Lamar Papers.
    Hugh McLeod Papers.
    John H. Reagan Papers.

Tulane University Library
  Albert Sidney Johnston Papers.
  Samuel Walker Papers.
  William Walker Papers.
University of Chicago Library
  Stephen Douglas Papers.
University of North Carolina Library
  J. F. H. Claiborne Papers.
  Duff Green Papers.
  William Porcher Miles Papers.
  John Quitman Papers.
  Alexander Stephens Papers.
  John Wheeler Papers.
University of Virginia Library
  James Madison Papers.
  John Quitman Papers.
  Virginia Letters Collection.
  William Sidney Thayer Papers.

C. PAMPHLETS

An Authentic Exposition of the K. G. C. by a member of the Order.
  Indianapolis, 1861.
Freidel, Frank, ed. *Union Pamphlets of the Civil War, 1861–1865.*
  Cambridge, Mass., 1967.
*K. G. C.: A Full Exposure of the Southern Traitors; The Knights of
  the Golden Circle.* Boston, 1860.
Pomfrey, J. W. *A True Disclosure and Exposition of the Knights of
  the Golden Circle.* Cincinnati, 1861.
Thrasher, John S. *A Preliminary Essay on the Purchase of Cuba.*
  New York, 1859.

D. PUBLISHED WORKS

Angle, Paul M., ed. *Created Equal?: The Complete Lincoln-Douglas
  Debates of 1858.* Chicago, 1958.
Baker, George, ed. *The Works of William H. Seward.* 5 vols. Boston,
  1884.
Basler, Roy P., ed. *The Collected Works of Abraham Lincoln.* 8 vols.
  New Brunswick, 1953–55.
Beale, Howard K., ed. "The Diary of Edward Bates, 1859–1866."
  *Annual Report of the American Historical Association for the
  Year 1930.* 4 vols. Washington, D.C., 1931–33. Vol. IV.
Boucher, Chauncey S., and Robert P. Brooks, eds. "Correspondence
  Addressed to John C. Calhoun, 1837–1849." *Annual Report of the*

American Historical Association for the Year 1929. Washington, D.C., 1930. pp. 125–533.

Brooks, R. P., ed. "Howell Cobb Papers." *Georgia Historical Quarterly,* VI (1922), 35–84.

Chittenden, L. E., ed. *Debates and Proceedings in the Secret Sessions of the Conference Convention.* New York, 1864.

Cluskey, M. W., ed. *Speeches, Messages and Other Writings of the Hon. Albert Gallatin Brown.* Philadelphia, 1859.

Donald, David, ed. *Inside Lincoln's Cabinet: The Civil War Diaries of Salmon P. Chase.* New York, 1954.

Fitzhugh, George. *Cannibals All, or Slaves Without Masters.* Edited by C. Vann Woodward. Cambridge, Mass., 1960.

Ford, Worthington Chauncey, ed. *A Cycle of Adams Letters, 1861–1865.* Boston, 1920.

Gower, Herschel, and Jack Allen, eds. *Pen and Sword: The Life and Journals of Randal W. McGavock.* Knoxville, 1959.

Helper, Hinton R. *The Land of Gold.* Baltimore, 1855.

Hicks, Jimmie, ed. "Some Letters Concerning the Knights of the Golden Circle in Texas, 1860–1861." *Southwestern Historical Quarterly,* LXV (1961), 80–86.

Johannsen, Robert W., ed. *The Letters of Stephen A. Douglas.* Urbana, 1961.

McKee, Thomas H., ed. *The National Conventions and Platforms of all Political Parties, 1789–1900.* Baltimore, 1900.

Manning, William R., ed. *Diplomatic Correspondence of the United States; Inter-American Affairs, 1831–1860.* 12 vols. Washington, D.C., 1932–39.

Moore, John Bassett, ed. *The Works of James Buchanan.* 12 vols. Philadelphia, 1908–11.

Murray, Amelia. *Letters from the United States, Cuba and Canada.* New York, 1856.

Nevins, Allan, ed. *Diary of John Quincy Adams.* New York, 1928.

Oates, Stephen B., ed. *Rip Ford's Texas.* Austin, 1963.

Official Proceedings of the National Democratic Convention Held in Cincinnati June 2–6, 1856.

Perkins, Howard C., ed. *Northern Editorials on Secession.* 2 vols. New York, 1942.

Phillips, Ulrich B., ed. "The Correspondence of Robert Toombs, Alexander Stephens and Howell Cobb." *Annual Report of the American Historical Association for the Year 1911.* 2 vols. Washington, D.C., 1913. Vol. II.

Pollard, Edward A. *Black Diamonds Gathered In The Darkey Homes of the South.* New York, 1859.

Quaife, Milo Milton, ed. *The Diary of James K. Polk.* 4 vols. Chicago, 1910.

Reese, George H., ed. *Proceedings of the Virginia State Convention of 1861.* 4 vols. Richmond, 1965.

Richardson, James D., ed. *Messages and Papers of the Confederacy.* 2 vols. Nashville, 1905.

————, comp. *Messages and Papers of the President.* 20 vols. Washington, D.C., 1897–1917.

Rowland, Dunbar, ed. *Jefferson Davis, Constitutionalist: His Letters, Papers, and Speeches.* 10 vols. Jackson, 1923.

Scroggs, William O., ed. "Walker-Heiss Papers: Some Diplomatic Correspondence of the Walker Regime in Nicaragua." *Tennessee Historical Magazine,* I (1915), 331–45.

Smith, Robert, ed. *What Happened in Cuba?* New York, 1963.

Smith, William R., ed. *The History and Debates of the People of Alabama.* Montgomery, 1861.

Stampp, Kenneth M., ed. "Letters from the Washington Peace Conference of 1861." *Journal of Southern History,* IX (1943), 394–403.

Sumner, Charles, ed. *The Works of Charles Sumner.* 15 vols. Boston, 1870–83.

White, Robert H., ed. *Messages of the Governors of Tennessee.* 7 vols. Nashville, 1952–67.

Williams, Amelia W., and Eugene C. Barker, eds. *The Writings of Sam Houston.* 8 vols. Austin, 1938–43.

SECONDARY SOURCES

A. MEMOIRS AND REMINISCENCES

Bigelow, John. *Retrospections of an Active Life.* 5 vols. New York, 1909–13.

Cox, Samuel S. *Union-Disunion-Reunion: Three Decades of Federal Legislation.* Providence, 1885.

Doubleday, C. W. *Reminiscences of the 'Filibuster' War in Nicaragua.* New York, 1886.

Foote, Henry S. *Casket of Reminiscences.* Washington, D.C., 1874.

Greeley, Horace. *The American Conflict: A History of the Great Rebellion in the United States of America, 1860–'64.* 2 vols. Hartford, 1864–66.

Harpending, Asbury. *The Great Diamond Hoax.* Edited by James H. Wilkins. 2nd ed. Norman, 1958.

Lea, H. C. "Walker's Last Campaign in Central America." 1881. Florida State Library.

Ratterman, Elleanore. "With Walker in Nicaragua: Reminiscences." *Tennessee Historical Magazine,* I (1915), 315–30.

Reagan, John H. *Memoirs: With Special Reference to Secession and the Civil War.* New York, 1906.

Thomas, Jane. *Old Days in Nashville, Tennessee: Reminiscences.* Nashville, 1897.

Walker, William. *The War in Nicaragua.* Mobile, 1860.

Wheeler, John H. *Reminiscences and Memoirs of North Carolinians.* Columbus, 1884.

B. BOOKS

Alexander, Thomas B. *Sectional Stress and Party Strength.* Nashville, 1967.

Bailey, Thomas. *A Diplomatic History of the American People.* 6th ed. New York, 1958.

Barney, William L. *The Road to Secession: A New Perspective on the Old South.* New York, 1972.

Baughman, James P. *Charles Morgan and the Development of Southern Transportation.* Nashville, 1968.

Bemis, Samuel Flagg, ed. *The American Secretaries of State and Their Diplomacy.* 10 vols. New York, 1927–29.

Bettersworth, John K. *Mississippi: A History.* Austin, 1959.

Boney, F. N. *John Letcher of Virginia: The Story of Virginia's Civil War Governor.* University, Alabama, 1966.

Butler, Pierce. *Judah P. Benjamin.* Philadelphia, 1907.

Caldwell, Robert G. *The Lopez Expeditions to Cuba, 1848–1851.* Princeton, 1915.

Callahan, James Morton. *American Foreign Policy in Canadian Relations.* New York, 1937.

Campbell, Mary R. *The Attitude of Tennesseans Toward the Union, 1847–1861.* New York, 1961.

Carr, Albert Z. *The World and William Walker.* New York, 1963.

Carr, Raymond. *Spain, 1808–1939.* Oxford, 1966.

Channing, Stephen A. *Crisis of Fear: Secession in South Carolina.* New York, 1970.

Claiborne, J. F. H. *Life and Correspondence of John A. Quitman.* 2 vols. New York, 1860.

Clendenen, George C. *Blood on the Border: The United States Army and the Mexican Irregulars.* London, 1969.

Cleveland, Henry. *Alexander H. Stephens in Public and Private.* Philadelphia, 1866.

Connor, Henry G. *John Archibald Campbell: Associate Justice of the United States Supreme Court.* Boston, 1920.

Bibliography

Corwin, Arthur F. *Spain and the Abolition of Slavery in Cuba, 1817–1886.* Austin, 1967.

Coulter, E. Merton. *The Confederate States of America, 1861–1865.* Baton Rouge, 1950.

Craven, Avery O. *The Growth of Southern Nationalism, 1848–1861.* Baton Rouge, 1953.

Dowty, Alan. *The Limits of Isolation: The United States and the Crimean War.* New York, 1971.

Dufour, Charles L. *Gentle Tiger: The Gallant Life of Roberdeau Wheat.* Baton Rouge, 1957.

Dunbar, Willis Frederick. *Lewis Cass.* Grand Rapids, 1970.

Eaton, Clement. *A History of the Old South.* 2nd ed. New York, 1966.

Ettinger, Amos. *The Mission to Spain of Pierre Soulé, 1853–1855.* New Haven, 1932.

Foner, Eric. *Free Soil, Free Labor, Free Men: The Ideology of the Republican Party Before the Civil War.* New York, 1970.

Foner, Philip. *A History of Cuba and Its Relations with the United States.* 2 vols. New York, 1962–63.

Forbes, Robert H. *Crabb's Filibustering Expedition into Sonora, 1857.* Tucson, 1952.

Fornell, Earl. *The Galveston Era.* Austin, 1961.

Freehling, William. *Prelude to Civil War: The Nullification Controversy in South Carolina, 1816–1836.* New York, 1965.

Fuess, Claude M. *The Life of Caleb Cushing.* 2 vols. New York, 1923.

Fuller, John D. P. *The Movement for the Acquisition of All Mexico, 1846–1848.* Baltimore, 1936.

Ganaway, Loomis Morton. *New Mexico and the Sectional Controversy, 1848–1861.* Albuquerque, 1944.

Garrison, Francis Jackson, and Wendell Phillips Garrison. *William Lloyd Garrison: The Story of His Life Told by His Children.* 4 vols. New York, 1889.

Genovese, Eugene. *The Political Economy of Slavery.* New York, 1965.

————. *The World the Slaveholders Made: Two Essays in Interpretation.* New York, 1969.

Goetzmann, William H. *When the Eagle Screamed: The Romantic Horizon in American Diplomacy, 1800–1860.* New York, 1966.

Hamilton, Holman. *Prologue to Conflict: The Crisis and Compromise of 1850.* Lexington, 1964.

Hanna, Albert J. and Kathryn A. *Napoleon III and Mexico: American Triumph over Monarchy.* Chapel Hill, 1971.

Hittell, Theodore H. *History of California.* 4 vols. San Francisco, 1897.

Hughes, W. J. *Rebellious Ranger: Rip Ford and the Old Southwest.* Norman, 1964.

Humphreys, R. A. *The Diplomatic History of British Honduras, 1638–1901.* New York, 1961.

Jaffa, Harry V. *Crisis of the House Divided.* New York, 1959.

Jordan, Winthrop. *White Over Black: American Attitudes Toward the Negro, 1550–1812.* Chapel Hill, 1968.

Katz, Irving. *August Belmont.* New York, 1968.

Kirwan, Albert D. *John J. Crittenden: The Struggle for the Union.* Lexington, 1962.

Klein, Philip S. *President James Buchanan: A Biography.* University Park, 1962.

Knight, Franklin W. *Slave Society in Cuba during the Nineteenth Century.* Madison, 1970.

Langley, Lester D. *The Cuba Policy of the United States.* New York, 1968.

Larson, Roy W. *New Mexico's Quest for Statehood, 1846–1912.* Albuquerque, 1968.

Leyburn, James G. *The Haitian People.* Rev. ed. New Haven, 1966.

McGowan, Edward. *The Strange Eventful History of Parker H. French.* Los Angeles, 1958.

Meade, Robert D. *Judah P. Benjamin: Confederate Statesman.* New York, 1943.

Merk, Frederick. *Manifest Destiny and Mission in American History.* New York, 1963.

Milton, George Fort. *The Eve of Conflict: Stephen A. Douglas and the Needless War.* New York, 1934.

Moore, Albert Burton. *History of Alabama.* University, Alabama, 1939.

Moore, John Bassett, ed. *A Digest of International Law.* 8 vols. Washington, D.C., 1906.

Morrison, Chaplain. *Democratic Politics and Sectionalism.* Chapel Hill, 1967.

Nevins, Allan. *The Emergence of Lincoln.* 2 vols. New York, 1950.
_____. *Ordeal of the Union.* 2 vols. New York, 1947.

Nichols, Roy. *The Disruption of American Democracy.* New York, 1948.
_____. *Franklin Pierce: Young Hickory of the Granite Hills.* Rev. ed. Philadelphia, 1958.

Osterweis, Rollin. *Judah P. Benjamin: Statesman of the Lost Cause.* New York, 1933.

Overdyke, William Darrell. *The Know-Nothing Party in the South.* Baton Rouge, 1950.

Owsley, Frank Lawrence. *King Cotton Diplomacy: Foreign Relations of the Confederate States of America.* Chicago, 1931.

Perkins, Dexter. *The Monroe Doctrine, 1826–1867.* Baltimore, 1933.

Potter, David. *Lincoln and His Party in the Secession Crisis.* New Haven, 1942.

Quisenberry, Anderson C. *Lopez's Expeditions to Cuba, 1850 and 1851.* Louisville, 1906.

Rainwater, Percy Lee. *Mississippi: Storm Center of Secession.* Baton Rouge, 1938.

Ranck, James Byrne. *Albert Gallatin Brown: Radical Southern Nationalist.* New York, 1937.

Rauch, Basil. *American Interest in Cuba, 1848–1855.* New York, 1948.

Reed, Merle E. *New Orleans and the Railroads: The Struggle for Commercial Empire, 1830–1860.* Baton Rouge, 1966.

Rhodes, James Ford. *History of the United States from the Compromise of 1850.* 9 vols. New York, 1900–28.

Rippy, James Fred. *The United States and Mexico.* New York, 1926.

Rister, Carl Coke. *Robert E. Lee in Texas.* Norman, 1946.

Roeder, Ralph. *Juarez and His Mexico.* New York, 1947.

Rolle, Andrew F. *The Lost Cause: The Confederate Exodus to Mexico.* Norman, 1965.

Russell, Robert Royal. *Economic Aspects of Southern Sectionalism, 1840–1861.* Urbana, 1923.

Salter, William. *The Life of James W. Grimes.* New York, 1876.

Schultz, Harold S. *Nationalism and Sectionalism in South Carolina, 1852–1860.* Durham, 1950.

Scroggs, William O. *Filibusters and Financiers: The Story of William Walker and His Associates.* New York, 1916.

Shanks, Henry T. *The Secession Movement in Virginia, 1847–1861.* Richmond, 1934.

Sitterson, Joseph Carlyle. *The Secession Movement in North Carolina.* Chapel Hill, 1939.

Smith, H. Shelton. *In His Image, But . . . Racism in Southern Religion, 1780–1910.* Durham, 1972.

Spencer, Ivor. *The Victor and the Spoils: A Life of William L. Marcy.* Providence, 1959.

Stampp, Kenneth M. *And the War Came: The North and the Secession Crisis, 1860–1861.* Baton Rouge, 1950.

Strode, Hudson. *Jefferson Davis: American Patriot.* New York, 1955.

Sydnor, Charles S. *The Development of Southern Sectionalism, 1819–1848.* Baton Rouge, 1948.

Takaki, Ronald T. *A Pro-Slavery Crusade: The Agitation to Reopen the African Slave Trade.* New York, 1971.

Tansill, Charles. *The Canadian Reciprocity Treaty of 1854.* Baltimore, 1922.

Tyler, Alice. *Freedom's Ferment: Phases of American Social History to 1860.* Minneapolis, 1944.

Wallace, Edward S. *Destiny and Glory.* New York, 1957.

Wallace, Ernest. *Texas in Turmoil, 1849–1875.* Austin, 1965.

Warner, Donald F. *The Idea of Continental Union: Agitation for the Annexation of Canada to the United States, 1849–1853.* Lexington, 1960.

Webb, Walter Prescott. *The Texas Rangers: A Century of Frontier Defense.* 2nd ed. Austin, 1965.

Weinberg, Albert K. *Manifest Destiny: A Study of Nationalist Expansionism in American History.* Baltimore, 1935.

Wells, Damon. *Stephen Douglas: The Last Years, 1857–1861.* Austin, 1971.

Williams, Frances Leigh. *Matthew Fontaine Maury: Scientist of the Sea.* New Brunswick, 1963.

Wiltse, Charles M. *John C. Calhoun.* 3 vols. New York, 1944–51.

Windrow, John Edwin. *John Berrien Lindsley: Educator, Physician, Social Philosopher.* Chapel Hill, 1938.

Woodford, Frank B. *Lewis Cass: The Last Jeffersonian.* New Brunswick, 1950.

C. ARTICLES

Bass, John M. "William Walker." *American Historical Magazine,* III (1898), 207–22.

Bridges, C. A. "The Knights of the Golden Circle: A Filibustering Fantasy." *Southwestern Historical Quarterly,* XLIV (1941), 287–302.

Broussard, Ray. "Governor John A. Quitman and the López Expeditions of 1851–1852." *Journal of Mississippi History,* XXVIII (1966), 103–20.

Bryan, Edward B. "Cuba and the Tripartite Treaty." *Southern Quarterly Review,* IX (1854), 16.

Callahan, James Morton. "The Mexican Policy of Southern Leaders Under Buchanan's Administration." *Annual Report of the Ameri-*

can Historical Association for the Year 1910. Washington, D.C., 1912. pp. 135–51.

Campbell, Mary R. "The Significance of the Unionist Victory in the Election of February 9, 1861, in Tennessee." *East Tennessee Historical Society's Publications,* No. 14 (1942), 11–30.

Coatsworth, John H. "American Trade with European Colonies in the Caribbean and South America, 1790–1812." *William and Mary Quarterly,* XXIV (1967), 243–61.

Crenshaw, Olliger. "The Knights of the Golden Circle." *American Historical Review,* XLVII (1941), 23–50.

Curti, Merle. "George N. Sanders—American Patriot of the Fifties." *South Atlantic Quarterly,* XXVII (1928), 79–87.

————. "Young America." *American Historical Review,* XXXII (1926), 34–55.

Diket, A. L. "Slidell's Right Hand: Emile La Sère." *Louisiana History,* IV (1963), 177–205.

Dunn, Roy Sylvan. "The KGC in Texas, 1860–1861." *Southwestern Historical Quarterly,* LXX (1967), 543–73.

Durden, Robert R. "J. D. B. De Bow: Convolutions of a Slavery Expansionist." *Journal of Southern History,* XVII (1951), 441–61.

Ely, Roland T. "The Old Cuba Trade: Highlights and Case Studies of Cuban-American Interdependence during the Nineteenth Century." *Business History Review,* XXXVIII (1964), 456–78.

Ferris, Nathan L. "The Relations of the United States with South America During the American Civil War." *Hispanic American Historical Review,* XXI (1941), 51–78.

Fitzhugh, George. "Cuba: The March of Empire and the Course of Trade." *De Bow's Review,* XXX (1861), 30–42.

Fornell, Earl W. "Texans and Filibusters in the 1850's." *Southwestern Historical Quarterly,* LIX (1956), 411–28.

Franklin, John Hope. "The Southern Expansionists of 1846." *Journal of Southern History,* XXV (1959), 323–38.

Gibson, George H. "Opinion in North Carolina Regarding the Acquisition of Texas and Cuba, 1835–1855." *North Carolina Historical Review,* XXXVII (1960), 1–21, 85–201.

Green, Fletcher M. "Duff Green: Industrial Promoter." *Journal of Southern History,* II (1936), 29–42.

Gunderson, Robert G. "William G. Rives and the 'Old Gentlemen's Convention.'" *Journal of Southern History,* XXII (1956), 459–76.

Hanna, Alfred J. and Kathryn A. "The Immigration Movement of the Empire as Seen Through the Mexican Press." *Hispanic American Historical Review,* XXVII (1947), 220–46.

Hart, Charles Desmond. "Why Lincoln Said 'No': Congressional Attitudes Toward Slavery Expansion, 1860–1861." *Social Science Quarterly*, II (1968), 732–41.

Henry, J. Milton. "The Revolution in Tennessee, February, 1861, to June, 1861." *Tennessee Historical Quarterly*, XVIII (1959), 99–119.

Hudson, Randall O. "The Filibuster Minister: The Career of John Hill Wheeler as United States Minister to Nicaragua, 1854–1856." *North Carolina Historical Review*, XLIX (1972), 280–97.

Hill, Lawrence F. "Confederate Exiles to Brazil." *Hispanic American Historical Review*, VII (1927), 192–210.

James, D. Clayton. "Tribulations of a Bayou Boeuf Store Owner, 1853–1857." *Louisiana History*, IV (1963), 243–56.

Janes, Henry L. "The Black Warrior Affair." *American Historical Review*, XII (1907), 280–98.

Johannsen, Robert W. "Stephen Douglas and the American Mission." In *The Frontier Challenge: Responses to the Trans-Mississippi West*. Edited by John G. Clark. Lawrence, 1971, pp. 111–40.

Johannsen, Robert W. "Stephen A. Douglas and the South." *Journal of Southern History*, XXXIII (1967), 26–50.

Kenny, William Robert. "Mexican-American Conflict on the Mining Frontier, 1849–1852." *Journal of the West*, VI (1967), 582–91.

Klement, Frank. "Carrington and the Golden Circle Legend in Indiana during the Civil War." *Indiana Magazine of History*, LXI (1965), 31–52.

Long, Durwood. "Alabama Opinion and the Whig Cuban Policy, 1849–1851." *Alabama Historical Quarterly*, XXV (1963), 262–79.

Lythgoe, Dennis. "Negro Slavery in Utah." *Utah Historical Quarterly*, XXXIX (1971), 40–54.

McPherson, Hallie M. "The Plan of William McKendree Gwin for a Colony in North Mexico, 1863–1865." *Pacific Historical Review*, II (1933), 357–86.

Maury, Matthew Fontaine. "Valley of the Amazon." *DeBow's Review*, XIV (1853), 449–60, 556–67, XV (1863), 36–43.

Melvin, Philip. "Stephen Russell Mallory: Southern Naval Statesman." *Journal of Southern History*, X (1944), 459–76.

Merk, Frederick. "A Safety Valve Thesis and Texan Annexation." *Mississippi Valley Historical Review*, XLIX (1962), 413–36.

Moore, J. Preston. "Pierre Soulé: Southern Expansionist and Promoter." *Journal of Southern History*, XXI (1955), 203–23.

"Nicaragua and the Filibusters." *Blackwood's Magazine*, LXXIX (1856), 314.

Patterson, William J. "United States Aggrandizement, 1850–1860: The Walker Expeditions as an Illustrative Case." *Proceedings of the South Carolina Historical Association* (1947), 9–20.

Pratt, Julius. "John L. O'Sullivan and Manifest Destiny." *New York History*, XIV (1933), 213–34.

Ramsdell, Charles W. "The Natural Limits of Slavery Expansion." *Mississippi Valley Historical Review*, XVI (1929), 151–71.

Rippy, James Fred. "Anglo-American Filibusters and the Gadsden Treaty." *Hispanic American Historical Review*, V (1922), 155–80.

————. "Border Troubles Along the Rio Grande, 1848–1860." *Southwestern Historical Quarterly*, LXX (1967), 91–111.

————. "Diplomacy Regarding the Isthmus of Tehuantepec, 1848–1860." *Mississippi Valley Historical Review*, VI (1919–20), 503–31.

————. "Mexican Projects of the Confederates." *Southwestern Historical Quarterly*, XXII (1919), 291–317.

Rister, Carl Coke. "Carlota: A Confederate Colony in Mexico." *Journal of Southern History*, XI (1945), 33–50.

Scroggs, William O. "Alabama and Territorial Expansion Before 1860." *Gulf States Historical Magazine*, II (1903), 172–85.

————. "William Walker's Designs on Cuba." *Mississippi Valley Historical Review*, I (1914), 198–211.

————. "William Walker and the Steamship Corporation in Nicaragua." *American Historical Review*, X (1904), 792–811.

Sears, Louis M. "Slidell and Buchanan." *American Historical Review*, XXVII (1922), 709–30.

Shalope, Robert E. "Race, Class, Slavery, and the Antebellum Southern Mind." *Journal of Southern History*, XXXVII (1971), 557–74.

Shearer, Ernest C. "The Callahan Expedition, 1855." *Southwestern Historical Quarterly*, LIV (1951), 430–51.

Stout, Joe A., Jr. "Henry A. Crabb: Filibuster or Colonizer?" *American West*, VIII (1971), 4–9.

————. "Joseph C. Morehead and Manifest Destiny: A Filibuster in Sonora, 1851." *Pacific Historian*, XV (1971), 62–70.

Tate, Merze. "Slavery and Racism as Deterrents to the Annexation of Hawaii, 1854–1855." *Journal of Negro History*, XLVII (1962), 1–18.

TePaske, John J. "Appleton Oaksmith: Filibustering Agent." *North Carolina Historical Review*, XXXV (1958), 427–47.

Tyler, Ronnie C. "The Callahan Expedition of 1855: Indians or Negroes?" *Southwestern Historical Quarterly*, LXX (1967), 574–85.

————. "Santiago Vidaurri and the Confederacy." *The Americas*, XXVI (1969), 66–76.

Urban, C. Stanley. "The Abortive Quitman Filibustering Expedition, 1853–1855." *Journal of Mississippi History*, XVIII (1956), 175–96.

_____. "The Ideology of Southern Imperialism: New Orleans and the Caribbean, 1845–1860." *Louisiana Historical Quarterly*, XXXIX (1956), 48–73.

_____. "New Orleans and the Cuban Question During the López Expeditions of 1849–1851: A Local Study of 'Manifest Destiny.'" *Louisiana Historical Quarterly*, XXII (1939), 1095–1167.

Van Alstyne, Richard. "British Diplomacy and the Clayton-Bulwer Treaty, 1850–1860." *Journal of Modern History*, XI (1939), 149–83.

Ward, Hortense Warner. "The First State Fair of Texas." *Southwestern Historical Quarterly*, LXX (1967), 163–64.

Weaver, Blanche Henry Clark. "Confederate Emigration to Brazil." *Journal of Southern History*, XXVII (1961), 33–53.

Wilgus, A. Curtis. "Official Expressions of Manifest Destiny Sentiment Concerning Hispanic America, 1848–1871." *Louisiana Historical Quarterly*, V (1932), 486–506.

Wyllys, Rufus Kay. "Henry A. Crabb—A Tragedy of the Sonora Frontier." *Pacific Historical Review*, IX (1940), 183–94.

_____. "The Republic of Lower California, 1853–1854." *Pacific Historical Review*, II (1933), 194–213.

D. UNPUBLISHED WORKS

Bell, William H. "Knights of the Golden Circle: Its Organization and Activities in Texas Prior to the Civil War." M.A. thesis, Texas College of Arts and Industries, 1965.

Cotner, Thomas E. "Diplomatic Relations Between the United States and Mexico Concerning a Tehuantepec Transit Route, 1823–1860." M.A. thesis, University of Texas, 1939.

Douglas, Lucia. "The Interest of Texas in the Nicaragua Filibusters." Typescript, Barker Texas History Center Archives, University of Texas, Austin.

Everett, John Samuel. "John A. Quitman's Connection with the Cuba Filibusters." M.A. thesis, George Peabody College for Teachers, 1928.

Gordon, Thomas Tolson. "Reminiscences." Typescript, Barker Texas History Center Archives, University of Texas, Austin.

Hamsa, Charles F. "William Walker's Mexican Adventure." M.A. thesis, University of Nebraska, 1968.

Lawson, H. Royston. "William Walker: His Early Life." Typescript, Tennessee State Library and Archives, Nashville.

Leard, Robert Benson. "Bonds of Destiny: The United States and Cuba, 1848–1861." Ph.D. dissertation, University of California, 1953.

Maisel, Jay Max. "The Origin and Development of Mexican Antipathy Toward the South, 1821–1867." Ph.D. dissertation, University of Texas, 1955.

Neighbors, Alice Atkinson. "The Life and Public Works of Charles Arden Russell, 1846–1878." Typescript, Barker Texas History Center Archives, University of Texas, Austin.

Smith, Barbara Lois. "Narciso López and Southern Annexationists, 1849–1851." M.A. thesis, Mississippi State University, 1964.

Tyler, Ronnie C. "Runaway Slaves and Border Diplomacy." Paper delivered at the meeting of the Southern Historical Association Convention at Houston, November 19, 1971.

Urban, C. Stanley. "The Idea of Progress and Southern Imperialism: New Orleans and the Caribbean, 1845–1861." Ph.D. dissertation, Northwestern University, 1943.

Wilson, Thomas Ray. "William Walker and the Filibustering Expedition to Lower California and Sonora." M.A. thesis, University of Texas, 1944.

Index